Sue Ingleton is an award-winning professional actor, director, dramaturge, writer and stand-up comedian. She has worked at Melbourne Theatre Company, Sydney Theatre Company, Belvoir St., La Boite, Malthouse and La Mama, and has toured Australia, New Zealand, USA, UK, Europe and Malaysia with her ground-breaking one-woman shows. Sue is a recipient of the Sydney Myer Individual Performing Arts Award, the Gloria Dawn/Gloria Payten Award, a Perrier Award Nomination at the Edinburgh Fringe Festival, multiple Arts Council and Asialink Grants and winner of the R.E. Ross Playwright's Award. Sue has performed and directed for Adelaide International Arts Festival, Montreal Juste Pour Rire, Melbourne International Comedy Festival, Festival of Fools – Penzance & Amsterdam, and the New York International Theatre Fringe Festival. She has written eleven plays and two books and contributed to three short story anthologies. She is a shamanic healer and runs workshops in drama and creative writing and teaches women's studies. She has also become a 'Detective in Time' and it is women's lost history that she is searching for.

T0290490

Also by Sue Ingleton

'A Letter to Roxane', in *Mother Love 2:
More Stories about Births, Babies and Beyond*
(1997, edited by Debra Adelaide)

*The Passion and its Deep Connection with
Lemon Delicious Pudding* (1995)

'The Marriage Tree', in *Weddings and Wives*
(1994, edited by Dale Spender)

*Sue Ingleton's Almaniac
– a woman's guide to domestic insanity*
(1990)

'Geese', in *Ink:
The Follow Me Short Story Collection*
(1990)

'Suzanne Ingleton', in *Memories of Melbourne University:
Undergraduate Life in the Years Since 1917*
(1985, edited by Hume Dow)

MAKING TROUBLE

Tongued with Fire

An Imagined History of
Harriet Elphinstone Dick and Alice C. Moon

SUE INGLETON

First published by Spinifex Press, 2019

Spinifex Press Pty Ltd
PO Box 5270, North Geelong, VIC 3215, Australia
PO Box 105, Mission Beach, QLD 4852, Australia

women@spinifexpress.com.au
www.spinifexpress.com.au

Edited by Pauline Hopkins, Susan Hawthorne and Renate Klein
Cover design by Deb Snibson, MAPG
Front cover illustration is 'A Sketch at the Ladies' Gymnasium' by J.R. Ashton, from
The Australasian Sketcher, Saturday 16 July, 1881, p. 232. From the collection of the
National Library of Australia. <https://trove.nla.gov.au/newspaper/page/5740598>

Back cover photo of Alice C. Moon is from *The Bulletin*, 5 May 1894, p. 9.
From the collection of the National Library of Australia.
<https://nla.gov.au:443/tarkine/nla.obj-489099363>

Back cover photo of Harriet Elphinstone Dick [Harriet Rowell] was taken
ca. 1889–1898. From the collection of the National Library of Australia.
<http://trove.nla.gov.au/version/182675792>

Back cover photo of an envelope with a drawing by Alice C. Moon is used
with the permission of the descendants of Florence Parker.

Typesetting by Helen Christie, Blue Wren Books
Typeset in Adobe Caslon Pro
Printed by McPherson's Printing Group

A catalogue record for this
book is available from the
National Library of Australia

ISBN: 9781925581713 (paperback)
ISBN: 9781925581744 (ebook: epub)
ISBN: 9781925581720 (ebook: pdf)
ISBN: 9781925581737 (ebook: kindle)

This project has been assisted by the Australian Government through
the Australia Council, its principal arts funding and advisory body.

CONTENTS

"One thing only I believe in a woman –
that she will not come to life again after she is dead;
in everything else I distrust her till she is dead."

Antiphanes, 4th century BCE

"And what the dead had no speech for, when living,
They can tell you, being dead: the communication
Of the dead is tongued with fire beyond the
language of the living."

T. S. Eliot, *Little Gidding: Four Quartets*

The Search Begins

I wouldn't even have attempted to venture into the unknown world of biography writing unless I was being horse-whipped from beyond the grave – a gravestone inscription in fact. Dragged kicking and screaming to the laptop by two very dead women, I've had to qualify this work as *An Imagined History*, for there are very few proofs; no letters, no direct descendants both women being childless, no personal communications, only some newspaper stories, advertisements and sections of a thesis written in 1985 as source material – but I do have a direct line to spirit and *they* do talk to me and guide me.

From 1996 onwards, before the advent of Trove, it was Me alone in the sacred, silent Libraries of Men being continually led, like another Alice, down the wrong rabbit holes. Me photocopying pages of microfiche documents of Lois Young's brilliant 1984 thesis on feminism, physical/sex education and dress reform.[1] Me, tapping away at my laptop with my undisciplined typing or trying to decipher my own hasty handwriting. Me flying off to Brighton, Sussex 1997 and 2014 searching out the wonderful, quite mad amateur historians who had answered my newspaper pleas. I name them before they pass themselves into history: the delightful, erudite David Sawyers along with his brilliant wife, Truus; the charmingly docile Roy Bruder, a distant relative of Harriet's family and his quick-witted wife, Divine Ann, me sitting with her on her Hove patio sharing G&Ts and laughing hysterically about marriage with men. Then there were the online connections to amateur historians: Roy Grant who sourced information for me from his home in Budapest via his fellow history ferrets in the UK – there's a secret society out there! But be warned, fellow biographers! Research is a matter of wearing blinkers so you don't get seduced to creep off down a mysterious, alluring alleyway in history.

What I'm attempting here is to create a barely documented history of two English women who, in love, bravely immigrated to Melbourne, Australia in 1875. Harriet Elphinstone Dick (neé Rowell – she changed her name) and Alice Caroline Mercy Moon first settled in Melbourne. Fourteen years later they separated when Alice moved to Sydney to pursue another career. Harriet, bereft, followed her. But in 1894, Alice, aged 37, suddenly died. Harriet, emotionally damaged by the split from her partner's life and almost destroyed by her sudden death, eventually returned to Melbourne where eight years later, she too died.

The Victorian fin-de-siècle. Difficult times of revolution from within society and extraordinary changes from without, and the 'New Woman' appeared as a tag for the women who struggled for freedom and recognition. This era of women's history has rarely been scrutinised, in truth which era has? What achievements my women gained both in England and Australia disappeared very quickly from the public record lest they threaten or intruded upon the works of man.

These two women began a revolution in Australia that exposed the patriarchal laws that controlled and governed women's bodies; laws which crippled women physically, through their attire and mentally, through the denial of an education which reduced them to lives of servitude and procreation. My women were early pioneers of physiotherapy, healthy diet, gymnastics and swimming for women and girls, biodynamic farming, journalism, breaking the barriers of women creating their own businesses and most importantly they were lesbians living openly together – the final bastion against the Patriarchy. Quite a rollcall for the times and for the Australia that they chose to live in.

Historically, the patriarchy does not so much fear the lesbian but rather chooses to believe that they do not exist – how can a woman have sex without a man, or indeed survive alone? If that historical lesbian in western civilisation did manage to live her life openly in the company of her lover, she did it as her 'companion' and was able to disguise her illicit relationship precisely because she both fostered and proved the patriarchal law that she couldn't get a man. As for a sexual relationship, the Victorian repression of any sexuality meant no questions asked, but the reality was that men could not conceive of the sex act even being possible without a penis involved. So, in a strange way it was possible for lesbians to live openly together, embrace, hold hands and kiss. Women do that sort of stuff – men don't.

It was simply bad luck if you fell in love with a bloke because none of the above behaviour was possible unless you married him! A married woman became persona non grata. The man was the head of the woman – she was headless – her property belonged to him but not his to her, same with any money she had. She was forbidden to have her own bank account without her husband's signature, she lost her children if she sued for divorce, it was forbidden by law for her to sign any legal documents and yet she was expected to pay taxes on all things without voting rights. It became very simple for men to commit their wives to insane asylums on the basis of their 'hysteria' disguised as his simple displeasure with her. Ownership of property was finally granted to women at the end of the century amidst outrage from men that she would become sexless and households would disintegrate. Most male outrage about women's rights usually centres around their control of their vaginas and the value of their servant capacity. Women's bodies are the terrain on which patriarchy is erected.

Just a quick comment here about the mythology of the 'weaker sex'. It was always to man's advantage to promote woman as physically and mentally weak, weaker than man and he had a lot of dancing around to do to convince her of that – one of the first images that comes to my mind is the seminal caveman armed with a club, dragging 'his' cavewoman by her hair into his cave. Firstly, the cavewoman was actually physically stronger than the man, after all it was she who owned the cave, got the food and gave birth to the people of the tribe. She alone would bleed and not die, she alone understood her body and the life that it created and fed, whereas the caveman was dull and stupid and had no idea how she got that baby thing in the first place and he was confused that he could never make milk from his teat. This 'weakness' of the female sex has got to be the greatest, most insidious, most successful lie of the patriarchy.

For each of us as women, there is a deep place within, where hidden and growing our true spirit rises … Within these deep places, each one holds an incredible reserve of creative power, of unexamined and unrecorded emotion and feeling. The woman's place of power within each of us is neither white nor surface; it is dark, it is ancient, and it is deep.

—Audre Lorde, 'Poetry is Not a Luxury' 1985

So, why me?

I'm renting in Melbourne while working on *Mercury* for ABC-TV plus teaching drama at the Victorian College of the Arts and trying to pay the bills. My youngest daughter, 14-year-old Roxane, is living with me and life at home is generally a battlefield.

My role was the Sporting Editor of the paper, *Mercury*. Bored with 'background acting' and needing something to read, I gazed up at my fake Sports Editor Reference Library on the shelf above my fake desk. *The Australian Biography of Sport* called out to me. I took it down, a heavy tome which immediately fell open at a page drawing my gaze to the name: Harriet Elphinstone Dick – a champion swimmer who emigrated from England in 1875 with her friend, Alice C. Moon. Perhaps I smelt the ocean, but I swear I heard a seagull's cry as a familiar ritual shudder went through my bones alerting me to the fact that these two women were calling to me from that place beyond the grave. It's happened before.

My award-winning show, *Near Ms's* in 1989–1990 had driven me into the wastelands of women's history and apart from the thrill of the resulting performances, the three years of intricate, labyrinthine work that I had undertaken to research it had transformed me from an activist into a Detective in Time. The thrill of the search, the smell of truth as I neared an undiscovered fact, the threading of the needle with yet another piece of yarn connecting the incredible quilt patches of so many lives. The pain of researching a book in a library of men's history to find abusive notes written in margins by disgruntled male scholars, such as, 'If she's so famous why haven't I heard of her?' My answer: Why? Because your grandfather eradicated her, that's why. I refrained from writing that though.

But having done *Near Ms's*, I wasn't that interested in making yet another play about 'lost female lives'. I noted their names and the fact that the book had opened on that page; I never ignore signals from Spirit. But that was all.

Christmas break at the end of that year, Roxi and I were driving back to Taylors Arm, our northern NSW home. In Sydney, we detoured to Old South Head Cemetery to try to maybe find the grave of Alice Moon. It was the 8th of December, a shining Sydney day. The cemetery was deserted. I do love cemeteries. In all my travels if I had the time, I'd visit the cemeteries of the country towns I was performing in, usually at dawn or at sunset. Reading inscriptions on gravestones would often make me weep or laugh out loud.

And now I must step you, dear reader, across the line between fact and fiction. I believe there exists in the ether a kind of 'dead zone' and if one looked through a microscope at that line one would see there were in fact two lines – the Fact line and the Fiction line and one would then see a space between, a no-go zone, the 'timeless moment'. It is in this zone that the spirit world operates. T.S. Eliot put it perfectly in *Four Quartets*:

> And what the dead had no speech for, when living,
> They can tell you, being dead: the communication
> Of the dead is tongued with fire beyond the language of the living.
> Here, the intersection of the timeless moment
> Is England and nowhere, Never and always.

Should the writer/researcher be in contact with or at least open to the existence of this Spirit world then the hidden facts, the invisible truths can sometimes hurl themselves at you like meteors from deep space. Such a meteor was about to hit me that December day in Old South Head Cemetery.

Roxi and I decided to split up. With no guiding maps, I started at the bottom and sent Roxi to start at the top, walking the rows looking for the name, so eventually we would meet in the middle. About 15 minutes in and she screamed from the slope above me, "I've found it! I've found it!"

Thrilled, I ran uphill to where she was literally dancing on a grave. And there it was. Number 120. There was the name. Such a shock to see Alice Moon's name printed large and clear beneath a plain white cement cross surmounted on three tiers, a bit like a wedding cake. The cross was actually severed at both its base and below the cross piece and was just balancing there. Suddenly Alice existed. Suddenly she was there.

A grave is a strange thing. It holds the history of a whole life and all its secrets as well. I finally understood the meaning of 'Silent as the grave'. The inscription was raised on the face of the plinths.

ALICE C. MOON

DIED 21ST OF APRIL 1894

AGED 37 YEARS

And then Roxi drew my attention to the sides of the plinths.

"Look Mum, there's more names!" How weird! The left-hand side displayed a woman's name and on the right-hand side, two more names of women. Three strange women lay entombed with Alice, all dying on various dates between 1949 and 1977.

On the left side:

FLORENCE

AGNES PARKER

27TH JULY 1949

REQUISCAT IN PACE.

Alice Moon's gravestones.

On the right-hand side:

EDITH

LOUISE LEARY

DEC. 1969.

Also on the right-hand side:

SELMA STEWART YOUNGER

DIED 15·10·1977

I was utterly confused and excited. Who were these women who has passed such a long time after Alice, yet chose to lie with her forever? What was their connection? I returned to the front then I noticed there was some writing below Alice's death date, hidden by grass and dirt. Roxi found a piece of rock and I scraped away to reveal the inscription.

"When He giveth quietness, who then can make trouble."

—Job C.34 V.29

I felt the ground shift under me. I felt a kick in the gut. The kick of betrayal or of ghastly discovery? Who would write such an accusation on a gravestone? The meteor had found its mark.

I had been chosen to find out what had happened to Alice. And what was her connection to these other women? I knew she had no relatives in Australia so how come they had become so closely connected to her as to be buried with her, albeit many years later? Surely they weren't randomly dropped into the earth beside her, they must have all known her which means they must've died at an elderly age. And what of Harriet?

Seagulls were screaming overhead. The die was cast.

Suddenly the searcher in me wanted to weep – I was alive when two of these women were alive! I could've spoken to them! But our history is lost to us! Women's lives made invisible.

I wrote letters to the newspapers in UK and Australia, no internet – no google, no emails, no mobile phones, just letters with those things called stamps and the snail mail. The following month I got mail. In envelopes. It was like opening treasure chests, a gallimaufry of information ranging from the Brighton Swimming Club, Rowell family descendants in the UK and in Western Australia and other crazy Searchers simply mad for the chase!

1996 proved to be a cathartic year for Roxi and I. The year that broke my heart. The year I sent her back to her Dad to live in the safety of his north coast home.[2]

Alert and alarmed. That was me after the graveyard visit. Alice became the trigger for the book and Harriet appeared to be the tagalong story and yet their love story is the strongest thread in the quilt.

Obituary photo, The Bulletin, *5 May 1894, page 9.*

I think it was the Mitchell Library that first offered up to me the gleanings of a harvest I was yet to gather. Death notices for Alice Moon were easy to find as I had her death date right there. There were many. She was a well-known figure in the world of writing, she was a journalist, a 'pen lady' and was published in the *Sydney Morning Herald* and in *The Australasian Sketcher* and *Freeman's Journal*, some publications that I never knew existed. The death notices were pretty similar. Sudden death, shock, grief, too young, unexplained death, were repeated in all notices. One notice gave me the information that, at the time of her death she was engaged in work with a scientist "which had now come to a standstill."[3] Upon reading that, the alarm bells again rang. Who was this scientist? Was my Intuition yelling at me that he was connected in some way with her death? Yes, of course! I knew it in my gut! So then I had to find him. 1890s, Sydney, a scientist. Again I found myself scouring the pages of the *Australian Dictionary of Biography* (*ADB*). There were two scientists who were possibilities regarding Time but only one met the criteria of Place.

John McGarvie Smith. Bacteriologist. Living in Woollahra a few blocks away from Alice in Double Bay. Thus began my quest to link him to Alice. I kept a cool head but perhaps not an open mind; when you know, you *know*. My subsequent thorough and detailed research into this man has at times made my blood run cold. I've traced the history of his work, his variety of skills and diversified education, his private life and the public comments about him. He had cut quite a figure and had done celebrity-type illustrated magazine and newspaper interviews. The *ADB* (an entry which I have since proven to be full of falsehoods) detailed his career which ranged from scientific experiments in developing a vaccine for anthrax,[4] training in metallurgy, the creation of snake vaccines and investigations of city waterworks but nowhere could I find a connection, no letters, no writings, not one reference that would link him with Alice Moon and her death.

Despite my lack of evidence, I gave him a pseudonym and wrote him into the story. At no time have I ever doubted a connection. But not actually being able to prove it, I felt completely blocked in moving forward and completing the work. How could I accuse one so famous? The McGarvie Smith Institute, unquestionably funded by Smith, stood legitimately in memory of the 'great and noble man'.

In decades of excavating the lost lives of women I have come across far too many 'great and noble men' who were tyrants, embezzlers, abusers, liars and miscreants. In today's world there are insufficient digits on both hands to count these honourable liars, despite the fact that they hold or once held high office. The self-interested blind eye of Dominance is turned on these men and they are welcomed into society, their sins forgiven and forgotten.

> I have had my belly full of great men (forgive the expression). I quite like to read about them in the pages of Plutarch, where they don't outrage my humanity. Let us see them carved in marble or cast in bronze and hear no more about them. In real life they are nasty creatures, persecutors, temperamental, despotic, bitter and suspicious.
>
> —George Sand, 1895

And so, despite all the scenes that emerged in the creative writing involving Smith and how he could have been implicated in Alice's death, even finding a documented boast some two years after of how he could dissolve tasteless snake poison into a glass of water, the journey faltered, became unreal and too damned hard.

In conference with David Sawyers in 2014 on my last visit

to Brighton, UK, he challenged me, "Name him. Trust your intuition!" But even so as a true historian I just couldn't do it without finding something that showed a possible connection. Thus it was on the night of the Winter Solstice, 22 June 2016, that I was drawn to my computer to search again, my inner voice guiding me to go back and again read all those obituaries which, years before, I had copied out into documents or copied direct from digitised newspapers (may the gods bless TROVE!). One particularly long obituary finished at the bottom with naming all those who were present at the burial of Alice. She died on the Saturday and was buried on the Monday after a coronial inquest on the Sunday which found she died of heart failure. The list was long and included some names I'd never heard of and for that reason I suppose I'd just never bothered to read past them to the very end, but on this night, I read all the names. And there, the near to last name to be printed: J. McGarvie Smith. He was at her funeral. To watch her be buried, silenced forever. He *was* my scientist.

My body went into meltdown. My brain exploded. My breath stopped. Ah, ah, ah! I ran outside to be under the cold stars on that magical night, the night that heralds the rebirth of the Light and I shouted to the stars, "Got you, you bastard!" How could I have missed this? How could I have wasted so many years? Is timing everything? Was I meant to sweat it out? I must have had this document since at least 2004! Enough. The last piece of the jigsaw puzzle had been found. "Now just get on with it," they called down to me.

A last word: only last month, August 2018, in revisiting the research with my editor, she sent me a copy of the very same obituary in *The Leader* (5 April, 1894) wherein I had found his name at the funeral. But her obit published in *The Sydney Daily Telegraph* (24 April, 1894) was word for word the one from *The*

Leader except for two extra sentences. They referred to Alice working with the scientist, John McGarvie Smith as his pupil! Named. I ponder why the gods led me to such a merry chase over so many years? Was it just to test my faith in my intuitive powers, for I had ended up, having travelled a maze of imaginings, at the same point of confirmation! Yes, it was necessary, because I have learnt to listen to the words tongued with fire.

CHAPTER 1

Highett, Melbourne

JULY 1902

In a darkened room, brown holland blinds are half-drawn against the bright winter sun which pours through slightly billowing cotton curtains. Pulling back from the window, which evokes both the time and space for us, we find we are in the bedroom of Harriet Elphinstone Dick and it is she who lies in a near-death state in the single bed. At the age of 50, Harriet has suffered a heart attack. Two women are in the room. One sits on a small chair drawn close to the bed, leaning in, grief keeping her body stiff, her breath as shallow as that of the woman whose hand she holds. She is Margaret 'Peggy' Montgomery, Harriet's intimate partner.

"Her hand is so cold," says Margaret.

Annie Seely, although she has known Harriet longer than Margaret, respectfully holds herself back and says comfortingly, "Who will ever remember her, Peggy? Even I do not know the full extent of her work. She never wrote anything down. I don't think they kept those newspaper clippings? There were so many instances …"

Annie's voice trails off as Margaret is not listening. She looks around the unfamiliar room and her gaze settles on a silver-framed photograph cut from a newspaper which stands on the dressing table. It is of a younger woman whose rebellious gaze and boyish haircut send out a challenge to the observer. Ah, she thinks, I never saw her like that, so changed and that glorious hair so sacrificed. How could she do that?

"I can't believe her strength is just ebbing away," whispers Margaret, "after all these years, her amazing strength, just slipping away." She will not release the hand.

"She was never the same after she came back to Melbourne," offers Annie, "Oh Peggy, you should've known her when she –"

"Oh hush, she's saying something," Margaret leant her face close and hears, "sea … skulls?"

The light appears to focus on Harriet's pale face and her last breath is released as her spirit lifts to join the gulls.

CHAPTER 2

Brighton Beach, England

1860

A pale English sky. The shrieking cries of haphazard seagulls drown out the playful cries of a few young children bent down in concentration on the pebbly shore. The impatient scavengers call and swoop above the waves of a rough colourless sea, one gull in particular has its eye fastened on an object below. Not an object but a young girl, about eight years old who stands alone at the edge of the frothing waves, her heart is in her mouth as she confronts the foaming, swirling water. She senses the power hidden beneath the waves that curve across the pebbles, reaching out to catch her by the ankle, to drag her in, to drag her under.

"Come on!" screeches the gull above her head. It's a challenge, and sturdy little Harriet Rowell takes it. She holds her breath and thrusts her little legs into the briny. Above the roaring around her, she catches the voice of her elder brother, George, already in the water.

"Come on Harry! You can do it!"

A little further out, ten-year-old George is waving encouragement but gasps in fright as he sees his little protégé go under but in an instant she's up and fighting with all her might, her heavy, baggy costume her only obstacle. Suddenly she gets the hang of it, suddenly she's on top of it, she's carried, supported by the water, her little toes flex in squeamish delight, she gulps salt water, coughs, then breathes properly, she thrashes her arms.

"Kick your legs, Harry, kick your legs!"

With every ounce of her concentrating upon staying afloat, she cannot make a sound. Her arms thrash about. The white gull swoops low overhead, she looks up, her eyes alight with joy, her little heart pounding, her soul in flight. With George just ahead of her, she succumbs to a wave that carries them both in to shore. She's beached. She's exhausted but utterly enthralled. She has faced the terror and won! She struggles to her feet and runs up the gravelly beach but is caught up in George's arms. "Bravo Harry, you're a Swimmer now!"

He wraps a heavy cotton sheet around her shivering body but she doesn't feel the cold or the sheet against her goose-bump skin. Her eyes are ablaze and her heart is beating so fast it feels like she is on fire. The seagulls cry their approval, and we are up there with them, following their erratic flight path as time moves forward. Let us follow one gull wheeling away, leaving the beach and rising above the Grand Junction Road, across towards the Steine, Brighton's showpiece boulevard of beautiful Victorian terraces, new homes to the rising professional classes which enjoy the uninterrupted views of the central, cast-iron fenced parkland with its grand fountain, bandstand and gazebos. It used to be where the fishermen all laid out their nets but today they are long gone, banished back to the shore. Today it is in its botanical infancy but with vision one can imagine how in one hundred years hence the trees will have grown and the gardens will bloom and the grand boulevard will be known as Old Steine.

The Steine has been well laid out with its wide road accommodating horse-drawn coaches, private broughams and commercial carts, while the side footpaths allow couples to promenade and young bloods to flirt with chaperoned young ladies who always walk together, maintaining their aloof superiority. Occasionally barrow market stalls sell ices in the hot weather and cockles and mussels all year round. Our gull is taking a circular route high above the rising structure of the luxurious Grand Hotel, which will cater for the enormous influx of well-to-do visitors who can now flock to Brighton on the train. She flies down past Poole Valley where Creak's Baths stand but not for long, they are soon to be replaced by Brill's Baths in East Street; she dives low over the roof of Cowells' 'Ye Olde Bunn Shoppe', drawn no doubt by the smell of newly baked bread. Finally, she arrives at her destination, number 17 Castle Square, Brighton's busiest and noisiest intersection which marks the end of North Street and the beginning of the Steine. Number 17 is in a row of four-storey terraces situated just around the corner from the romantically designed Royal Pavilion. Our eavesdropping gull is happy to land on the sill of the first-floor bay window, which sits above the awnings of the lower street level shops. The sign above the shop of her choice pronounces 'Rowell's Clock Factory'.

We have travelled from 1860 to the year of 1863 and the Rowell family consists of the father, Phillip, and his beloved wife, Harriett, two years his senior, known as Marmie to her children of whom, so far, there are six surviving infants; the eldest is 12-year-old George whom we've met, then Harriet, now a self-contained ten year-old and then, in descending order of age, each of two years separation, come Thomas, John, Richard and infant Emma. Marmie lost her firstborn child, Eleanor, to diphtheria when she was four or five and she will have four more children within the next eight years: Alice, Frederick, Edward and Edith.

Rowell's Clock Factory with Brill's Baths in foreground.
Before the move to Castle Square. The name Rowell's Clock Factory is
visible on the high central building.

The parlour of the Rowell household is neatly but not lavishly furnished. Let us venture into the parlour where a soft pale light from the afternoon sun filters through the lace curtains, trapping some dust motes in the folds of the dark green, slightly worn, velvet drapes. Two men, one who is sitting at a small circular polished table examining a gold fob watch while the other, Phillip Rowell's visitor and owner of said timepiece, strides casually about the room on the well-worn carpet, choosing to come to rest in the only pool of sunlight afforded by the one large window. He is Dr Justus, the family physician. His wealthy lifestyle is marked by a distinctive paunch, flushed cheeks and well-manicured nails which shine as he fingers the chain lying across his belly where the watch that now rests in the hands of the watchmaker usually hangs. Phillip has his jeweller's eyepiece in and has expertly removed the back of the timepiece. He is examining it thoughtfully while wondering to himself why it is that Dr Justus thinks he has a right to drop in casually on a Saturday afternoon to have his watch fixed and probably not expect to pay for such a service, while he himself would have to make an appointment, wait, and pay to see the grand man despite suffering from any illness that may at any moment prove fatal. Phillip does not look up at his visitor until the parlour door is flung open and a whirlwind of a daughter flies into the room and stops abruptly at the sight of the doctor, whom she rarely sees but whose personal smell of tobacco and alcohol she dislikes immensely.

Harriet hesitates, her purpose foiled by the grand man's unexpected presence. She is taller now that she is ten and she has forsaken petticoats and layers of heavy pinafores to wear her brother's cast-off knickerbockers, garments that are all but worn out. Dr Justus draws deeply on the cheroot that he is smoking and blows the smoke into the air just above Harriet's head.

"Well now, it's little Miss Rowell, in a hurry as usual? And what d'ye think ye be in that attire? A young lad?"

"No, Dr Justus. I'm a swimmer!" Harriet has no qualms in replying honestly to his demeaning question.

Justus snorts into his beard, "Oh a 'swimmer' is it? And where might ye be doin' that, I pray? In the scullery sink?"

His laughter is caught short as Harriet, wondering if that was an attempt to be funny, replies, "No sir, in the sea!"

"The sea!"

Justus coughs and spins round to attack Phillip who quickly looks back down to his business with the watch, disguising his grin with a frown.

"Good grief Rowell, is the child mad? Swimming is a most unhealthy and dangerous activity for a female, and for one so young! Have you no sense?"

"No, no, Hubert, please don't misjudge me but you see, she's just different. Likes to throw away her clothes and jump into the briny with her disreputable brothers."

"And you condone this? Good grief man, the sea's a most treacherous demmed place. The human body was not designed for such an element. Do we have fins? Do we grow gills? Certainly not!"

"You're right, sir. I've tried locking her up but the noise of her shouting would bring the horse guards down – if we had any. But my dear sir, I cannot argue with natural born talent. Her brother George has already proved his worth, winning in competitions above his age. They don't have races for girls but one day they surely must. It's the seawater she thrives in. And you're right – I wouldn't be surprised one morning to find her grown a set of gills."

Harriet sends her father a puzzled look, locking me up? Gills? In answer he flashes her a frown, which tells her not to be rude. Dr Justus leans into the watchmaker, breathing his foul, tainted breath right into his face, perhaps forgetting momentarily that, to say the least, he is imposing on this man's hospitality and goodwill not to mention his day of leisure.

"My dear Rowell, you must cease this foolhardy attitude to your daughter's well-being. It's a proven medical fact that women have been made sterile by far less than submersion in the inhuman, cold water of the ocean. It could affect her brain, sir! I'm a doctor and I've treated cases of hysteria in women, brought on by prolonged wading even in the calm waters of Lake Windermere. The mere fact that adult women today even venture to dip themselves into the sea is enough to cause anxiety amongst us, but she is a mere child, man."

"Yes, yes, I'm sure you've a point there but she does look well though don't you think, Doctor? And there are other opinions to be heard on the matter. Have you not made yourself aware of the work of Dr Answitter who, as you no doubt know, created the Creak Baths, the Turkish bath houses and the like? He's quite renowned."

"That's not the point, Rowell. Things happen inside women's bodies that we cannot see, nor yet properly measure; we can only guess at the horrendous entanglements and mess that they can get their organs into, let alone one so young who is yet to even come fully into the workings of her own soul. We are their guardians, Rowell and it's a great responsibility that we have brought upon ourselves and it is our duty of care that makes us the men we are meant to be."

Let us allow the self-satisfied, pompous voice of Dr Hubert Justus to fade away as we see young Harriet running down across the pebbly beach to the sea, while above her the lowering sky is full of wheeling, crying gulls. She imitates their cry, her strong little legs running, barefoot … watch now as they become the legs of a young woman, running, running.

Harriet is 17 years old. She stands at the end of the West Pier, clutching her billowing skirts around her, lifting them up from her strong shapely legs. The sea is below, the wind in her face. She is a striking looking girl, with thick dark hair tied into a bun at the nape of her neck but with two separate braids, which wrap around her forehead. Her dark eyes are shining. She cries to the elements, her arms outstretched to heaven.

"Yes! Yes! Oh, yes!"

It is a call that will be answered by the gods. She is about to meet her angel in white. Fourteen-year-old Alice Moon is watching.

CHAPTER 3

The West Pier

BRIGHTON, 1869

Harriet walked slowly back along the pier towards the shore, having already noticed the young woman in white who was leaning on the railings gazing out to sea. Rather apprehensively she passed her but then, slowing down, she turned back. The young girl was gazing intently at her as if it was she who had made her hesitate and turn.

"Hello. You must think I'm a bit crazed calling out to the sea like that?"

"Not at all. I do crazed things myself, all the time."

"You do? That's a great comfort then."

"I'm Alice."

"I'm Harriet. How do you do?"

"Well, thank you. I've seen you swimming in the sea. You're very brave."

"Or rather very crazed!" Harriet laughed and joined Alice on the railings. "I've been swimming since I was eight. My brothers are quite mad for it and so am I."

"Aren't you afraid in the water? All those mysterious creatures swimming about you and the tides and the huge waves? What a challenge!"

"Perhaps, but that never enters my head. Anyway, the only mysterious creatures are men and they're not frightening at all. It's the power of swimming that excites me. It's total freedom. And I'm quite strong you know."

"I should think you were. I should like to become as strong when I grow up."

"How old are you now?"

"I'm 14."

"Not long to go then. I'm 17. You should start to learn now."

"I think I should rather learn in Brill's Baths not the briny!"

"I go there regularly. We could meet there if you were to be allowed. I usually go with my brother, George. Do you have a brother who could accompany you?"

"No, but I have my sister, Myra. She could perhaps give me permission. I say, could you come to my house and meet her? She could quiz you about it all."

"I'd be delighted. It would be better to do that, to assure her that I can take care of you."

"I'm sure you can take care of me, Harriet. Come tomorrow afternoon for tea and cake? I live at Number Nine, The Steine."

"Thank you. I'm honoured, Alice. Alice …?"

"Alice Moon."

"Perfect! And I'm Harriet Rowell."

"Also perfect!"

And with that Alice swung herself off the rails and ran leaping down the pier to the beach and up the stairs to the Grand Road. Harriet's heart was pounding, she felt suddenly out of breath. And she hadn't even been swimming.

CHAPTER 4

A Visit

THE STEINE, 1869

A day later, Harriet stood in the front portico above the steps of the beautiful four-storied terrace house, Number Nine, The Steine. At one side of the heavy panelled door was a brass plate inscribed: 'Dr Henry Moon M.D.' She rang the bell. Within seconds the door was opened by a neatly dressed parlour maid who, upon hearing her name, dropped a quick curtsy and swiftly guided her into the front drawing room. Harriet felt a thrill of anticipation. The room, indeed the whole house, had a delightful smell of fresh flowers and quiet wealth. The furnishings were in stark contrast to her own home and she quickly registered the social status of the family Moon. Under the bay window sat a beautiful ottoman settee of embroidered pale green brocade. Two comfortably proportioned leather armchairs were on either side of the marble mantle and fireplace and opposite an inlaid polished walnut sideboard with a gilded mirror above. Upon the polished floor lay an enormous carpet of Chinese silk. A minute later, Harriet turned as her name was softly spoken to meet a tall, very striking woman who had entered the room, her hand extended in friendship. Close behind her came Alice, dressed in a simple grey serge gown with a white pinafore over it, her face flushed in excitement. Harriet felt most peculiar as if her insides were melting. Confused, she believed this woman to be Alice's mother, even though she was perhaps a little too young. But before she made a fool of herself Alice had leapt forward, "Harriet, this is my sister, Myra. Myra this is she – Harriet Rowell!"

Myra laughed, accepting her young sister's garrulousness.

"Yes, my dear. Harriet Rowell, welcome to our home. Suffice to say I already know so much about you. Alice calls you the Lady of the Sea, because as I understand it you actually swim with ease in its rough waters?"

Harriet blushed. "Oh, dear me no, not with ease, not really. It's a challenge, I assure you. The sea water baths though are a different story."

"Yes, Myra. Harriet thinks I might benefit from learning to swim. Not in the sea of course but at Brill's Baths. Do you think father would allow it?" Alice was being very polite and Harriet could sense that underneath this calm request lay a desperate fear of being refused permission.

"We can only ask him, dearest. But right now, let us have some tea and find out more about you, Harriet."

Myra smiled and led the way through the tall folding doors into the second parlour where afternoon tea was already laid out.

It was a glorious meeting, a time out of time that for Harriet seemed like the start of a new journey. She kept them enthralled with her radical ideas about women's dress reform and the lack of opportunity for women in education and careers. Alice eagerly announced she was definitely going to go to the Brighton School of Art. They had only been open ten years but already they had agreed to allow women to study there so long as they were

No. 9. The Steine today.

segregated from the men. They would never be allowed to do life-drawing classes with naked men of course, but as Alice pointed out, who'd want to do that anyway? Myra blushed and signalled that her language was inappropriate. Alice's enthusiasm was not at all childlike but was bursting with adolescent sensuality and Harriet quickly felt uncomfortable with what was physically happening to her intimate bodily parts; this is a young girl, just a girl, I cannot allow these feelings to overcome me, this is so wrong, she is invading me. I must find a resistance to this. How can it be that I'm falling under some kind of spell? It is forbidden. But she was entranced and if indeed it was a spell, she had no resistance to it. Stalwart as ever, she maintained her usual controlled presence, a trait that would follow her all her life.

In the days after this meeting, Harriet called often to the house at number nine. She met the rest of the family: Alice's father, Dr Henry Moon, was a rather severe man but Harriet sensed he was warm-hearted and it was immediately obvious that he adored Alice. Alice's mother, Caroline, had only died the year before at the young age of 47 leaving Henry a widower for the second time. His first marriage had produced seven children, five of whom were still alive when he had married Caroline Gardiner. By the time Harriet met the Moon family it was reduced down to Myra, Alice's half-sister who was eight years her senior and her young sister, Grace, five years her junior. Alfred, her half-brother, had recently migrated to New Zealand and then there had been her older brother, Nathaniel, who had tragically passed away in 1866.

CHAPTER 5

Friendship

BRIGHTON, 1871

After being told the family history and absorbing the names of those living, dead or simply absent, Harriet understood that Alice's childhood had been quite different to hers. Although she herself had lost a sister whom she never knew, to diphtheria, it seemed after that one death, Harriet's entire family had maintained extremely good health. Alice, on the other hand, had seen her mother die and she had witnessed a succession of siblings get married or simply move away. There was a governess, Jane Wise, who was still living with the family in that capacity, tending to the younger siblings, but Alice was hungry for knowledge and Harriet soon learnt that there was more than one string to this fascinating creature's bow.

Dr Moon was easily convinced to allow Alice to attend swimming lessons with Harriet at Brill's Baths. Disappointingly for Harriet, Alice did not take to the water with the same affinity as she had for the sport, but Alice was still interested to learn about the gymnastics that Harriet was training in: the Swedish Ling Method devised by Per Henrik Ling.

Alice was in hero-worship mode, while Harriet, utterly enchanted, had simply succumbed to the wicked and amusing Alice, who by the age of 16 had blossomed into a lithesome and beautiful woman with cat-like energy and feline mysteriousness. She moved with agility, her long dark locks fighting all fashionable restraints flew loosely about her face, while her deep grey-blue eyes, heavily lidded and thick-lashed, contained a light that charged every word she said with special meaning. After swimming lessons, Harriet always walked her home but they often detoured, around the Steine or across into the Brighton Pavilion. Sometimes they walked the shoreline almost to Shoreham and back. They talked for hours. Their intense conversations were always around the untenable position of women in society, the subject of dress reform along with the challenge of freeing up women's bodies, and the bias against women entering any of the exclusive male professions.

"I just cannot abide the corset!" Alice would shout aloud. "The daily advertisements that threaten us with the impossibilities of being able to stand up without being encased in iron are truly taking me to the edge of distraction!" Alice, in her frustration, began stomping along the pavement like a soldier on a parade ground. It put Harriet into a sudden fit of laughter, the effect of which upon Alice was one of horror. She swung round, stopped short, her hands on her hips, "Surely you don't disagree?"

"Oh, my dearest, no, no, no. I agree! I agree! It's just that you become so militaristic when you get incensed like that!"

"It's only natural, Harriet. We are at war. Don't we all understand this?"

"Yes, we are at war, you are right, and their target is our bodies and our weapons can only be our minds and our words!"

"Myra wears corsets all the time! She swears she cannot stand upright without them. I take her to task daily. Just one day, Myra, I plead, just leave them off for one day."

"But she won't, will she? It's not just habit, it's that she has been educated to believe that her body is weak. You should show her our exercises. Why don't you do that? Convince by example?"

"I will try. Yes, but she is nearly 25, surely her bones are set?"

"I believe we can take any woman's body and set it straight. I have to believe this. I know my work is going to be about saving women from themselves, from the rule of men's minds who need to keep them in these prisons of iron. We need to get women on their own, away from men, so that together we can talk freely and share what we know without that incessant male voice shouting us down and demeaning our intelligences."

"You are a champion swimmer. Isn't that what you want to teach?"

"No. I am going to be a teacher of gymnastics one day. I shall make women's bodies strong and free. Meanwhile swimming is certainly my passion."

"I haven't yet shared with you my true passion, have I?"

"Goodness, am I prepared for this?" Harriet was taken aback.

Alice stopped walking and turned to face her.

"Here's the thing. When I was 13, Pa gave me my very own microscope. He said, 'If you were born a man you would have made an extraordinary doctor of medicine with your enquiring mind and your quick intelligence'."

"Oh dear." Harriet sighed.

"Then of course you know me! I had retorted, 'I don't see any obstacles to my mind, unless they're in your mind, Pa?' Well, that was a bit rude, I must admit, but he wasn't angry. He simply rose up and handed me a small wooden box saying, 'This is for you, my sweet Alice. You may now put that extra-ordinary brain of yours to the test!'"

"I immediately knew the contents, Harriet! The box was heavy, it had to be the very thing I'd imagined. Unhooking the brass clip, I lifted the lid and there gleaming in all its splendour lay a microscope, *my* microscope. I was speechless, almost in tears. He was so pleased. Oh Harriet, I have seen the minutiae that exists in the very cracks of life! And I've learnt to make my own slides too. Have you ever looked at your own blood?"

Harriet gasped, incredulous, shaking her head. Who really was this extraordinary young woman?

"Yes, blood. It's amazing. The whole world is amazing! And you know how I love art. I know I could be a wonderful artist too but it's such an uphill battle for us. Men just walk into a studio and work away and the waters part for them. We have to beg. We're not allowed to gaze upon a naked body, not a male one of course but not even a female body."

"You can draw me if you wish."

"Really? But I would never ask that of you."

"And you didn't. I'm offering. I could pose for you, somewhere?" They both burst out laughing. "By all the saints," murmured Harriet, "how frustrating that we don't have anywhere that we could go, do we?" Neither of them knew of a safe place.

Alice was thus encouraged to investigate and question the world of living matter. Like many similarly inclined women of the time, she depended on a parent to provide the private means for study. This lifelong fascination with bacteriology and science was to contribute, I believe, to her untimely early death.

One fine morning, after a month of lessons with Alice in Brill's Baths, Harriet rang the doorbell at number nine The Steine. The parlour maid opened the door and smiled.

"Yes ma'm? Oh, good morning Miss Rowell."

Harriet assumed a very formal air but with a slight grin, "Good morning Helen. I wish to see Miss Moon please."

"Certainly, Miss Rowell, come into the parlour if you please."

Harriet crossed the carpet and entered her favourite room in the Moon household. The maid had disappeared up the stairs to summon Alice. There was no yelling in this household, not with the number of servants they had to do their bidding. In a minute Alice was heard leaping down the stairs, no decorum there, thought Harriet, obviously Myra was not within hearing distance. She burst into the room and Harriet felt the sunshine come in with her.

"Good morning, Miss Moon."

"Good morning, Miss Rowell."

"It's a very fine morning, Miss Moon, and I thought it might be a good day to take that most important swimming lesson I have promised you."

"Oh, my goodness, so quick!" Alice was genuinely aghast. Was this the day she had been dreading? "Am I ready for the Sea? Yes. I must be brave! I shall get my costume."

"And something to wrap yourself in afterwards."

Brighton Beach. It was a clear day. The water was grey-blue and little bouncy whitecaps were scooped up in the breeze while seagulls wheeled and fought for space above Harriet and Alice, who were deep in conversation at the water's edge. Harriet was talking Alice through the different experience of swimming in the sea, reminding her of the strokes she had taught her in the Baths. They were dressed in bathing costumes, such over-abundant frilly things, neck-to-bloomered knee. There was no one on the shore. They were alone. Alice was still apprehensive but once challenged, felt rather brave.

"Just remember you must not panic. I shall be there beside you. Now you will remember what I've taught you, won't you?"

"I'll be utterly wonderful, do not fear."

"I have every confidence in you and what I know you can do, but I do fear a little." She turned her gaze to the horizon. "It's a bit unsettled out there today."

"Oh please, don't change your mind, Harriet! You promised me this, after all my lessons, you promised me I could attempt the briny!"

"And I keep my word. All right, but please, don't be foolish."

Harriet plunged into the cold waters and Alice bravely followed. Harriet's swift strokes took her quickly out from the shore. She turned to watch Alice's progress behind her. Hesitating at first, Alice raced in, leapt over waves, shrieking a little at the shock of the cold. There was a distinct unpleasantness when their garments became heavy and wet and clung to their skin. They were restrictive and cumbersome, ah if only they could have experienced the freedom of what was to come – lycra! Alice's stroking was still awkward and slightly panicky, for suddenly the sea was so different to the controllable waters of Brill's Baths, yet she was managing to be on top of rather than under the waves.

"Wonderful! Keep coming to me!" Harriet's calls of encouragement were whipped away on the breeze.

They were about two yards apart, Alice keeping afloat more with dog paddle than swimming strokes. Harriet realised Alice had almost instantly forgotten all the training she had given her. She trod water calling out instructions.

"On your stomach now, kick your legs out behind you and lift your head up, let your body float, lift your tummy!"

"All right, all right! I'm trying to remember it!" Talking and swimming at the same time proved difficult. Alice swallowed two gulps of seawater.

Harriet stayed with her, then turned and stroked a little more, loving the thrust of the waves. But Alice, after suddenly taking in another large mouthful had gone under. Harriet was stroking powerfully ahead, sure that Alice was making up the distance behind. Going under for the third time, gasping for air, perhaps a cry was uttered but in reality, she was silent. Harriet turned just in time to see Alice's head going under for the last time. Swiftly she swam back and dived. Underwater she grasped the sinking Alice, drawing her up to the air. Alice coughing, gasping for breath while Harriet's strong arms crossed, life-saving fashion over her breasts and under her chin. Harriet now supported her across her own body. Alice was conscious, her coughing slowly eased. Their heads were very close. Harriet's hand was gently appreciating the shape of Alice's face. The rescue was over. Alice closed her eyes, floating safely on her back, encircled by Harriet's strong arms and as Harriet gently turned her body to face her, their lips met, their mouths joined in a surprising kiss. Their forbidden secret was revealed to them both.

CHAPTER 6

Lovers

BRIGHTON, 1874–1875

"Why do you look so pleased with yourself, Miss Moon?" It was some 12 months later that Harriet and Alice strolled together arm-in-arm along The Steine. Summer was coming to an end but the twilight still lingered until 9 pm. They were not alone, as many couples also took advantage of the promenade at this time of the evening.

"I feel like Little Jack Horner who sat in a corner." Alice smiled wickedly as she slipped her hand into Harriet's.

"Ah, the one who put in his thumb and pulled out a plum?"

"That's him, and you are my Plum! In fact, I've got the whole pie to myself and I'm going to eat it all!" Gently she raised Harriet's hand to her mouth and kissed her palm. "Very tasty!" She licked her lips but Harriet patted her hand and quickly, almost embarrassingly placed it away out of sight.

And so, Alice grew up a little more and attended the Brighton College of Art, as well as applying her enquiring mind to the small scientific conundrums that her father often placed before her. Harriet continued teaching at Brill's and other establishments.

The two women made private vows to each other and although Alice let the swimming drop away, she instead became Harriet's out-of-water enthusiastic supporter and attendant. There were secret plans afoot to leave England together and emigrate to Australia, an idea that began one day after Harriet had a conversation with Fred Cavill at the Brighton Swimming Club which went something like this:

"Have you ever thought of going out to the colonies, Miss Rowell?"

"To Australia? The idea never crossed my mind, Mr Cavill."

"I would give it some thought if I were you. I myself intend to go as soon as my wife is well and has completed this last confinement."

"Your whole family will go?"

"Yes. Certainly, yes. We shall go to Sydney. I believe there is a strong swimming fraternity there. I cannot think of a better place in which to let my sons grow up. They are going to be champions in a new world! I believe it's a land free of prejudice."

"Is there a land free of prejudice anywhere?"

"Well now, that's a true enough question, Miss Rowell, but let's just say that I believe that with your ability there's no telling how far you could go."

"The weather there is certainly more conducive for the outdoor life …"

"And there are many strong young lads there just waiting for a woman like you to come their way!"

"I'm only interested in *my* way at present, Mr Cavill, and it's a rare man who's ever interested in that, wouldn't you agree?"

"Ah, you're a difficult woman, Miss Rowell!" and Cavill laughed good-naturedly at the quizzical look his comment brought to her face. She remained silent.

∞

The idea to emigrate was planted. To both Harriet and Alice it seemed like the perfect answer. They would escape the ghastly class and religious restrictions of Victorian England and travel together to the colonies, to the new world where every opportunity would be available to them. Their love would go unnoticed. But they knew it would be difficult to convince Dr Moon. Alice was 18 and perhaps expected to be married by now. How could they convince her father that she would be safe, travelling with an unmarried woman not much older than she?

"If your poor mother were alive to hear this it would break her heart."

"Oh Pa, don't use those silly analogies here. Mother is at peace and surely she's in the best place to help me and guide me now?"

Myra sat clasping her hands in her lap, unable to drink the tea before her. Dr Moon leaned forward in his leather chair, also with his hands clasped firmly before him. Myra spoke calmly, "Alice, what will you do there? Your safety is at stake. You have no family there, no friends …"

Alice jumped in before she could go any further, "I have Harriet! She is both to me. I will teach art. I am qualified you know!"

"What if you were to meet an Irish rogue, you may want to marry him!" Myra quickly stifled a laugh then reconsidered her thought. "Oh heavens, there are so many disreputable men out there, so rough and of criminal nature."

"I can look after myself, Myra. I'm nearly 19, and I assure you I will not be marrying an Irishman!"

"And what of Pa, what will he do without you, Alice?" Myra was hoping that Henry would agree with her.

Alice leapt across the carpet and kneeled at Dr Moon's feet. "Oh Pa, you'll be fine, won't you? With three daughters to look after you here?"

Her father stirred himself from his reverie. What was he imagining? "Yes, yes. I'll be fine." He knew better than to oppose this recalcitrant daughter once her mind was made up.

"There you see!" Alice placed a kiss upon his brow and stood up tall. "I shall return one day, don't you fear. It's going to be such an adventure!"

Myra rose from her seat, "I never was one for adventure, Alice."

"Not even a dream or two, Myra?"

But Myra had turned away to hide her tears. Alice was at once by her side. The sudden realisation of what she had just said, of how much it would have hurt her beloved half-sister, the one who had taken on the selfless role of mother to all the family, hit her. What dreams had she had to give up for them all?

"Oh dearest, don't cry." Alice too had tears now.

"I shall miss your – gaiety." Myra smiled. They held each other tight and Alice was suddenly aware of what she too was going to truly miss.

It was a slightly different story in the Rowell household. There they all sat in the parlour, Marmie and Father, George, Frederick, Alice, and Edith. Harriet stood determinedly in the centre of the room, in gladiator mode. The younger girls were speechless while Freddie leapt around, conjuring images that were frightening to Marmie and disgusting to Harriet.

"Gosh, Harry you may see a shark in the water! They say they tear people from limb to limb. The water turns red with their blood!"

"Frederick! Please. Silence." Phillip Rowell's head was spinning.

"Harriet – Phillip?" Marmie tried to appeal to them both. But her husband couldn't begin to imagine where his daughter would be. Couldn't deal with such an idea of distance and her absolute absence. He put his hand to his forehead.

"Never, never, never would I have thought."

"Gosh, Harry, can I come too?" Freddie was back.

"We're leaving from Gravesend on 6 December." Harriet was positively stoic. "We have booked our passage."

"Phillip, have I no influence here!" Marmie was appealing to her husband to deal more purposefully with it, "I'm so worried about young Alice; she is so unstable, so – wild. What sort of future do they expect for themselves?"

"My dearest wife," said Phillip grasping her beloved hands in his. "Harriet will always do what she wants. And she is of an age where it is hard to prevent her! You've surely learnt that by now, my dearest."

George, who up until now had been silent and scribbling notes on a notepad stood up. "I'll come with you to see you both to the boat."

Harriet grasped his hands in hers. "Thank you, Georgie, that would be lovely. I feel as though this is my true destiny, you understand, don't you, Georgie? Perhaps I'll be able to help build a world where women can just be free."

"Between you and Queen Victoria – and Alice, my dear – I'm sure things will change. Live and let live, y'know!"

"Harry," Freddie was jumping around again, "if you see a bushranger you must promise me that you'll get his autograph for me!"

Harriet burst out laughing, as did Marmie. George grabbed his young brother and swung him round.

"Now that Harry's made the first move I'm up for it too. I'm going to come out soon too. Australia! You wait. I'll bring my gun. I sense there's a great lot of hunting to be done there. All those unknown species to souvenir!"

"Ugh, George. Live and let live, remember?" Harriet crossed the floor and kneeled down and hugged her beloved Marmie, holding her thus for a long time.

CHAPTER 7

The Challenge

BRIGHTON, 1875

Then one day in September 1875, only a few months before their planned departure for Australia, Harriet decided to prove something beyond the Brill's Baths entertainments and races. She and her swimming friend, Helen Saigeman who was actually more intimate with her brother George, decided that they, as accredited teachers at Brill's, should put their reputations to the test and attempt a long-distance swim from Rottingdean to Brighton, a distance of 3.2 nautical miles.

There's nothing so strong as an idea whose time has come. At that very same time it so happened that in London there was a young, 14-year-old swimmer called Agnes Beckwith who was about to attempt a long distance swim in the river Thames. A report of that swim, undertaken five days before Harriet and Helen's attempt, appeared in the *Brighton Gazette*.[5]

It was game on. Remember though, that Harriet and Helen were swimming in rough open seas whereas Beckwith was in the river, surrounded by rowing boats.

Their day arrived. Thursday 9 September 1875 and the women were prepared. They had advertised the upcoming event. Because of the changing wind and weather, it had been decided just the day before that the swim would not commence from Rottingdean but from the opposite direction, starting at the mouth of the Shoreham Harbour and along to the West Pier in Brighton. Phillip Rowell and George would attend to the women from a rowboat, with George prepared to swim alongside them for support and as a rescue or first aid party, if need be. Mr Giles, the swimming master of Brill's Baths, was in attendance in another boat, also prepared for a rescue if needed. The men set off early, rowing down to Shoreham. Harriet and Helen were taking the coach. A huge crowd had already built up along the Brighton Promenade. A pleasure boat was also leaving the harbour at Shoreham, full of well-wishers and spectators. Marmie sent the younger children off to the West Pier on the Brighton foreshore to await the end of the race. She held Harriet close to her before her departure and spoke to her in her soft, assured voice.

"Dearest, never hesitate to put yourself at risk, nor to push yourself to your extreme limits, for there you will find your truth, there you will find a strength that you, as a woman, will need to find daily in your life. Never accept that there is only one well-trodden path for you; the bars of a cage will never suit you. Marriage and children are that cage, that one path and you must choose at that fork in the road. When you were born, I prayed for a daughter, but in the pain of your birth I felt the pain of all women coming through me, the pain of being a woman and I gave you all my strength then and I survived that – and there you were, lusty and strong and healthy and female. To be true to yourself, my daughter, will bring to me the greatest of all rewards. I will be waiting on the beach for you. You will swim this race and you will win. You will endure it for yourself alone and we will all bathe in that light. Now kiss me and be onto the coach to Shoreham. Pa and Georgie will be nearly down there in the boat."

Let us imagine that fabulous day. Come down now to the pebbly beach at Brighton. The West Pier was where they would finish the race and this recent addition to the foreshore was very impressive. There was bunting along the pier and noisy crowds on the beach and up on the Grand Esplanade. Little stalls had sprung up which had enough goods for sale to both feed and entertain the spectators apart from the Lady Swimmers who were the great drawcard. The crowd had certainly dressed up for the occasion. The Brighton Pier, further up the shoreline, had its usual complement of visitors enjoying the fine, autumn day. A funfair was in full swing. The arcade was crowded.

"What're they all doin' down there at the West Pier, Jenny?"

"Must be the swimmers, Marj, the lady swimmers. They're swimmin' in from Shoreham, would you believe!"

"What? They're *swimmin'*! – What? *In the water?* From *Shoreham?* Never! Coo. They must be barmy! Coo."

"Let's go and 'ave a dickey!"

Let's follow our shopgirls, Jenny and Marjory down onto the crowded beach. They walked awkwardly, breathless from their tightly laced corsets whose steel stays dug into their ribs, each one holding her long dress and layers of petticoats up, all the while just managing to stay upright as their boots sank into the pebbles. They joined the crowd.

Mrs Rowell was standing on the beach with two of her sons beside her, Frederick, 15, Edward, 11 and her young daughters Alice, 14 and Edith, the baby of the family, who crossly refuted this title, insisting she was nearly ten. Farewelled by a throng of well-wishers who surrounded them, Harriet and Helen had taken the coach to Shoreham. An even bigger group of horrified men and women had held back, disgusted at the display of what they predicted to be the seeds of society's disintegration and the eventual demise of the human race, most believing that immersion in cold water destroyed a woman's child-bearing capacity. This crowd now moved down to the shoreline to get the best view of the end of the race. There were newspaper journalists and sketchers already at work drawing the crowd.

Standing a little apart, dressed in white, Alice Moon waited at the entrance of the pier. Cool and aloof, dressed much like the other women, except that we see she wears no shoes and a softly falling shift which obviously advertises that she is not wearing a corset. Her toes stretch and squeeze in the stony pebbles. One gay young blood, getting into the swing of things, the excitement of the moment, approaches Alice with jollity.

"What ho, there! Come to see the freak show, eh?"

"I wasn't aware that we were going to be looking at men?"

"What?" His grin soured, as he understood what she has just said to him. His chum however thought he could do better.

"All alone are we?" He swaggered up to her side.

"Absolutely," she replied. Will they never give up?

"My poor poppet!"

"How you mistake me, sir! I am not yours and I am certainly not a poppet. I am a woman and I am not poor, but exceedingly well-off and certainly in a class above you." Her eyes gleamed with the light of a crusader and she whipped around and was gone before he could think of a reply.

The hours passed. Finally, a cheer went up at the far end of the beach. Mrs Rowell, who had been tight-lipped, suddenly relaxed and her eyes shone and her breath eased. Her sons yelled and started to run. Freddie called out exasperated.

"Oh, do come on, Marmie! She's coming! She's coming! She's landing on the pier!"

"Yes Marmie! She's won!" echoed young Edward.

Mad excitement as people stumbled across the beach, women clumsy in their high heel boots and delicate pumps, talking as they ran.

"It's damn near a six-mile swim you know!"

"Bloody miracle if you ask me, old chum."

"They're not real women –"

"No! They're amazons!"

"I hear tell they got an engine strapped aroun' their waist?"

"It's not natural, whatever way you look at it."

"I could believe a man to stay afloat but I read it was impossible for a woman."

"I've had it on good authority that the effort unsexes them."

And so it went.

CHAPTER 8

Harriet Elphinstone Dick

BRIGHTON, 1875

Harriet was 23 years old. I'll let her tell you about the swim and then you can read the verbatim accounts of this historical event:

Arriving at the harbour mouth at Shoreham where we have been advised it is to be the best place to start, I see there are many people waiting and watching for us. The residents from Hove and Shoreham have put out the word, no doubt, that lady swimmers were going to drown in front of their eyes. That'd guarantee a crowd.

Pa and Georgie are there in the boat, my would-be rescuers. I see dear Mr Giles is there too. I think he rather wished he were in the race as well. Marmie's words are ringing in my ears. How wise and wonderful she truly is. How gentle and strong. I will never have her gentility, or her humility. There seems to be no room inside me for those emotions. Not today anyway! Helen and I grasp hands and then amid cheers and cat-calls we plunge forward. Immediately the lapping waves are hitting us both as if trying to force us back to the shore.

But I know how to deal with that. Stroking strongly, I get away as fast as I can and quickly reach the deeper sea where I can sense the rhythm of the energies that are pulling the tides and I can become at one with this glorious water. I ask permission of it to cut my way through and I can sense it surrendering in agreement. Helen is there with me at the beginning. We know each other well. We stroke together. The sea is certainly rough today, even though the sky is clear. I do not think of the cold.

The voices above or beside me, the calling out of my name, calling Helen's name, Georgie's voice, the sound of the oars stroking quite close, all begin to fade as I feel a loss of sensation in my ears and I've become only rhythm of arms and shoulders, thighs rolling, legs stroking. The temperature of the water and my own heat seemed to have equalized. I'm melting into the sea, I no longer receive messages from my brain, nor instructions from the boat, am I falling into unconsciousness? But I have never felt so alert, so in tune with the universe around me. It's true that one can reach a state of supreme bliss in the body and mind, they melt together; any fear or pain combine into some amazing form of light, no, of ecstasy! I just keep on, on. It's almost effortless but maybe from the outside the view is different. George is there, has begun to swim beside me. Am I failing? I don't feel as though I've changed. He's shouting encouragement but he sounds so far away. Helen comes back to my mind and I wonder where she can be. There's more shouting. My body exists in outer space! Now Georgie is shouting again. "You've done it, you're here, Harry! Harry you're there!"

I open my eyes and my ears. West Pier is right in front of me and I feel Georgie and Pa lifting me out of the water and into the boat. We dock at the pier and I stagger out onto its wooden surface. Out of the element now and my legs are quite weak and my skin feels like ice. How did I ever do it? I'm walking now with Georgie, I think he is holding me up! He has placed a cover around me. The beach is crowded with people shouting and clapping. Alice waits at the end of the pier. My Alice. Dressed in white, she glows like an etheric being. I look back to find Helen. But it's only George who is there behind me and then I see Pa, who is gasping for breath pulling the rowboat in to shore. Too much rowing for the old boy! But Helen isn't there. Georgie answers me when I ask about her?

"Harry, she had to quit. She got too cold and exhausted. You're on your own. You've won. On your own!"

People throw blankets on me but I'm an Amazon! I feel nothing but joy and my whole body is tingling, electric. Where is Marmie? There she is, the boys are dragging her down to meet me. Oh Marmie, Marmie, I manage to whisper to her as she holds me tight, smaller than me but strong, so strong. "It's true what you told me!"

The noise is incredible. There are newspaper people asking me questions and there are men sketching me and children touching my blanket and my angel, Alice, stands a little way back. I send her a smile, oh, it feels as though my heart has leapt out of my body!"[6]

Alice stood away from the crowd. She felt her heart leap airborne from her body, towards the goddess who now stood on the beach, blankets tossed aside, she could almost be a naked Aphrodite, not some wimpy Botticelli maiden but strong and agile, her flesh glistening and her dark hair like sealskin on her proud head. That's my lover. Harriet Rowell. She is magnificent. I shall draw her like this.

Harriet sought her angel in white. Alice pushed forward through the crowd, slipping easily between the burly men and their big boots and the parasols and crinoline skirts that dragged on the pebbles, the chattering and giggling and the mumblings and hurrahs. With her beautiful bobbing hair curling around her face, her braids coming loose, she was utterly ravishing to Harriet, not really feminine in the way of her friends, no, she glistened; it's her energy, full of light and fearless, thought Harriet. By the heavens, she is like a tiger and I am a lioness! Harriet grasped the outstretched hand.

"Hello, Harriet Rowell."

"Hello, Alice Moon, let me introduce myself," responded Harriet.

"Introduce yourself? Whatever do you mean, Plum?"

Breathing deeply not just from exhaustion now but from the liquid feeling in her legs, afraid that after all the hours of exertion it will be this young woman in white who will make her crumple to the ground, it was time to reveal her new secret.

"Miss Moon. From now on I shall be known as Harriet Elphinstone Dick!"

A look of surprise on Alice's face. Her eyebrows raised and suppressing a quirky grin, "Goodness, Plum! What on earth has come over you?"

"A new name and a new life, my dear!" Unable to stop herself, she laughed out loud and turned to the waiting throng, "Write it down lads, the name is Harriet Elphinstone Dick!"

Marmie, standing a little aback stared at her daughter in amazement. Others crowded round, asking for Harriet's name. Somewhere in the crowd someone called, "I think she calls herself Miss Dick?"

"Well, I know the woman, my dear sir, and I know she's watchmaker Rowell's daughter!"

"P'rhaps she's adopting a form of her married name?"

"She's not married, old son, and not likely to be either."

"Who'd want to bed a fish, eh?"

No one understood why she changed her name to Harriet Elphinstone Dick. (Me least of all-and I've tried! Suggestions welcome.)

*Portrait of Harriet which carries an inscription
to Alice Moon on the back.*

It was Saturday, 11 September 1875 and the Rowell family was gathered around the table pouring over the copies of the *Brighton Herald*. Phillip gazed appreciatively at a sketch of Harriet swimming her last yards through the rough seas and murmured his appreciation. The brothers Rowell were all talking at once, comparing papers, two or three copies of each paper to study. They were in a state of high excitement. Freddie's excitement rose above all others.

"Our Harry's a bloody genius!"

"Do not use that dreadful language under my roof, Frederick and certainly not in the presence of your mother!"

It was Edward now shouting, reading out loud from the paper, "Miss Dick, Miss *Dick*! Gosh, Harry, what a smashing name! 'Miss *Dick* landed at West Pier. Miss Saigeman had not, we believe, previously bathed this season in the sea where the water is ten degrees colder than it is in the baths' – ha, ha serves her right, the land-lubber, 'but Miss *Dick*'," he again snorted, "'has been accustomed to its temperature, enabling her to remain in it longer than was deemed advisable for her fair companion'."

Edward's voice fades as we move to the back of the house to the kitchen of 17 Castle Square where Harriet and Marmie were having an argument.

"Harriet, I just cannot understand why you have chosen to deny your own name? What is the meaning of this strange appellation that you have broadcast to the world?"

"Marmie, with all due respect I am 23-years-old. I have chosen a name that I will henceforth be known as, professionally. It is the name I have long admired. Elphinstone Dick! I will carry this name with me to the new world."

There was nothing more to argue about.

CHAPTER 9

Leaving Home

BRIGHTON TO GRAVESEND

T he next months flew by; October, November and suddenly it was December and Harriet and Alice were packed and farewelled on Brighton station. Dr Moon had taken Alice aside on that final night at The Steine.

"I've written to an acquaintance of mine, a Professor Halford who has taken up the Chair of Chemistry at the University of Melbourne. I've asked that he should look after you in whatever way he can and I advise you to make contact with him, my love, so that you do not lose your connection to science. He may also prove to be a strong advocate for you should the need arise. Otherwise I have no one I know in Melbourne." Alice saw his consternation and understood completely what it must be like for him to cut her loose to the unknown without a lifeline.

The family came to the farewell and it was really then that Alice understood how her going away, so far away, was breaking her father's heart. Myra stood strong by his side but Alice knew that he was thinking about Caroline, her mother. I must remind him of her, she realised. How hard I have made this for him.

"Pa, I will come back for a visit, I promise. Give me two years."

He had nodded and held her close for another longed-for minute. George Rowell scooped them all into the carriage as the whistle was blowing and then the train pulled them slowly away from family and all things known and loved.

Until the building of Tilbury Docks on the opposite side of the Thames River, between 1882 and 1886, Gravesend was the Thames' first port of entry. Thousands of emigrants, as well as large numbers of troops in many wars, embarked from here. The entrance to the Docks is somewhat awkward, situated as it is on the sharp bend of the river, often causing the need for tugboat assistance, as do the larger ships moored at Tilbury landing stages. There have been many tug companies based at Gravesend: among them the Sun Company, the Alexandra Towing Company and today, the Smith Howard Towing Company. East Indiamen traditionally stopped here at a point known as Long Reach to lighten their loads before sailing up the Thames to moorings at Blackwall.

The train journey from Brighton to Gravesend was a time for Harriet and George to talk. He had it fixed in his head that he would shortly follow them out to Australia. He promised Alice that he would keep in touch with the Moon family and keep in touch with both of them with all the news from home. Alice, before she left, had felt a premonition about her father's health. She had spent long hours talking with Myra and then with Henry himself. If anything were to happen, should his health deteriorate, she would come home. She had received from Henry a large amount of money, deposited into an account for her at the Bank of England.

"Take it as an advance on your inheritance." Henry had a way of keeping his gaze upon you, revealing much without saying about how he was feeling. He squeezed her hand, then looked away stating matter-of-factly, "You need it now."

The Docks were like all busy places at that time. Noisy, dirty, awash with water and faecal matter, screaming gulls and roaming dogs, shouting men loading carts, trucks on rails and horses and their waste matter everywhere. Cabbies and coaches all backed up waiting to unload. People were already boarding up the main gangways while the other gangways were heavily in use with men laden with bails, boxes and trunks making their shaky way up to the decks of *The Newcastle* steamer. There was much conversation going on around them; they overheard many sad tales about sailing across the Indian Ocean and about getting past the now infamous Shipwreck Coast of the Southern Ocean on the leg from Perth to Melbourne. They were told of weekly reports documenting lost lives and smashed and sunken vessels all common knowledge to sailors. *The Newcastle* was sturdy and steel-hulled but that was no guarantee.

People, not the least Harriet and Alice, were well rugged up on this cold, white day, a few weeks short of Christmas.

"You'll toast us all on Christmas Day won't you, my dears?" cried George as they made their way up the gangplank.

"And you to us, dear brother," called Harriet, but her voice was carried away on the wind.

So much excitement as people bade their last farewells, called and shouted to those loved ones that they may never see again. Flowers and handkerchiefs were tossed to those below but whisked away by the wind, never reaching their destination. From the passenger deck the two women squeezed a place on the rails to wave to George. He was hard to find in the masses below. The gangways were hauled up and at last Harriet could pick him out, a singular man, moustached with sideburns and a strained look on his face, but smiling as best he could and waving furiously. Harriet felt her throat tighten. My big brother. No one to watch out for me now, my Georgie. The boat foghorn blasted a mournful wail. Three times, like a cry for help from a prehistoric creature. As if she could read her thoughts, Alice snuggled close to Harriet, her fur muffler drawn up around her face.

"Say goodbye to the cold, my dear Plum."

Harriet waved frantically to George blowing him kisses. "Kisses for Marmie," she called as she blinked back some tears. Alice on the other hand was excited and definitely not crying. The gulls still wheeled above and called their farewell. Harriet's gaze followed their flight and softly she whispered to them.

"Farewell cousins."

CHAPTER 10

Arriving

MELBOURNE, AUSTRALIA, 1876

T hey departed England on 6 December 1875 and they set down their luggage in the Port of Melbourne on 26 March 1876. They survived a trip that took three months on the boat, two of which they could have happily done without. The crossings were rough and the accommodations were pretty much the same.

The Victoria inward passenger lists 1839–1923 stated that Alice Caroline Moon, age 25 (she was really 20), was born in England in 1851 (really 1855). Harriet was listed as Miss Emily Howell (Harriet Rowell). The category was listed as travel and migration. They probably increased their ages to avoid any questions about their plans or why they travelled together.

The weather on that March day at the Port of Melbourne, then called Sandridge, was wild and blustery, a day of puffy white clouds and sunshine with the temperature a mild 55 degrees Fahrenheit. A brusque autumn day in Melbourne. The ship's passengers took hours to disembark, all seeking assurances for the collection of their luggage from their porters, all in trepidation that once on land they wouldn't know what to do and be at the mercy of louts and pickpockets. Probably all true but Harriet and Alice were not going to harbour thoughts such as these. They'd had months to prepare for this moment. The voyage had been long and often arduous but the exotic nature of the ports at which they had stopped had compensated for any seasickness or other discomfort they may have suffered. They were adventurers after all, travellers of the world! At last it was their turn to descend the gangway and clinging to their bonnets against the gusts of wind and glad of their sturdy shoes on the swaying timber gangway, they descended, down into the thronging crowds below who were still waving and shouting to the new arrivals.

"It's glorious!" screamed Alice as she danced in front of Harriet and turned back to give her a joyful embrace.

"Keep moving along there, ladies," growled the attendant on the deck. Sailors and other passengers regarded them with either dismay or amusement. When Alice set foot on *terra firma* she let out another delighted shriek.

"We've landed! I want to see a kangaroo! And a bushranger!"

"There's plenty a' them out d'ere, ma'am. You best watch out for Captain Starlight!"

"Heavens, Plum! Did you hear that! Captain Starlight!" Alice shrieked with delight.

One very snooty couple, who had felt nothing but embarrassment the whole voyage from these two outrageous 'disgraces to their sex', disembarked behind the pair with loud, derogatory comments and shocked glances. As the luggage was stacked on the quayside, numbered in deck order, Harriet and Alice waited to claim their trunks alongside the disgruntled couple. As the woman pushed Harriet aside to get to her trunk, a large, cheeky gull landed on that very trunk and caught Harriet's gaze, giving her the 'sideways eye'.

"Well cousin, you know me then?" whispered Harriet with

a secret smile and the gull shrieked, lifting itself off the lady's trunk, leaving behind a little gooey message of endearment on its leather surface.

"Oh, dear me, what a rude welcome!" cried Harriet, blushing for the appalled owner.

"I think I'm going to like it here!" laughed Alice. The disgruntled couple stared in dismay at the large gift from above, slowly dribbling down the leather.

Leaving Harriet to guard their trunks, Alice was already on the move enquiring after transport to the city of Melbourne. She was pleased to find out that there was a rail line all the way from Sandridge to the city and she purchased tickets for them. It took a few hours to take their leave of the port and get settled into their appointed carriage which quickly became crowded with an entire family, newly arrived like them. Pale and exhausted, the mother, who was obviously with child, clutched her two skinny young boys of about six and eight to her swollen stomach and squashed herself up against her husband, Mr Bill Grimshaw, who was a farrier and openly shared that he had sold up his business in Shropshire and put all his eggs in one basket, hoping for a new and better life for his family. They were all squeezed in beside and between Alice and Harriet whose spirits were high, so thrilled were they with the rawness of it all, the wide-open spaces, the huge sky, the strange smells of eucalyptus, the brown colours of the vegetation and the cries of different birds that they would not have minded if they were forced to sit on each other's laps. Entranced, they all watched a wild flock of white cockatoos rise from the treetops, like messy, screeching clouds. Screaming parrots, just flashes of red and bright blue swooped through the air but as the train rocked along and the rising shape of Melbourne came into focus, they both had private moments of panic! Where will we live? How will we survive?

Then they caught each other's eye and burst out laughing for they knew they were having the very same thoughts. Over the heads of the two lads beside them, they clasped fists in a salute which ended in a deep embrace and laughter much to the embarrassment of farrier Bill and his missus, but not the boys who innocently delighted in sharing their joy. The good wife was bearing up well despite the discomforts of her pregnancy, her demanding children and the noise of the train and other passengers.

They emerged from Spencer Street Station into the crowded hustle and bustle of Melbourne city. It was in the Australian Hotel in Spencer Street where they were to first lay their heads. Bill Grimshaw's large family could not be accommodated there and most probably it was out of their price range. They were last seen bundled into a cab which took them back over the bridge to another hotel on the south side of the river. Alice had watched with dismay as the poor woman, a look of lost dreams on her face and clutching the youngest boy on her hip, had to wade through a muddy path to gain entry to the cab. I'm blessed not to have children, Alice reminded herself.

Melbourne, like Australia, was young, raw, rough, and wide open. Its laws were British and man-made. Perhaps Alice and Harriet had not expected the level of development that greeted them. Tram-trolleys were pulled by horses, streets were wide and unsealed and generally traffic was anarchic. Some houses were huge while others were workers' cottages. Hotels did a roaring trade alongside the mad building frenzy of banks, mutual societies, civic buildings and department stores; commercial wagons mucked in with hansom cabs, sulkies and broughams as people on foot and barrow boys vied for space on the muddy, always dusty sidewalks, except that they found in most parts of the central city of Melbourne that sidewalks were paved. They discovered that the majority of the buildings were Victorian in splendour, benefitting no doubt from the recent gold rush and influx of foreign capital. Everywhere they turned, there were horses, horses, horses and everything that went with them – stables, drinking troughs, hay and manure.

Smoke, gas, poor lighting, animal manure and raw sewerage made it a mad place for women to be wearing four layers of underwear including corsets, bustles, iron hoops, wicker cages, floor-length skirts, blouse, jacket, cape, high-heeled boots and ridiculously oversized hats. Harriet, in lieu of corsets, claimed the right to wear whatever hat she chose, usually much to the distaste of Alice who preferred to be hatless.

Their first weeks living in the hotel allowed them to get to know the simple grid layout of Melbourne. Harriet immediately obtained a copy of the Melbourne daily paper, *The Argus*. Both she and Alice were keen to familiarise themselves with the doings of Melbourne, its politics and its cultural offerings. They later spent many hours wandering through the elegant and generously proportioned streets of Melbourne. Such a change from the narrow lanes and thoroughfares of Brighton. They gazed into the ornate Bijou Theatre and, right beside it, the Opera House in Bourke Street. They visited the Melbourne Town Hall and booked tickets for an orchestral concert. But really their immediate concern was to find accommodation of their own and to move out of the Australian Hotel which had been recommended to them by a fellow passenger on the voyage, a man returning to Melbourne whose own experience of the hotel seemed a reliable basis on which to stay there. It had proved to be clean and safe although they found Spencer Street to be rather a wild place and had not ventured out at night at all. The main modes of transport were horse-drawn trolley cars or private hansom cabs. Harriet was loathe to spend money whereas

Alice, who had never had to even think about money, was more careless and *laissez-faire* with her pounds. Prices seemed to be much higher than Brighton and Harriet complained a lot.

"We are so far away Plum, it's only natural that all these things may have to come from England – and therefore we pay." Alice ordered another coffee and Harriet sat tight-lipped.

CHAPTER 11

A Home

CARLTON, 1876

Through an agency and for a reasonable rent they found a house – 158 Elgin Street, Carlton.[7] It still stands today, a small, single storey, single-fronted brick cottage, the middle one in a row of three and one block from Lygon Street, a main thoroughfare which provided a trolley bus to the centre of the city. Carlton was a working-class suburb situated a mile north of the Melbourne Town Hall boasting many hotels, or public houses – 'pubs' as they were known.

Both women noticed the difference between the behaviour of the male clientele compared to home. The men often held drunken abusive brawls on the footpaths, shouting and punching wildly at each other. This drunkenness could lead to men being run over by carriages as they swayed across streets, oblivious to traffic. They witnessed one such event in nearby Lygon Street, while shopping at two in the afternoon. "How can they be drunk at this hour of the day?" they wondered. A gentleman heard the remark and added as he passed, "Dear Ladies, they are never sober."

It wasn't only men who suffered loss of limb in street accidents, women too and oftimes young barrow-boys and street urchins. Although Harriet and Alice never went out at night, they did notice the street gangs, or larrikins as they were called, lounging about the pubs or bakeries, demanding favours from passers-by.

It didn't take long for their lives to settle into some sort of pattern. They attended church on Sundays, usually taking the trolley bus into the city to St Paul's parish church on the corner of Swanston and Flinders Streets and then enjoying a coffee at the Coffee Palace, or simply walking around in the church grounds and soaking up the sunshine.

Harriet soon found herself at a loose end, but Alice lost no time in placing an advertisement in the local gazette advertising her skills as a teacher of art. Two people had called and left their cards and booked in their daughters. Alice converted the small front room of the terrace house into her studio and teaching room. She cleaned the pine floorboards and lacquered them. Then she found a source of rush mats from enquiries made at the Coffee Palace in the city. The mats came from Africa and she had noticed them out the back of the building on her visit there. They looked wonderful and were almost at a giveaway price so that she didn't mind having to replace them when they became discoloured or dirty. Although Harriet enjoyed helping Alice and her new enterprise, she missed the exhilaration of physical exercise – she needed to swim! Upon their arrival that day at the Port of Melbourne she had had a chance to take in the extent of Port Phillip Bay and in betwixt the unloading and dealing with entry forms and signatures, with the shouting and shoving, the hustle and bustle of hundreds of people disembarking from *The Newcastle*, she had managed to take one long uninterrupted look down the bayside beaches towards a place, she was later informed, was named St Kilda.

A small sign on the wall of 158 Elgin Street announced Misses Moon & Rowell – Artists. Right now, the door opens and a young lady emerges onto the street with her middle-aged mother close behind, their bustled and floor-length dresses just managing to fit through the narrow front doorway. The lass is clutching her artist's satchel and is looking rather hot and numbed after her lesson, due no doubt to her tightly-laced corset causing her as much frustration as her limited talent. Alice appears behind them and politely farewells them, then closing the door, goes into the front room where the easel is set up, scowls and swears as she proceeds to dismantle the frame and pack it away. "My God, any more of this and I will retire to the madhouse."

There was the sound of a key in the lock and Harriet swirled in, "Did I just pass Miss Barr-Smith with her ignorant mother in tow?"

"The Miss-*I-have-no-imagination*-Barr-Smith, if you don't mind!"

"Stop doing that and get your swimming costume, my love. We're off to St. Kilda!"

CHAPTER 12

Swimming

ST KILDA, 1876

Alice, glad to get out of the house, was happy to accompany Harriet anywhere. Armed with their swimming costumes and drying sheets packed into a hold-all, they were ready to attempt the waters of the Southern Ocean which fed the bay. On the train to Sandridge, Harriet could barely contain her excitement.

"This is the day I've been waiting for, my dear! I can sink into the seawaters of the bay or attempt an entry into one of the few bathing baths said to lie along the St Kilda foreshore."

Alice would have preferred to spend her free time venturing into the city to visit the State Library and Museum or to attend lectures at the Assembly Hall and later to enjoy coffee in the Coffee Palace. She was not dependent on Harriet to accompany her, neither did she ever hesitate to venture out alone. In fact she saw it as her citizen's right in this new environment. Despite her personal refutation of class and social mores she had found Melbourne at times to be even worse than Brighton; those of the upper classes were arrogant and flaunted their wealth.

"Which reveals them to have had very poor and humble beginnings, my dear," pronounced Harriet after one particularly rude encounter in the queue at the State Art Gallery ticket box. A notice on the wall of Hegarty's Railway Baths, St Kilda:

> In consequence of the proximity of the Esplanade and the houses bordering on the same, gentlemen using these baths are particularly requested not to unnecessarily expose themselves. Instructions have been given to the police to take action against any persons who may offend in this way.

Harriet and Alice read it with amusement. Two men waltzed past them on their way into the baths.

"Hope you've got your costumes, gentlemen!" quizzed Alice, wickedly.

"Why don't you peep through the fence and find out, Missie," challenged the bewhiskered would-be aquatic genius.

"Oh, there's *little* of interest to us in there, sir," laughed Alice, indicating the man's trousers or the baths – probably both.

The two chums never got her double entendre, laughing and punching each other, sparring even as they went through the turnstile.

"You do insist on baiting men, don't you, Miss Moon? It will certainly get you into trouble one of these days."

Harriet was covering her anger. Alice on the other hand was snorting in delight at the pathetic masculine display put on for their benefit.

They continued walking along the foreshore until they reached their destination: Kenney's Ladies' Baths.[8] They paid and entered. Only a few women were in the water, none were actually swimming, rather they were just flopping about. Alice was content to watch Harriet take to the waves. Unhesitatingly, Harriet dived in and began breaststroking cleanly through the seas. Once she started swimming she could not stop, so exhilarated and charged was she. Gradually everyone's attention was turned on her, including a certain Mrs Kenney. She beckoned a young boy to her.

"Go get your father, be quick about it." She returned her gaze to the fast-stroking Harriet.

Captain Kenney was a short, suntanned, athletic man who had an eye for the melodramatic and always dressed like a sea captain, even though he had never had a proper commission, except for the hulk of the sunken boat that had given his bathing ship baths its name. He watched Harriet's performance with interest and greeted her as she finally stepped out of the water. They made a deal. He would pay Harriet to give swimming lessons to ladies and their children, and in return also with a small payment, he would showcase her talents in the forthcoming swimming carnivals that he planned for the summer. He also agreed to pay for advertising her classes in *The Argus*.

The sea change had occurred. Harriet and Alice celebrated with ice creams on the St Kilda pier and a donkey ride across the sand. Alice, true to form and to the tourists' horror, sat astride the donkey hitching up her skirts to expose her long bare legs while digging her heels into its tough little hide.

∞

It is some months later. At home, Alice reads *The Argus* aloud to Harriet.

"Listen to this, Plum. The New South Wales parliament has rejected a bill to allow women the right to own property on the grounds 'that it would undermine the God-founded institution of matrimony.' A similar law was easily passed in England in 1870! Apparently, they passed it here too, in Victoria. Thank heavens we don't live in Sydney. Och! Listen, this man says the legislation would 'debase women morally, converting them into the position of bread-getter, instead of, as heretofore she had been, the crown of her husband …' His crown! Ha."

She continued to read aloud, "'The legislation made a wife independent of her husband and therefore, it would be fatal to her happiness'. He asked what would become of a family reared to believe that the mother was the mistress of the house, rather than the father, master? 'It would be destroying the most valuable thing God ever created.' As to holding life insurance policies on their husbands, he says that would be the cause of crime."

"Ha. Of course. They all would murder their husbands and collect the money. I find the idea of marriage utterly appalling," continued Alice.

"We agree on that, my love."

Alice and Harriet had enough experience – just being women – to know what they were up against. Women were considered – and indeed trained – to be the sexual property of men and were kept in terrible ignorance of their own internal organs and their bodily functions. Euphemisms for women's parts hid their reality and deliberately contributed to the general total ignorance of female sex organs and their reproductive purpose. Sex education was pleaded for by many female educators. Masturbation, named 'self-abuse', was scientifically proven to lead to insanity. It was believed that each stage of the female reproductive cycle could be mentally unbalancing – puberty, pregnancy, post-parturition, lactation, uterine and ovarian disorders – until finally she reached menopause which was the last nail in her coffin! No wonder men did not want women to study medicine and become doctors whence they would find out their own truths. The times demanded that nude statues be draped, that men were not allowed to witness women in swimming competitions, that if a woman rode a bicycle it would unsex her. Perhaps it was in this age that the incredible 'disappearing act' of the male sex organ – promoting the 'all-powerful mysterious penis' – began. The Church, whose doctrines and edicts were born from the minds of men, had to accept that its long-held powerful sway over woman had to be shared with the State. The influx of secular laws during the eighteenth and nineteenth centuries, grounding the power of the judiciary and the parliament firmly in the male corner, proved to be a firewall to women's rights. Those rights first of all embraced the necessary recognition of their humanity, that the human race was not of one sex – the male – but of an equal duality. There is a correlation with the masculine view of science – based on the search for the single building block of the universe – debunked today with the discovery of quantum theory.

As that society evolved it became clear that there were masculine ideals for one class of women only and the rest – the 'lower classes' – were ignored. If a woman married she gave up all independence; she could not sign a contract or own property. Divorce meant she forfeited all rights to her children. Women and their children were bound, in their bodies, minds and souls, by both religious and patriarchal laws. Being bound to men and their system and kept in a perpetual state of ignorance and fear concerning the function of their bodies, they became so exhausted from continuous childbearing that they had little time or energy to battle for their rights, let alone understand the extent to which those limited rights existed.

So many families were devastated when young mothers, in huge numbers, succumbed to badly executed backyard abortions. Birth was just as dangerous in the lying-in hospitals where male doctors, who had replaced female midwives, would move from a disease-ridden patient straight to a birthing woman with no knowledge about the transition of germs and thus creating the horror of puerperal fever. In nineteenth-century England, women screamed and begged not to be taken to lying-in hospitals for fear of the death that lay within. At one stage they were burying two women to a coffin to hide the numbers of fatalities.[9]

Any creative energy women may have had, had been sapped by the demands of a society that had double standards. Some women managed to produce creative works, other than children, but usually only if they were of independent means and lived a life of spinsterhood. When both the Church and State turned a woman into less than a slave (a slave at least could be granted freedom), many women opted to stay outside the system altogether. Harriet Dick and Alice Moon rejected both men and marriage. Their story reveals a large undocumented historical undercurrent of the lives of women who lived outside the mainstream of culturally acceptable family life.

CHAPTER 13

Christmas Dinner

CARLTON, 1876

At the end of the first year of their arrival, they were still living at 158 Elgin Street, Carlton. A lot of traffic passed the front and it was really too noisy for them but they knew it was temporary until they found something quieter and more permanent. Alice paid the rent.

Alice poured brandy over a steaming plum pudding. She set a match to the brandy and carried the flaming pudding from the kitchen to the dining room and set it upon the damask tablecloth where the remains of a traditional Christmas lunch were in evidence. Harriet, flushed not only with wine but also because of the unbearable temperature in the room, applauded the pudding. The windows were open. A hot north wind blew into the room, the curtains billowed. Outside the magpies were warbling and blowflies were buzzing, thudding into the wire screen.

"Thanks be, we have the wire screenings at last. Listen to those awful creatures."

"I'll get the brandy butter – I do hope it is hard, we'll have to eat it really quickly or it'll melt. The ice chest doesn't stand a chance in this heat."

"Have we got cream?"

"Yes Plum, we've got everything."

Alice returned, balancing along her arm the cream jug, the brandy sauce jug and the brandy butter in a dish.

"You would have made a wonderful waitress."

"Don't worry, I may still have to. Although I'd rather own a tearoom than serve in one."

"If you owned it, you'd be serving all day long."

"That's probably true. Would you cut it now? The flame is out."

Harriet cut the pudding and served out two portions. After lavishly pouring cream and brandy sauce and scooping brandy butter on her plate, she tucked in and bit hard.

"Oh, ouch, very nice! I have already found a florin! Bravo. How many did you put in?"

"Only one."

"And it's mine! Aha!"

Alice helped herself to her pudding. She spooned and saw something silver, half sticking out. She cut across a bit more to make sure she had the trophy.

"Aha! The wedding ring!" She held the small, silver wedding ring up. "A ring symbolises so many other more important things."

Harriet poured more wine and made a toast. "To our first Christmas in the madness of this hot, hot wilderness called Melbourne!"

"And may we have many more." Alice drank deeply, not only flushed from the heat of the day, but also from the heat of the kitchen where she had cooked the all-but-demolished small roast goose.

"I wonder how Father is. They'll be eating hot goose and plum pudding in the middle of the snow. How sensible!"

"Not yet, they won't. They're still asleep, snuggled in bed. Ah the cold, cold nights of Christmas Eve. I never realised how precious they were."

"This ritual makes no sense at all, does it? We should be indulging in cold compote of fruit and slices of smoked ham with delicious mustard, but here we are sweating over a steaming pudding! Would you like a brandy, Plum? If there's any left over?"

Harriet rose quickly. "Yes, my love, I'd love a brandy and there is, I believe, at least half a bottle untouched."

Harriet returned from the kitchen with the brandy and placed it on the table. She took two glasses, not brandy balloons for they had not yet purchased such luxury items, and poured a measure into each. She whistled, 'O Come, All Ye Faithful'. Alice unbuttoned her blouse – neither women wore corsets, just camisoles – and fanned herself with a silk Chinese fan. Harriet gazed at her, admiring her beautiful glowing, now lightly tanned skin. Standing close behind her, she dipped her finger into her brandy and leaning in, slid it across the rise of Alice's breast leaving a snail trail of brandy on her skin revealed above her camisole. She dipped again and traced a line from one shoulder to her cleavage and from the other shoulder to her cleavage. Alice arched her back.

"Mmm, that is so cooling."

"Versatile brandy."

CHAPTER 14

The Challenge

ST KILDA, 1877[10]

Captain Kenney's Bathing Ship Baths:
Ladies' and Gentlemen's rules of bathing, etc. No mixed bathing.
All men must wear costumes suitable for modesty.

It is a sunny Saturday in St Kilda. Photos of the period show The Esplanade at the end of Fitzroy Street with very few houses, wide streets, cows grazing in paddocks and a trolley line. An event is underway. Patrons swarm the promenade desperate to join the queue and pay their entrance fee. There are groups of excited women, some young, some middle-aged. It is a festive occasion. A band is playing popular tunes of the day. On the foreshore and the promenade vendors are selling lemonade and ices. A spruiker is at the ticket booth. He is gaily attired in boater and blazer – it is, in fact, Captain William Kenney himself. There's no way he could find another to do a better job of it! Kenney spruiks:

This will be the last of two great matches between the famous lady swimmer from England, Miss Elphinstone Dick and our very own champion of the waterways, Jack McGonigal. See the superior, masculine strength of McGonigal matched by the feminine wiles of Miss Dick. Each has vowed to beat the other! A test of physical endurance such as you will never see again, ladies and gentlemen!

Come along now, you misses down there. Come along and cheer the lady on. Miss Dick won the first match by a technicality, a *technicality*, gentlemen, have you ever heard of such a thing! This time there'll be no technicalities! They'll swim 'til they drop!

The crowds were enormous. They pushed their way out along the pier walkway that Kenney had recently built for the public's convenience, rather than having to get the push-me pull-me boat. From all walks of life, they swarmed along the unsteady decking. Listen to the conversations, like this one between May and Lottie, two shop assistants from Collingwood who had made the trip by trolley and train.

"Lottie! Do 'urry up. There'll be no room left if you don't 'urry up!"

"I feel so nervous, you don't think the men will be naked do you, May?"

"Don't be daft, they'll have fig leaves pasted on!"

"Ooh May, you've a tongue on you!"

There are far more men than women in the crowd, mostly young lads, many sporting the attire of the larrikin who are no doubt out for blood. They have come because of the last match, held back in December of 1876, when McGonigal was beaten by this Miss Dick even though there had been a protest. She had claimed McGonigal had cheated and there had been an uproar when Captain Kenney awarded her the match. The men are out for revenge and to see 'fair play' done. Enough that a woman was even daring to swim, let alone against a man! It had been said that Kenney had only allowed the two of them to compete in the match, refusing any other competitors a space.

"He's set this up right sure," complained one larrikin to his mate.

"Well it's paid off chum, look at the money rolling in here!"

A well-dressed group of matrons were walking into the bathing enclosure, speaking excitedly as they carefully squeezed their way through the crowds, to secure a position on the railings right at the edge of the viewing platforms that surround the water. In the middle of the water at the moment was the greasy pole and the competition was in full swing. Young men trying to walk the pole, crawl the pole, creating an enormously entertaining amusement for the crowded galleries calling encouragements.

"Why, Frances, there's even more folk here this time than the last!"

"Oh, I do wish I'd seen it! Elizabeth, where did he actually get out of the water?"

"Well, my dears, do you see that buoy down there? He just got out of the water and walked around that buoy, and of course she filed a complaint – that he had interrupted his swim ..."

"But Elizabeth, he also changed his stroke!"

"My dear Frances, yes certainly he did, halfway through, but Miss Dick was supremely constant!"

"That's right, Mary."

Frances was breathless with excitement, turning each way to listen to her two friends on either side describe the swimming match that she had missed. "And so, what did she do?"

Elizabeth jumped in before Mary could answer her. "She complained of course! And would not be pushed aside. And they upheld her protest! She was pronounced the winner!"

"Oh, look my dears! There she is! I do declare look, look, over there with Captain Kenney himself and the youngest Kenney boy."

"He's going to be a champion, I'll wager." Elizabeth knowingly replied.

"You'll wager, Lizzie? I'm glad your Harold is not here to

listen to that sort of talk!"

"Poosht! Whilst we are here we can be whoever we want, Mary!"

Mary blushed, embarrassed, but Frances chuckled. There was no more time for chat for all eyes were on Harriet Elphinstone Dick who had emerged onto one of the platforms, robed and smiling and talking to Captain Kenney and a few other women, one of whom was Alice, as always dressed in white, her petite figure draped almost in the roman style.

"Oh, she is very striking looking," observed Frances.

"Quite magnificent really and not at all afraid of showing herself like this, quite revealed!"

"Such a strong body, but most feminine really. I feel my stays digging into me in a most painful way right now."

"You need a larger size, my dear. At our age we cannot afford to become slack."

Over to their left stand young May and Lottie, their eyes glued to the arrival of Harriet.

"Is that 'er, Lottie?"

"I s'pose it must be. She's not that tall, is she?"

"Naoo. I'd 'ave thought she would need to be more tall like – for the water. Oo's that lady in the white dress? She don't look like she's wearin' any stays?"

"Niver she is, I swear. I wonder 'ow she stands upright?"

Harriet stood erect and supple. She removed her cloak, handing it to Alice and flexed and stretched her arms and swung them around. Then she touched her toes and massaged each leg, oblivious of the crowd and the jeering that was now coming at her from all angles. Men jeering about her swimming attire, about her legs, her arms, her ability to cheat and her very sex. No matter how layered her swimming costume it cannot hide her magnificent build.

A young man, Nigel nudges his chum, Pike, another young blood.

"The Amazon's return, eh Pike?"

"My dear Nigel, she's positively slab-sided!"

"Thank god I forbade Polly from coming to this! The poor girl would've fainted at the sight of that! God keep our women corseted!"

"And closeted!"

He leant forward shouting loudly, "Bring on our man and let's have done with it!"

"Hear, hear," came a chorus of robust male voices. More shouting and whistles and cheering. The women started to timidly clap and exclaim, "Hoorah!" as Harriet walked forward in her bathing costume. Most of them had never seen a woman's bathing costume, let alone a woman wearing one so boldly, nor had most of them ever seen a costumed man either. Their reactions went from wide-eyed wonder, to embarrassment, giggling and shame.

Nigel commented on the young lasses who were cheering a little more boldly now. "You'd wonder what they're all excited about! Really!"

But one elderly gentleman standing behind them was happy to take them to task. "You young bloods ought to appreciate the sight, we never had anything so fine to look at when I was a young 'un."

Pike took Nigel under his elbow and shifted him away. "Poor old bugger probably still fancies Lady Godiva on her bloody horse!"

The cheering settled down as Captain Kenney got up to speak through his megaphone. The band ceased playing and a hush fell over the expectant crowd.

"Ladiees and Gennellmen! Captain Kenney's compliments to you all! At last we come to the highlight of this exciting

Swimming matches at St Kilda.
The Australasian Sketcher *with Pen and Pencil*
(Melbourne, Vic.: 1873-1889), Saturday 11 May 1878, page 17.

Saturday's matches and as promised it will commence at approximately a quarter to three. The famous lady swimmer and teacher of the fine art of swimming, Miss Elphinstone Dick, there she is ladiees and gennellmen, will compete in the return match against her rival, Mr McGonigal. Today they will be competing for this magnificent silver cup valued at ten guineas! Yes!"

The crowd applauded as he held up the cup.

"Ladiees and Gennellmen! This is a match that seemed to be left unresolved in their last meeting, a match that promises once and forever to lay to rest the very vexing question of man's supremacy over woman in the sea. These two champions of the sexes shall battle it out in the water. The best swimmer over two miles, *two miles* ladies and gentlemen! And there shall be no leaving of the water, no changing of the strokes, and no physical combat in the briny!"

That brought a big laugh and the cheers rose again as impatience hit the crowd. Young men who continually eyed the ladies in the crowd, especially those who appeared to be unaccompanied by a male, shouted and roughly jostled each other, showing off before any young ladies who would raise their eyes to them. Not many did.

Harriet's face was calm and her mouth set. She breathed regularly through her nostrils allowing each breath to expand her chest. Her clear eyes narrowed as she gauged the length of the baths. Inhaling deeply down to her stomach, her diaphragm working rhythmically, her hands flexing and her feet stretching as she rose up onto her toes and down again. Alice's hand was on her back.

"Remember me," she whispered, "I'll be here, waiting."

"Take your places!" shouted Kenney into the megaphone.

McGonigal was there with two supporters, one who was rubbing his shoulders while the other looked with venom and a touch of pity at Harriet and Alice.

"Miss Elphinstone Dick!" announced Kenney.

The crowd cheered, many booed, some even yelled, "Bloody disgrace to womanhood!" but the young women cheered and clapped, much to the chagrin of their male chaperones.

"McGonigal!" shouted Kenney.

Loud roars of encouragement from the stronger male voices in the crowd. Aggressive cheering and hooting in favour of McGonigal.

"No contest!"

"Watch out, lady!"

"It's a man's sport!"

"On your line there. At the count of three you will begin."

Harriet was a picture of calm determination, McGonigal more like a bull at the gate.

"Best keep out of my way, Lady!" he whispered harshly to her.
"One …"

A hush fell on the crowd.

"Two …"

The young women in the crowd all held their breath.

"Three!"

Harriet was like a tiger leaping for its prey. They both hit the water. McGonigal thrashed away like a mad man. He led out across the water, his hands beating the surface as if to hurt it, as if to show who was its master. Harriet embraced the water becoming at one with it, her smooth breaststroke hardly making a ripple. All the surface movement was due to McGonigal's thrashing display. The crowds cheered enthusiastically. At this point, none of them realised the race would go on for three and a half hours and that their enthusiasm would eventually wane!

The swimmers reached the first buoy with Harriet trailing McGonigal by a few feet. She turned at the buoy and saw Alice's figure on her horizon. Alice, her angel in white. McGonigal's face in and out of the water, he pummelled the sea as if it was his enemy. Whereas Harriet belonged to it, she stroked it and her pace was even and her breaststroke action continued to calmly cut a gentle swathe through the waves that were of McGonigal's making. Time passed slowly as the crowd's energy slackened; the women were hot and shaded their faces, the men leant disconsolately, every now and then energising themselves to shout encouragement. The clock tower on the ship's structure showed it was now two hours and they were still swimming.

Captain Kenney kept up a magnificent commentary for the whole time, whipping up the crowd's enthusiasm when he felt it waning. The band had ceased playing their encouraging ditties. They'd had enough. McGonigal had swum nearly two miles. Miss Dick had almost done one and three quarter. McGonigal was leading. Some of the crowd had dispersed, but most of the ladies who had not had to obey their bored husbands and leave, were still enthusiastic.

"She's like a fish, Mary. I've never seen anything like it."

"She must be so tired by now, Frances. I know I am."

Elizabeth pronounced quite loudly, "McGonigal looks like the tired one. Have you noticed him having those rests? She just doesn't stop, but he does. Look, there now, look he's stopped again!"

Indeed McGonigal was treading water, looking round for Harriet, trying to work out where she was. He was near exhaustion. The clock showed nearly a quarter past six. A murmur rose from the crowd. Something was wrong in the water. Alice's eyes followed Harriet. McGonigal's trainer was heard to whisper harshly to a chum, "Gawdstrewth! What's happenin' to him now?"

The trouble in the water belonged to McGonigal. He was coughing, having trouble breathing. Someone tossed a life buoy into the water. His trainer was preparing to go to his aid. Two men eventually entered the water to come to his rescue and he was pulled from the water to collapse on the boards where a doctor was waiting to help resuscitate him. Alice's eyes were fixed on Harriet.

"Come on my love, come on, Plum, this race is yours now!"

Harriet swam evenly through the water, down to the marker buoy turned and came back to the starting point, another 240 yards. Calmly and strongly she came on to the cheering of the slightly hysterical women in the crowd, all of whom had lost any sense of decorum. The majority of males were disgusted, their egos destroyed, their eyes full of disbelief.

Harriet emerged from the water onto the boards unaided and unpuffed. Alice embraced Harriet, not minding that her gown was soaked through by Harriet's dripping costume. With a wave and a victory handclasp above her head, Harriet acknowledged the cheering of the crowd and the 'bravos' of the women. Wrapping the robe tenderly around Harriet's shoulders, their eyes met.

"My love," said Harriet, "I never lost sight of you."

Women rushed to descend the steps and crowd around her. Our well-mannered trio of matrons pushed and thrust their way into her presence, Frances in her haste and in a most unladylike fashion nearly tripping up her friend, Mary. A few newspaper journalists crowded in upon the Lady Swimmer alongside a few men also keen to shake her hand. It was her victory. Harriet stepped up to Captain Kenney. The crowd cheered. Captain Kenney seized the megaphone and called for calm.

"Ladiees and gennellmen! May I have your attention please! The race is over, the race is won, I do declare, by Miss Dick, who remained swimming for the greater time. Mr McGonigal will be all right. Have no fear, he is but temporarily unconscious. Miss Elphinstone Dick has proved beyond doubt her great ability in the water, her greatest ever long-distance swim. No other woman has ever equalled such a feat as you have seen here today at Captain Kenney's Bathing Ship Baths!"

The crowd roared and Kenney milked it for all he could. His wife handed him the silver cup.

"Congratulations Miss Dick! This silver cup is now yours! And remember ladies – Miss Dick teaches swimming at Captain Kenney's Baths!"

Pike of course was disgusted at the announcement.

"Goddammit man, McGonigal swam much further."

"Absolutely, Pike," agreed Nigel, blowing his nose and adjusting his boater, "who was measuring that, eh?"

But the elderly gentlemen had found them again and happily had the last word. "The only thing they're measuring him for now, old chums, is a coffin."

Exhausted and jubilant, Harriet sat at last in the changing room where a cup of hot tea was put into her hands.

"You'll be famous now, Plum," Alice said as she bent to massage her cold legs to bring the warmth back into her limbs.

"My Love," and she placed the teacup down, "I need a whiskey!"

That was January 1877. The following year, 1878, Harriet remained teaching at Kenney's Baths having given up encouraging Alice to increase her prowess in the water. Alice was not a swimmer. Frustrated, her mind turned to other pursuits, the teaching of art to untalented young women no longer one of them. Any plans were interrupted by the arrival of a postal clerk at 158 Elgin Street.

"There's a telegram for you my love," said Harriet, arriving back home from teaching at St Kilda. "I intercepted it at the door." Alice read the telegram, dated April 1878. It was from her half-sister, Myra.

"Oh Plum, Pa is not well. Myra feels I should come back while there is still time …"

"Then we shall both return. I shall book a passage straight away. But Alice, our future is here, we both know that."

"Yes, yes. I will find my place in that future somehow, Plum."

"I know you will, my love."

"And when we return we will burn these dreadful easels," added Alice triumphantly.

"But what will we do? My teaching swimming won't keep us both alive."

"Plum, my love," replied Alice with a smile, "we will open a ladies' gymnasium! You have the training for all that and I have the money! I would love to get hold of these young women and rip their corsets from their bodies!"

It's good to be reminded at this point in the story that disease and illness were numerous, but women suffered from a special fatigue of body and mind. They were sick from having their internal organs crushed by wicked corsets – a fashion invented by men and the Church not just to give women the tiniest waists in the world, but to convince them of the inherent weakness of the female sex. Without these ghastly cages they could not safely stand upright, remaining feeble of both body and mind.

From their earliest teenage years, girls were crushed into shapes that defied nature. These contraptions of torture gave them curvature of the spine, internal organ failures, menstrual difficulties and breathing problems which contributed to them contracting tuberculosis and stomach diseases. Corsetry was made from iron stays, sometimes stitched with leather to make their cages 'supple' and to protect the bruising and ulcerated flesh caused by the iron which wore into flesh; sometimes the 'cages' were made from whalebones that should have been left inside the whale and, like their foremothers, those Chinese women of the lotus-hook feet, they suffered it all to make them acceptable to their male rulers:

> "… the head of every man is Christ; and the head of the woman is the man."
>
> —St Paul, Corinthians

Women and the general population were kept in terrible ignorance of their internal organs and their bodily functions. Biologically, they were considered the weaker sex and their destiny was stigmatised as purely physiological – they were there to provide the children for a patriarchal society that had put an imaginary womankind on its pedestal. In reality it was to get women out of the way.

CHAPTER 15

A Return Visit

ENGLAND, 1878–1879

Alice and Harriet returned home to England on 6 May 1878, sailing on the *Durham*.[11] They stayed in England until December of that year. Harriet used the time to study elementary physiology, anatomy and medical gymnastics under the celebrated Dr Bernard Roth (physician to the London Institution for the Treatment of Deformities), from whom she gained a Certificate of Competency. Henry Moon rallied a lot and even though he was not completely well, the arrival of Alice was a great relief to all the family until they very soon learnt that she in no way planned to stay. Australia was too exciting, and the women's movement there was way in advance of Britain and especially parochial Brighton.

Harriet, of course, fell into the beloved arms of Marmie who in her wisdom had already intuited that her daughter would be returning to the colonies and that perhaps this was the last time she would have with her. Sadly, she was right: Marmie died in March 1891, never to see her beloved daughter again. The months flew by in Brighton and they had barely enough time to renew old acquaintances before they were boarding The Assam en route to Melbourne via Point de Galle, Ceylon.

They arrived back in Melbourne in March 1879, loaded with all the appliances used in the treatment of curable deformities and with a plan that would secure their fame and destiny. Using funds from her father's gift, Alice would pay to open a Ladies' Gymnasium in Melbourne and three months later, on 30 June 1879, that is precisely what they did. Another three months later, Alice's father, Dr Henry Moon, passed away. He died on 7 October 1879 leaving Alice a large fortune, on top of the new gift he had already given her on their return visit. There was always going to be enough money to fund The Ladies' Gymnasium. Principal: Miss H. Elphinstone Dick. 'Rational Gymnastics' had arrived.

CHAPTER 16

The Ladies' Gymnasium

MELBOURNE, 1879

It is the thirtieth of June 1879. A neatly gilded sign on the wall inside number five of the Mutual Provident Society building in Collins Street West announces: "The Ladies' Gymnasium. Principal, Miss H. Elphinstone Dick." To the left of their rooms is J.M. Coote. Tea Importers, and to the right, Anderson & Marshall Importers & Shipping Agents.

Night. The opening celebration is winding down. It has been a simple affair and a roaring success. Harriet is very good at publicity! Weeks of renovation saw the installation of the gymnastic apparatus made by a Mr Turnbull of Harker Street, Fitzroy. The floor is covered with coconut matting, padded underneath so that besides being springy to the foot, any pupil who accidentally 'came to the ground' had little chance of being injured. The installation included wall ladders, climbing ropes, mats, an exercise 'horse', Indian clubs and dumbbells as well as the storage cupboards built to house them and a divided changing room which also stored first aid equipment. The pièce de resistance – a piano – took pride of place against the far wall. Harriet and

Alice gave a demonstration of club swinging and rope work to the accompaniment of their pianist, Mr Harcourt Lee, and also moved through a series of Ling exercises designed to show how the female body could be strengthened and maintained in good health. 'Violent gymnastic feats', however, did not form part of Harriet's scheme of physical instruction. She preferred a gradual development of the muscles which would induce her pupils, after they had undergone a course of instruction with her, to continue healthy exercises themselves.

"The love of exercise by which a country-bred girl is so strongly distinguished from her town-bred cousin arises from the habitual exertion which is incident to rural life, and if Miss Dick can instil similar tastes into her Melbourne pupils she will undoubtedly accomplish good work for the future mothers of Victoria. It is satisfactory to learn that Miss Dick has in establishing her gymnasium received strong encouragement from many of the leading ladies of the colony. Lady Bowen, before her departure from the colony, wrote expressing her interest in the undertaking and Mrs Moorhouse and Mrs Thornton have given their patronage to what the former lady recognises as 'a useful and valuable institution'. Among the deformities she is prepared to treat under her system (only, however, after consulting a medical man in order to ascertain whether the deformity arises from muscular contraction or weakness, and not from disease), are lateral and other curvatures of the spine and stiff and weak joints, contracted chest, high shoulders, infantile paralysis and other deformities that can be cured or benefited by movements."[12]

The response from those who attended the invitation-only opening night was sufficiently rapturous to almost guarantee that the gymnasium venture would be successful.

Everyone had departed and now they were alone. Alice played the piano while Harriet danced. They had drunk a lot of champagne and even now Alice was swigging at a bottle of ale. She belched openly amidst laughter and stopped playing and singing as, seductively, she swayed toward Harriet, who was poised like a panther waiting to pounce. Alice's dance and song was wonderfully provocative and erotic, evoking a fantasy of the seven veils with hand towels. They both ended up in a sweet embrace and much laughter.

"Now all we need are some clients," sang Alice.

"No," replied Harriet, her eyes narrowing, "first we need some patrons."

The first quarter began at the end of June 1879 and thereafter quarters coincided with those of private girls' schools from which many of their clients were to come.[13] Alice was a full partner right from the beginning, financing the whole enterprise. Apart from providing the gradual accumulation of equipment and upgrading of facilities, she was also an instructor. It wasn't long before they rented another space beside their own, a sure sign of the success of the gymnasium. Harriet set out to court the ladies in high places. Not only were these women wives of wealthy and respected men of the colony, but they were also well known for their benevolent activities and their work for women's rights.

Women's rights. A phrase that was new to the ears of men – and women. Along with the rise of the middle classes, changing property laws and financial independence for many, came the cry from women for equal rights and the vote. The loud voices of women signalled the beginning of the end of thousands of years of oppression by one half of humanity over the other.

Although Alice and Harriet were never deeply connected to the suffrage movement, they certainly were outspoken in the areas of women's rights over their own bodies and minds.

In Australia, the suffrage movement led the world with the women here receiving the vote many years before their American or English sisters. The women of Victoria began the Shilling Fund, raising money to build the Queen Victoria Hospital, the first hospital exclusively for women. In 1880, a year after the establishment of their gymnasium, some women were admitted to the University of Melbourne but not to the medical faculty. The names of Vida Goldstein, Alice Henry, and Dr Constance Stone, among others, raged from the mouths of men but were sung from the mouths of women. It was a time of huge change, pain, frustration and courage.

Using a few contacts, Harriet began her search by introducing her work into private girls' schools from whence, she knew, she would get her gymnasium clientele. She was very clever at selling the ancient Greek idea of, 'a healthy body means a healthy mind' to the headmasters and headmistresses, who, in general, were keen reformers and lovers of the 'Classics'. *Mens sana in corpore sano.*

The first class at the ladies' gymnasium began with eight girls. An hilarious but painful scene. The girls and their mothers had a lot of trouble coming to terms with the fact that the girls must first take off their corsets and change into the soft gym tunics and, horrors of horrors, the knickerbockers that Harriet had provided! The scene was poignant and evocative as the girls and their mothers had to confront their own flesh, in the same room. Harriet and Alice, to break the ice, demonstrated their own prowess with club swinging and gymnastic exercises on the bars and the ropes. They put on a terrific show, illustrating their display with little scenes that they acted out; scenes of danger or emergency where an athletic attitude could save a life.

Most of the girls were thrilled, but one broke down into tears and left in the arms of her mother never to return, and two others were so embarrassed by their own bodies that they sat and wept in the corner, but still insisted on remaining to watch the others. One mother refused to let her daughter participate at all. The daughter, disappointed but obedient, left quietly with her mother. As they retreated down the hallway Harriet caught up with them pointing out that, "There was once a brave and courageous young woman, who knew that in order for the new world to get better for everyone, she would have to break some of the laws of the old world to do it."

"Well, she probably met a bad end," replied the straight-backed mother, her tiny waist savagely corseted under layers of bustle, skirt, petticoats and undergarments and as if that wasn't enough weight, she was also struggling under an enormous contraption of stiff buckram and layers of lace upon her head which consisted of enough feathers to clothe a bird.

"On the contrary, dear madam. Today she is our Queen, Victoria."

"I am afraid of breaking laws, Miss Dick!"

"Do not be afraid," said Harriet, smiling and holding out her hand, "for I will break them for you!"

The woman turned slowly and came back along the hallway with her daughter, who was hiding a shy smile. It was this mother, Lady Clarke, who became Harriet's most generous patron and first adult client.

Very soon there were over one hundred pupils enrolled in the gymnasium. The young women and girls were generally delivered to the premises by their mothers, most of whom stayed to watch. Harriet's efforts to find patrons, something that was ever necessary in those days for accreditation, viability and recognition in any business, let alone a business set up by two women, had been very successful. Among her patrons were Lady Clarke, Lady Vernon and Lady Loch.[14]

A morning class in full swing. The girls were working with the Indian clubs, long-handled and bottom heavy so that when swung in rhythm, they helped to exercise the arms and torso, building up muscle in a gentle way. The students all wore the special uniforms of bloomer-styled pants and tunic tops designed by Harriet. They were allowed the usual undergarments of camisoles and singlets but all must take off corsets if they were wearing them – of which 95% were. Today we would gasp in horror at the sight of these steel stays and whalebone corsets, bound around these young developing bodies.

One of the 16-year-old pupils has fainted. Her name is Sarah. She's collapsed on the floor. The girls around her receive a terrible fright although this form of physical debilitation is not unknown to most of them. Harriet is immediately at her side, holding her head and fanning her face. There are no mothers observing at this particular session.

"Get her over to the window, quickly. Florence, hold her feet."

Florence was flushed. "She wouldn't take off her corsets, Miss Dick."

"I told her it'd make her sick," offered Gladys.

Alice arrived with the smelling salts. Harriet held it under Sarah's nose and wiped her forehead with a damp lavender-soaked cloth. "Sarah. Sarah. Come on, come on."

Sarah's eyes slowly opened. Her face had more colour now. Harriet attempted to undo Sarah's corset. Under her breath, "Dear Mother Mary, when will they ever learn?"

"Oh, Miss Dick! No, no don't, don't take it off, please!"

"You cannot possibly work in this gymnasium wearing this monstrous piece of artillery."

Sarah was visibly frightened. "My mother won't allow this, Miss Dick."

"I'll deal with your mother, Sarah. Now just do as I say."

"I don't want them to look at me."

She nodded toward the other five or six girls who were huddled in a group, avidly watching. Alice turned to them and directed them to come with her to the ropes and the bars on the opposite wall.

"Off we go girls. Back to the bars please – get your legs going – swinging from the hips. Sarah's all right now."

Harriet got Sarah up on her feet and walked her to the privacy of the change room to the left of the entrance.

"Now, let's take it off. Allow me to assist you, dear."

"Oh, Miss Dick, I can't walk without it."

"Don't be ridiculous, Sarah. Turn around."

Harriet helped her to take off her tunic, which, once off revealed the vicious corset, laced and hooked, pressing into her thin camisole and the young flesh beneath. Gently, Harriet undid the hooks at the back, already afraid of what its removal would reveal. She stood back, shocked but not surprised. The camisole was stained in patches where underneath open sores had developed into ulcers and where dressings had been applied but were wet with the discharge.

"How can you wear this? You must be in so much pain!"

"Mother says all women have pain. We all have to bear it." Sarah crossed her arms over her chest.

"Much as I admire your mother," said Harriet, as she dropped the camisole back over the girl's head, "and would not contradict her in front of you, I have to tell you that this pain is not necessary!" She flung the corset into the corner. Sarah was aghast, she ran to pick it up.

"Oh no, Miss Dick, I'll have to put it back on before mother gets here."

"You'll not put it on ever again!" Harriet closely inspected the girl's back, adjusting her posture, taking note of how her spine had a slight curvature, to the left. The skin under her armpits showed cruel marks from the stays. "You're 16, aren't you Sarah?"

"Yes, Miss Dick."

"Have you begun your periods?"

"Oh, Miss Dick!" Sarah blushed and started to cry.

"Please Sarah, we are women together here, you must feel safe to talk about this with me, I'm your teacher." Sarah's face was crimson. Her head was bowed and she couldn't speak. "It's your gift to have this. It's the gift of life for all women. It's the evidence of your supreme power on the earth."

"It's not to be talked about. It's shameful and terrible."

"That's right, it's not to be talked about with just anyone, but I'm your teacher and I'm here to free you from these terrible bonds that keep you in pain. Again I ask, do you have your periods?"

"Yes. I have them." An almost inaudible whisper.

"Do they hurt?"

"Yes."

Harriet couldn't see her lips move but saw her tears.

"Can you indicate to me where?"

"Here." And she motioned to her belly.

"When you stop wearing that," she pointed to the corset, "the pain will ease, I promise. I will give you some exercises to do for the pain and there is a fine blackcurrant tea you can drink too. I will advise your mother. Now just wait here whilst I get you some ointment for your bruises."

"May I please sit down?"

"Yes, of course, my dear, but I want you to sit like this."

Harriet took her to a chair and showed her how to sit down, keeping her spine straight and her head high. Harriet placed her hands on her back so that she could feel the uplift as she showed her how to use her stomach muscles and her breath.

"I can't keep my spine straight – that is why we wear corsets!"

"No, my dear, your muscles will keep your spine straight, not corsets. Corsets prevent the muscles from working. Now just imagine that your head is controlling it all. The spine is hanging from the head. Your legs take the weight, like this and your neck is very long and open, like this. Now your head is light, full of air, floating above your body like a big balloon, see how your spine is like the string hanging from the balloon?"

Sarah slowly lowered herself onto the chair and allowed Harriet's sure hands to touch her back.

"God has given you a skeleton which is designed to hold you up, sit you down, swim you in the sea, run along the road, walk on the common, jump in the snow, dance in the ballroom, float in the bath, labour in the fields and labour in childbirth. Women's bodies are the most beautiful and powerful things on this earth! Why else would God have chosen us to bring forth mankind? We are the strongest, not the weakest sex."

"Please tell my mother, Miss Dick."

"I shall, Sarah. I certainly shall."

CHAPTER 17

Consolidation

MELBOURNE, 1879–1880s

To celebrate the end of the first year of their successful enterprise they bought tickets to see *HMAS Pinafore,* the delightful new musical composed and written by two unknown English composers, Gilbert and Sullivan, and starring James C. Williamson. It was known that James Williamson had had previous successful seasons in Melbourne and Sydney and that he and his wife, Maggie Moore, had also toured India, London and New York. Now that he was trained in theatre management, they were going to return to live in Melbourne.

Around this time Alice made her acquaintance with her father's contact, Professor Halford at the University of Melbourne. He was enchanted with her and her intelligent interest in bacteriology and science. It was just a short walk to the grounds of the university from their cottage, and in her spare time she took advantage of that, delighting in the atmosphere of the university and the thrill of Halford's generous attention, allowing her many a rewarding hour under his tutelage. She had permission to access the faculty library and was able to borrow a few scientific tracts from his own library. He had even once suggested that he could allocate her a place in his rooms where she could dedicate more time to her studies but she had to refuse, as the workload at the gymnasium and the schools was gathering force and quickly proving to be overwhelming and time consuming.

In the new year of 1880 many changes were coming to Melbourne. In January, Harriet and Alice read the accounts of the hanging of the infamous bushranger, Captain Moonlite, and the subsequent condemnation of this act in the first edition of the new weekly paper, *The Bulletin*, on the first of February. That same month both women were ecstatic to learn that for the first time the University of Melbourne was to admit female students.

"But not into medicine, Plum!" Alice was outraged. "God help the men if women were ever given a chance to learn about their own bodies!"

Melbourne was once again ahead of Sydney as there they did not admit female students until July 1881, and, like Melbourne, the University of Sydney Medical Faculty remained closed to women. 1880 was a bad year for bushrangers. Ned Kelly was captured in June and sent to trial in November, to be hung on 11 November.

In that same year they left the Elgin Street house and moved into a house at 11 Rupert Street, Collingwood. This was only temporary, for Alice soon bought a property at 2 St Heliers Street in Collingwood. This purchase, made possible thanks to Alice's wealth, meant they now owned their first real home and it was wonderful. Their four-bedroom brick cottage, hidden away amongst trees and rich undergrowth was idyllically situated close to the banks of the wonderful Yarra River. Today, one can walk down St Heliers narrow footpath past the Abbotsford Convent and imagine the once rustic feeling of the quiet little street surrounded by green fields where sheep and cows grazed, and old farm houses nestled sleepily along the Yarra. Today, these lands are occupied by the Collingwood Children's Farm and a large carpark while all the original houses of that past era have long been razed to the ground never to be replaced. Alice held onto this property for many years, naming it The Steyne in memory of her Brighton home. The Steyne, St Heliers Street was later occupied by Josephine McCormick, of whom we shall learn more shortly, and her mother Anna, right up until Josephine's death in 1924. I would surmise that Josephine had purchased it from Alice.

In 1884, Alice and Harriet moved the gymnasium out of the Mutual Provident Society building into premises directly opposite called Hansen's Buildings.[15] They worked non-stop in those first years. Harriet was always full of new ideas to extend their influence in the world. For example, she ran an essay competition in 1880 on the subject of physical education for girls. In the advertisements she had written, 'Health is the Best Wealth' as a prompter. Prizes were awarded and the judges were professors from University of Melbourne. Alice Henry, at 22 years old, won second prize. She went on to become a famous journalist, suffragist and trade unionist in America.

Schools were a major source of income for their gymnasium and from 1880 to 1892 they conducted classes in 16 different schools. They taught both junior and senior girls at Methodist Ladies College from 1882 until 1887 by which time Alice, who had given up teaching years ago, had sold her share in their business to Josephine McCormick who had become Harriet's assistant. One needs to imagine how hard they worked. The travel time to these schools alone would have taken a third of their day. I would hope that the schools provided the equipment otherwise they would have been carrying all manner of objects to and fro.

In those first three years, 1879–1881, they developed a wide range of classes catering for young women, ladies, boys under twelve, family groups of ten or more, school girls and business women. By 1881, there were nearly 200 pupils and in July 1881, *The Australasian Sketcher* article appeared. Their promotions sold the idea that girls needed moderate physical exercise for the good of the human race and studious girls needed it more than their idle sisters.

Harriet's use of the surname Dick in public and Rowell in private became confusing after she gave up professional swimming and started the gymnasium. A little later she phased out using Rowell completely.

In 1882 to 1883, Harriet and Alice were also advertising classes in calisthenics and gymnastics, every Thursday in Geelong.[16] Their timetable was exhaustive.

The Australian Health Society (AHS),[17] at 14 Collins Street West was a magnet for them and upon their return from England in 1879 and after opening their gymnasium they had both joined. The ideals of this society dovetailed perfectly with their own vision of 'healthy mind, healthy body' but also the AHS was a thread to connect them with future pupils. For many years Alice was on the society's council and their membership lasted from 1879 to 1883. Beginning in Collingwood, the society moved to Carlton in 1885.[18] They promoted advanced views on health for all beings and it gave Harriet and Alice an outlet, in both print and their lecture series, for their revolutionary ideas about dress reform, health and exercise, not to forget Alice's special interest in bacteriology. Josephine McCormick was also listed as an AHS member at the same time. I believe that this was where she first came into contact with Harriet and Alice. It was a meeting that would have huge repercussions for them all and was to steer Alice onto a path of no return.

With Harriet's persistence, they extended their influence into the Education Department by advertising their offerings in a series of lectures on physiology for lady teachers.

> "We have pleasure in calling the attention of lady teachers to a series of lectures on Physiology to be commenced on the 1st instant by Miss Dick and Miss Moon in the Ladies' Gymnasium, Collins Street West. As Miss Dick and Miss Moon have proved themselves successful teachers of candidates at the Education Dept, University and Health Society Examination, a large attendance may be anticipated."
>
> —*The Australasian Schoolmaster* (Aug 1882, p. 26)

Harriet and Alice gave a series of eight lectures in a course on physiology at their ladies' gymnasium in 1882 which "successfully prepared pupils in Physiology for the science (Education Department), Matriculation, and Health Society's examinations."[19] If one thinks of the world today and the popularity of gyms, fitness centres and personal trainers, it proves that there has always been a desire amongst many to enhance the performance of their bodies.

Perhaps dangerously, it was Harriet's desire to include in their physiology classes information for women concerning their reproductive systems. Up to this point physiology teachings were limited to learning and naming every bone and artery in the body, but studiously ignoring all information related to a woman's special organs and chief natural functions. Harriet was up against the strict teachings of the church and the ruling patriarchy which, worldwide, deemed the body (in particular the female body) impure. For a woman to have knowledge of its sexual functions was considered unnatural and sinful and best kept under the complete control of men. Poor hygiene, poor diet, and constant childbearing, led to major health problems for women. Those who tried to procure abortions demonstrated that ignorance did not guarantee chastity. Feminists of the day argued that sex education would safeguard the nation's morals and eradicate venereal diseases. They emphasised that knowledge rather than ignorance would prepare young women for marriage and motherhood.

For Alice and Harriet to run lectures which touched on such taboo subjects was not only brave but also challenging, as they insisted on doing it publicly, inviting the press to witness their work.

Touching on religion and the effect it may or may not have had on their lives I would easily guess that both women were acutely aware of the suffering that women had endured for hundreds of years under the yoke of the church. I would also surmise that their upbringings had been strictly within the tenets of the Christian faith. Though there is no corroborative evidence of this (except that Alice's burial was conducted by a Church of England minister), I deduce from what I intuit of their personalities that Harriet would have maintained an inner belief and an outward display of adhering to the faith, whereas Alice couldn't give a damn about appearances and would have fought it tooth and nail. Harriet was the wiser, knowing that to be living 'in sin' with Alice had to be kept hidden, not that that was hard. The structure of the patriarchal society of the day did not conceive that things like lesbians even existed. Where women lived together it was because no man had ever asked them to wed and thus, as spinsters, they were to be pitied. Alice continually baulked against this subterfuge by often openly displaying her sexuality in public. Harriet deplored it. She knew she had to guard her reputation and so, to all outsiders, their partnership had to be seen as a business one.

To document all their diversity of work, the gym classes, teaching at schools, giving displays, writing papers and giving lectures is a huge task and one which belongs to a more academic work than this professes to be. But here is just one example of their diversity: in 1880, a group of wealthy middle-class women created a club for working girls called The Girls Leisure Hour Club and Harriet took up a teaching job there which lasted until 1882. The classes were always held on a Wednesday evening. I say 'Harriet' even though Alice was also involved, but the Ladies' Gymnasium was always more of Harriet's enterprise than Alice's, and it was usually only Harriet's name that appeared in newspapers and thus garnered publicity. I have the sense that Alice knew her destiny was not to be teaching gymnastics until old age overtook her.

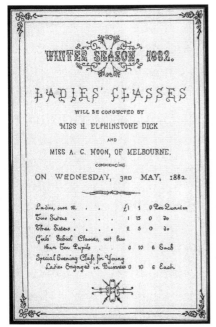
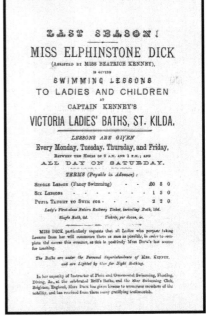

Advertisements for the gymnasium.

These classes ended in 1882, at the same time that the Ladies' Gymnasium received an invitation to work in Ballarat every Wednesday. The Ballarat Gymnastic Association had been requested by the Education Department to hold classes for male and female teachers and trainee teachers. The Association was allocated £50 per annum. Gustav Techow was allocated to teach the men and Harriet Elphinstone Dick and Alice Moon were given the job of teaching the women. So for two years every Wednesday, they took the train, a two to three hour trip of over 140 miles, to Ballarat via Werribee, returning to Melbourne the same night. As was her wont, Harriet increased the intake of pupils there by inviting Ballarat's schoolgirls as well as business women into the classes:

> Miss Elphinstone Dick, ladies' instructress at the Ballarat Gymnasium is winning golden opinions from her pupils. The ladies class is well patronised and the girls class is now so large that not more than two or three additional pupils can be taken unless arrangements are made for an additional class.[20]

It's easy to imagine their lifestyle. Not often home before dark, arriving exhausted and neither of them wanting to cook a meal at that time. No takeaways then! Living further out from the city gymnasium meant more travel time. There were some trains and there were tram trolleys but still the horses ruled. And how did they travel around to all the various schools? I can only surmise that they hired hansom cabs. They must have had equipment delivered to the schools where it stayed until their time was up. Or perhaps the schools had to buy their own equipment which would have made more sense. Later, once they had moved out to Beaconsfield in 1884, I cannot imagine them running classes every day of the week with the travel times of coach and train taking over two hours each way.

CHAPTER 18

Notoriety

MELBOURNE, 1882–1884

Nearing the end of 1881, Alice and Harriet found themselves becoming quite famous. The Ladies' Gymnasium had around 200 clients, mostly from wealthy and well-to-do families. Their school clientele had increased to almost burdensome proportions. Harriet proved to be a genius when it came to making influential connections and finding patrons.

"Plum! Let me read you this article in *The Australasian*!"

"What is it about?"

"Dress reform! Listen to this, 'What you find a burden in belief or apparel, cast off. Woman has always sacrificed her comfort to fashion. You have but a few years to live, be as free and as happy as you can for that time that remains. Fit yourselves for a higher sphere and cease grovelling in the mire. Let there be no stain of earth upon your soul or apparel.' That's a quote from the American, Amelia Bloomer – you remember her? She invented the Bloomers, back in the fifties. Aren't they the most inspiring words? Plum, we should have it printed on the wall of the gymnasium!"

"Who wrote the article?"

"It's the columnist, Humming Bee."

"Ah yes. It's a pity her articles are limited to the Ladies Column."

"She is quite the feminist journalist. I'd love to know who she really is."

"Now there's a term I'm not familiar with. Feminist?"

"Intriguing isn't it? From an English writer. Being used everywhere now. But look. Humming Bee has actually provided a pattern for the divided skirt, absolutely free! I shall order one immediately. She goes on to quote this article from *The Lancet*. Ah, it's man's reaction to our beloved divided skirt!"

Alice read aloud, "If women please to unsex themselves in dress as well as in habits of life and silly exploits of possible, but not prudent, intellectual and physical energy …' – silly intellectual and physical exploits! ugh! – '… they may be left to compass their own discomfiture without more than an ordinary warning; but when they appeal to the canons of health in support or defence of their vagaries, it is necessary to show the appeal is inadmissible. The divided skirt is clearly not likely to advance the interests or improve the health of the sex if it should be commonly adopted as the dress of the period. It is unnatural and must be productive of unwomanly ways which are to be deprecated.'

"Plum, we must answer this! To call our appeal to be unbound a 'vagary'. The arrogance of the male sex. Seriously – just to stand back and from a neutral position, look at these garments that men force us to wear. Oh wait," and Alice laughed uncontrollably as she read on, "Here Humming Bee gives another comment by the Church on the divided skirt! She is too marvellous! 'They are ungodly and unwomanly. The bible clearly says: The woman shall not wear that which pertaineth unto the man, neither shall a man put on a woman's garment for all that do so are an abomination to the Lord Thy God.' Oh, my dear Plum, how do they get away with it? Surely one look at their own priesthood would tell them that men have been wearing women's clothes for years! And look to the law courts of men! Gowns and wigs even, duplicating women's hair! And the hallowed mayoral robes of office and the Freemasons wear aprons, my dear! Seriously Plum, we must draw the attention of all women to these anomalies and to peel their eyes to truly see the way men force us to wear these horrendous garments."

"And also that most women acquiesce to wear, don't forget," reminded Harriet from the bedroom.

"Agreed. However, you will never see a man in a corset, even though they try to imitate us in everything else! Would a woman ever design this? Surely we are keeping the cotton mills of Manchester employed! The bustles and corsets! Bones, bones! Bones! Hours spent in dressing and needing help what's more. I will never again wear a corset as long as I live. Not even if I were asked to bow before the Queen."

"That might yet happen, my love. We're quite famous you know!"

From 1882 they held gymnastic competitions, awarding gold and silver medals which they paid for themselves. Juniors, seniors and former students were invited to enter. Swedish gymnastics was a cause not just a career. The prize lists show the calibre of girls; high-class families, prominent Melbourne families all demonstrated that it was socially acceptable to send your daughters to the Ladies' Gymnasium.

1883 and 1884 became a time of consolidation for their extensive schedules. Alice had already written two tracts for the AHS: 'Preservation of Teeth' (A.C. Moon), in issue number 11, February 1881 of *Australian Health Society*, and in 1882, issue number 16, 'Kitchen Physic' – with Mrs. Bartrop [SLV], a very basic pamphlet on kitchen hygiene, healthy food and basics like ventilation. (Remember, there were no refrigerators.)

In 1884, despite dropping their membership, Alice encouraged the Ladies' Committee of the AHS to run a lecture series, 'Talks to Wives and Daughters', aiming to reach a class of people who would not normally come in contact with the AHS lectures.[21]

Harriet gave a series of lectures 'For Wives and Daughters' at the Australian Health Society. 'Clothing First Help in Accidents' on 27 July 1883 and later, in the 'Meetings for Wives and Daughters' series on 13 September 1887, she spoke on dress reform and the prospect of replacing cumbersome and impractical underwear for children with one-piece combinations. She arrived with a skeleton to illustrate her lecture and an array of suitable alternative clothing!

The Hall is packed. Harriet wows 'em with an amusing, insightful lecture on the affects of high heel boots on the spine, the damage done to the whole body by steel stays, whalebone corsets and pillows stuffed in bustles. She offers patterns for combination garments for infants and children and introduces a new cloth called 'flanellette'. She finishes off with, "Are women born in whalebone jackets? Did heaven create Eve with a natural inability to hold up her fresh, fair body without the aid of Mrs Ford's latest patent? Is there reason in the eternal nature of things where your brother can stand erect and feel at ease, and you drop altogether unless you lean upon a long steel rod? I heard one woman say, 'I can't stand up straight nor hardly at all without my corsets' to which I replied, 'how very fortunate for you that you were not born until corsets were invented'."

It was also in that year of 1883 that the first woman, Lydia Amelia Harris, having enrolled in 1880, passed her final exams at the University of Melbourne and graduated with a Degree in Arts. In contrast to that achievement, the Archbishop of Melbourne, Dr Moorhouse, speaking at the opening of the Servants Training Institution was quoted as saying:

> A good servant's job is a much better opening for a young woman than a factory job. Learning to preserve their honesty and integrity and to control their tempers and manners they will become a perfect household treasure as both the servant then the wife and mother.

When Harriet read that she burst out laughing, "She starts as she is meant to continue – a servant, then wife, then mother!"

"But always a slave!" added Alice.

CHAPTER 19

The Tasmanian Connection Begins

MELBOURNE, 1881

Alice was relaxing at home after a late dinner and reading *The Australasian Sketcher*. She loved her house and its quiet bucolic atmosphere, especially its proximity to the Yarra River. She was friends with her neighbours, Arthur Snowdon, a solicitor and his family, and heading down towards the river on the other side, Max Kreitmayer, who ran the Melbourne Waxworks Museum. Their friend Josephine McCormick with her widowed mother, Anna, and Jo's older sister, Ellen, were renting a house but a few doors away. [22]

Probably around this time an important meeting occurs, a meeting that will seal Alice's fate. Josephine has close friends in Tasmania and by extension, in Sydney: The Parker-Leary family. [23] It is possible that Mrs Florence Parker has come across Bass Strait on the coastal passenger lines on a few occasions to stay with Josephine and her mother. Florence is an accomplished musician, married to Erskine Rainey Parker, a wealthy horse breeder from Longford near Launceston. She eventually gave birth to nine children one of whom, Reike, ended up living permanently in Melbourne with Josephine McCormick's family. It's perhaps drawing a long bow but I intuit that Josephine must have been the link who brought Alice and Florence Parker and her extensive family together, and that it was she who took Alice with her on a holiday to Launceston sometime in the early 1880s. There are no records that I can find of either of them travelling to Tasmania at that early date, but there is one record of Miss A.C. Moon sailing from Melbourne to Launceston in 1891. There must be more. There are many records of Miss McCormick travelling the same route almost once a year, sometimes twice in the early 1900s. But travel Alice certainly did, and she began a deep and lasting friendship with Florence (Leary) Erskine Parker. The Erskine Parker family owned the large estate Parknook, probably situated on what is now Lake River Road in Cressy near Longford. Some early Parker ancestors lie buried at St Mark's Lake River Church known as the Pisa.

Florence Parker's wealthy sister, Mrs Mary Rose Merewether, lived in Sydney. Florence perhaps assured Alice that should she ever up sticks and decide to move to the warmer climes of New South Wales, she would always be most welcome at her sister's home in Sydney. She insisted they would have an instant rapport. As she described the joys and creative life of Sydney, we can only imagine in Alice's eyes the old, familiar light of adventure and change to re-kindle again.

Let me briefly introduce the Leary-Parker-Merewether Family, and try to trace how Alice came to be so close to them, close enough so that much later she divided her estate between Josephine McCormick and Florence (née Leary) Parker and her sister, Mary Rose (née Leary) Merewether. And to have both Florence and her daughter, Selma Younger along with Florence's sister, Edith Leary, buried in Alice's grave with her.

113

Florence Parker.

Florence Agnes (Marmie) Leary was born in Balmain and married Erskine James Rainey Parker in Campbelltown in 1880 and went to live in his estate home in Longford, Tasmania, where all her children were born. By the end of her life she was a widow living in Sydney at Lynton, 294 Jersey Road, Woollahra and upon her death in 1949, was buried in Alice's grave.

Florence's children are worth noting here in order of birth: Lucy (Liebe), Charles, Leonora (Nora), Catherine (Kitty), Selma (Shez who was buried in Alice's grave), Frederika (Reike), Magdalene (Mona) and Mary Rainey (Molly).

Florence's siblings – the Leary family – should be listed too. Her older sister, Mary Rose (Dolly), whom I have already mentioned was married to Walton Merewether, a barrister ten years her senior whose family owned land from Edgecliff to Bondi. When Alice later left Melbourne for Sydney in 1891, it was to reside with them in their home, Lurlie, at 27 William Street, Double Bay until 1894. It was in this house that she died. The rest of the Leary siblings were Catherine (Kate) who was a witness on Alice's death certificate, Henry, John, Thomas, Clare Josephine Leary, Alfred, Edith Louise (Lulu, who was born in 1872 and died in1969 and is also buried in Alice's grave), and finally, younger brothers Joseph and Frank Leary.

It's important to know too, that three of the Leary siblings, Edith, Florence and Clare as well as Florence's daughter, Selma, all ended up living at Lynton, 294 Jersey Road, Woollahra,[24] the original home of Rose Scott – more on this later.

It is documented that Florence's daughter, Frederike (Reike) Parker, born 1894 (three months after Alice's death), suffered from a spinal condition caused by falling from a horse when very young. At the age of five she was brought to Melbourne for treatment with a specialist, Dr Arthur Jeffreys Wood, a graduate of the University of Melbourne and a leading paediatrician of his day. Treatment included an exercise program supervised by Miss Josephine McCormick.[25] But since Alice made her will in 1891 – presumably in Sydney where she was then living – in which she bequeathed everything to Florence Parker, Mary Rose Merewether and Josephine McCormick, this meant that her relationship with the Leary sisters was already deep and committed by that year of 1891. One could assume that Florence, an accomplished pianist and organist, may have found herself attending a concert in Melbourne and may have tried out the Ladies' Gymnasium, thus perhaps meeting Josephine? One must remember that travel in those days was long and often arduous. Boats, trains and steamers from Melbourne to Sydney and down to Tasmania, were the main means of transport. The Melbourne-Sydney rail connection had been established at Albury in 1883.

I can imagine Alice and Josephine taking off for a weekend on the steamer across the Bass Strait to Launceston and taking a coach through the charming Esk River Valley to the Parker Estate. Florence, who was always called Marmie (as was Harriet's mother – a common nickname given to mothers in the nineteenth century), was beautiful, courageous, talented and capable. She ran her homestead with ease and managed the upbringing of her many infants, teaching them both social and religious morals. She was a practising Anglican as, in her own way, was Alice. Their Sunday mornings would have been spent gathering the young 'uns into the traps and going to the tiny St Mark's Church for a morning service. Singing and prayers; after that home for a huge Sunday roast. Alice played the piano well enough to accompany Florence in duets. And apart from entertaining themselves, there was always riding to be done. Erskine Parker raised horses! Alice's upbringing from an early age had included riding lessons around the tan in the central gardens of The Steine, along with piano and drawing lessons at home with her private governess. Time spent with Florence was also time spent with her extraordinary children. Alice particularly loved the toddler, Selma and nicknamed her Shez, much to the infant's delight. A few days of this family life gave Alice a taste of the things she knew she would never have. There was another great attraction to Parknook. That was Florence's talking about her sisters 'Dolly' Mary Rose Merewether and 'Lulu' Edith Leary who lived in Sydney amongst a bevy of writers and artists, all female who were becoming known as the 'new women': leaders for change and rights for women. Did Florence encourage Alice to become a writer, perhaps move to Sydney? All these thoughts buzzed in her head on the return journeys on the evening steamer back to Melbourne.

Alice definitely spent much time travelling across to the east coast, specifically to Falmouth. In 1893, her story, 'Blos: a Tasmanian River Study',[26] set along the Scamander River, was published in the Christmas edition of *The Sydney Mail* and the *New South Wales Advertiser*. Her writing is both poignant and evocative of this fading seaside town. My research found that there was a large family called Singline whose patriarch's name was Blaustus, known as Blos. Josephine McCormick in all likelihood accompanied her on these excursions. Once she had shifted to Sydney, I'm not sure how many trips she continued to make to Tasmania.

In her will, Alice left a property named The Viney Hotel, Falmouth,[27] to Mary Rose Merewether, Florence's sister. Buying property was a popular venture for Alice as was buying shares. She had a brain for business and her personal wealth to experiment with.

CHAPTER 20

Watershed Moments, The Call of the Wild

1884

The year 1884 was to be a watershed year for Alice and Harriet. It is the year that Harriet, ambitious for a wider audience and recognition of her work, decided to move their gym displays and prize-giving ceremonies into the Melbourne Town Hall. Prior to that first display they had applied to the Melbourne City Council through its manager, Mr H. J. Samuels, for free use of the Town Hall on the grounds that no profit was to be made from their performance. They were refused, but after a lengthy correspondence, the Council agreed to charge them reduced rates at charity hire for seven pounds instead of ten pounds. Mr Samuels negotiated on their behalf. They could barely afford the seven pounds, but the publicity was important. The Town Hall maintained the reduced rate for three years. Harriet, with Alice, again generously paid for all the medals and prizes they handed out.[28]

The girls wore white skirts and blouses with light and dark blue trimmings. The two tones of blue were the colours of the Ladies' Gymnasium. The girls sang as well. Harriet paid for the hire of the Town Hall and didn't charge an entry fee. (On 22 October and on 30 October 1884 there was a cartoon in *Punch* based on Harriet's athletic prowess. It showed a beefy woman raising with one hand a rather skinny looking specimen of a man. The New Woman!)

In the Town Hall displays she didn't use beams or ladders or ropes as she did in her gym. These public displays were held between 1884 and 1890, usually performed in the afternoons around 3.30 pm, and they lasted about one and a half hours.[29] Harriet organised the space so that the audience sat on the stage or in the balcony, thus leaving the entire floor of the hall empty for the girls' routines. According to reports in the papers, their marching was precision-based and along with the beautifully orchestrated displays of Indian club swinging and ring-stress pulling, it was a grand spectacle. It must have looked terrific when you think of the girls in their blue and white uniforms – sailor blouses, pleated skirts and knickerbockers allowing them to lift their legs high and leap around, both exercising and singing along with a simple orchestral and piano accompaniment. Never before would the audience have observed such freedom of movement, nor such muscular display in girls of an adolescent age. Stays were of course forbidden! Weak muscles, spinal curvature (lateral), and under-developed lungs all resulted from the wearing of corsets, and all these conditions were treated at the gym. Leaving off the corset developed a taste for freedom! The audience of mostly mothers must have held their breath!

Sometime early in 1883, Professor Halford extended an invitation for Alice and Harriet to visit Beaconsfield where he had recently retired with his family to live out his old age. He suggested they stay at the Beaconsfield House and offered to arrange a booking for them.

"Plum, we're off to the country! An invitation to visit Professor Halford. He will arrange our accommodation and will gladly escort us around the district!"

"I cannot leave the gymnasium."

"Just for one day – well, two. We could go on a Friday afternoon, have Saturday and Sunday and perhaps even Monday and return on Tuesday!"

"Perhaps, when the schools are in recess for Easter. I suppose I could let the classes go on Monday but not Tuesday as well."

"Dearest Plum, you do need a break!"

Sketches at Miss Dick's gymnasium exhibition.
Source: The Australasian Sketcher, *19 November 1884.*

Athletics for Ladies – An alarming result
Better-half (to hubby) – "Oh dear, no; he's not going off to dinner by his
little selfy selfy, he's going to take his poor little wifey to the theatre
to-night, and to the derby on Saturday, that's what he's going to do."
Source: Melbourne Punch, *30 October 1884.*

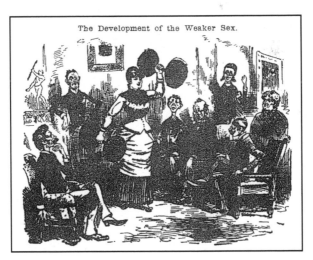

Sweet Girl Graduate –"These are the dumb-bells I used last year in
Miss Dick's gymnasium. Won't one of you gentlemen just put them up?
It's awfully easy." Source: Table Talk, *18 March 1886.*

CHAPTER 21

A Tree Change

BEACONSFIELD, 1883–1884

After much organisation on Harriet's part, the day finally dawned when they took the late afternoon train from Melbourne to Beaconsfield Station where after two hours of train travel they were met by Professor Halford in his trap. He took them along the scenic route and both women were utterly enchanted by the ride and the countryside. At every turn in the ascending road there were glimpses of the coastal landscape in the distance. The native forests of mountain ash and the singing and bell-like calls from invisible native birds transported the women to another entirely new world. Alice remarked how the air became lighter and purer the higher up they travelled. Harriet laughed, adding that her brain seemed to be functioning in a different manner. Five miles away from the station, the Professor halted the journey at his home for some refreshment. They met his family and gasped at the views from his windows.

"We are 1,200 feet above sea level here!" he boasted. "You can see all the way down to Western Port Bay."

They then continued with the Professor to their pre-arranged lodging at Beaconsfield House commonly called, 'The Big House', finally arriving at twilight. They bid the Professor farewell, thanking him effusively for his kindness. They saw the moonrise from the verandah. It was magical, casting great shadows from the ranges and down the gullies.

"Oh, smell that beautiful smell, what is it?" Alice breathed in deeply then exhaled as if she were in Elysium.

"Night jasmine," breathed Harriet, also quite overcome.

"It's exquisite, and Plum, look at the stars."

Harriet gazed upward following Alice's directive. A myriad of stars. Excitedly she pointed, "There's the great Southern Cross! It's so very easy to see it out here."

"Look at the Milky Way. The ancients believed it was born from the udder of Io, the sacred cow of the moon goddess."

"Really? Where did you read that?"

"My grandmother used to tell me stories when I was a child." Alice shivered as she drew her shawl around her against the damp night air. But in fact she was hearing the call of the wild. It was a tree change and she grasped it with both hands. Whether Harriet was fully supportive I don't know, but it was Alice's money and Alice's dream. The city of Melbourne was polluted, noisy, smelly. And all around her, the robust and boisterous presence of men and their belittling and patriarchal usage of women riled her. Money was never a problem for Alice, so I assume that Henry Moon had left her well cared for in that department. With such personal wealth, she never had to ask permission to follow her next dream. And so it was that in September 1883 she bought 20 acres followed by a further 40 acres in 1884[30] in A'Beckett Road, Upper Beaconsfield. Alice built a house there and they both moved out of Melbourne in 1884. Alice set about creating an organic poultry farm, while Harriet maintained travelling to

Melbourne to run the gymnasium with Josephine McCormick. Alice seems to have had a propensity for unravelling things as fast as she could. Or perhaps it was simply her restless nature, her continual search for being, that made her decision-making so abrupt and quite often ill-considered.

The McCormicks had moved into St Heliers Street in 1884, three years after Alice and Harriet. Josephine was involved in the gymnasium from 1880, and it would be safe to assume that Alice found the house for Josephine and her family. A house becomes vacant, Josephine and her family are looking for accommodation, Alice steps in? Whichever way it happens, Josephine, an athletic, clever woman, two years younger than Alice, vibrant and beautiful, became involved in the working lives of Alice and Harriet and was taking classes at the gymnasium. Josephine McCormick was to make a career of gymnastics, remedial massage and medical therapies and became quite famous for her successes in curing spinal deformities. She attended the gym regularly as an instructor, eventually entering in a partnership with Harriet when Alice left. Then, when Harriet left to follow Alice to Sydney, Jo ran the gymnasium on her own, eventually buying it from Harriet.

It was true that upon their first meeting, Alice had felt a deep attraction to Josephine that was both sensual and disturbing.

Alice had been with Harriet for more than ten years and their two personalities clashed often. Alice was quixotic, always in a hurry to change the world, quick-witted, often too quick to speak her mind. Without a second thought, she could be abrasively rude to men whereas Harriet was far more diplomatic, her energy always grounded, thinking ahead to the main game. Alice delighted in baiting men, she saw no man as worth kowtowing to and she repeated that phrase often. She had a sharp wit and a clever tongue and none of the men she confronted ever quite expected to get the vocal tirade or the unusual feminist put-down that could ensue. She was so ahead of her time both in her language and her boldness.

CHAPTER 22

Tuesday Evening, April Fools Day

1884

A Tuesday evening at home, Abbotsford. The house at Beaconsfield was still under construction. Alice was reading *The Australasian* magazine but her thoughts were all over the place. Has she come into my life to rattle me? Alice wondered to herself, for she had definitely read in Josephine's eyes the same spark of connection that she felt. I am content with Plum, am I not? I know I have become bored at the gymnasium and even though I love lecturing at the Australian Health Society – and that at least is giving me chance to write, but I do hate routine. Why does it always feel like a trap? Timetables and the same pattern day after day, going to the gymnasium, going to schools, dull little boys and constricted girls, carriages and trolleys, dirt and dust. Teaching at Ballarat has given just a change of scenery but by now, that is just another timetable to be obeyed. What does my spirit crave? Is it to be always wild and unpredictable, to be dissatisfied with repetition, and to want to demand chaos?

I love challenges. Plum used to be like that, back home, to see her swimming against those men, in the rough seas, that I could never do. She was so brave back then, especially when we first arrived here, those matches at Captain Kenney's Baths, she was amazing. But now she won't swim. Now she is so business-like. But we are doing good work, aren't we? We are rescuing young girls from a crippling life bound into those wicked cages. But oh, how can I reconcile my yearning for another life with Plum's staidness?

She turned a page to see an article on dress reform, her favourite subject. "Oh, good heavens Plum," she called to Harriet, who was in the bedroom packing their holdalls for their scheduled trip to Ballarat on the morrow. They had been teaching ladies' classes at the Ballarat Gymnasium, one day a week, for nearly two years. "Talk about crippling. Look at this article, Plum! Just look at this advertisement for the latest in corsets! Brown's dermathistic corset! Oh, the reality of this! 'Elegance, Comfort, Durability!' I'll say they're durable. They'll last as long as the steel hull of the *Durham*! Oh, but see now they have a new trick, they've encased the steel in leather." She read aloud to Harriet: "'The actual wearing out of a corset such as this becomes an absolute impossibility. This corset has met with almost unprecedented success. To its advantages of good cut, durability and suppleness, combined with support to the figure a further improvement has just been added which is calculated to bring the Dermathistic corset more into favour.'

"Horrors, but here's more drivel, 'Ladies who indulge', – indulge, how patronising! – 'in much healthful and exhilarating exercises as rowing, driving, lawn tennis, will find the leather facing being a sure prevention against bodice, busks or stays breaking whilst it renders the corset most delightfully pliable to the figure during the most active or violent exertions' – and there's appalling drawings of ladies rowing and horse riding and playing tennis."

"To the scrap-heap with them all, I say! Shall I pack your red jacket?" called Harriet from the bedroom.

"No thank you, I'll wear it. No wait, I think a button has come off."

"Do you have the button?"

"Of course not! I would've sewn it back on by now if I had it. Leave it. I'll take my grey one. I'll need to buy all new buttons. I'll never match the original. Made from bone. Ach! Bone again. Whalebone. You'd never suspect the pain underneath, the weeping sores. Remember that young girl last March?"

"How could I forget. Those ugly wounds around her beautiful young torso. Oh, these mothers."

"It's a version of medieval torture."

"Yes. I believe so. There was the Iron Maiden, a torture chamber. I once saw one in the Hove museum when I was a child; it was horrifying."

"And iron chastity belts!"

"Perhaps I need a chastity belt for you my dear, you are such a wild one!"

Alice felt a stab of guilt. Could Harriet read her mind? Had she been privy to the looks, the intimate energy that was passing between herself and Josephine when they were together? A bit too quickly she replied, "Ah, but that's where trust comes in, Plum."

"Yes. I trust you, of course."

But Harriet's heart was in her mouth as she said it. She had seen the looks that Alice shared with Josephine. In those moments she felt as though the ground upon which she stood was shifting. Her stomach felt hollow and her breath caught in her chest. I must not take her for granted, take nothing for granted. I must not try to control her wild nature for that is what I love about her. But I know one day it could take her away from me, and that, I could not bear.

Alice was at it again, her eyes ablaze. She was writing furiously now.

"What are you writing, dearest?"

"I'm writing about dress reform. I'll send it to *The Australasian Sketcher*. They may take it. Will you hear it?"

"I'd love to!"

She read her proposed article aloud to Harriet, "'It is a proven medical fact that 'stays' have a deleterious effect on all the organs of a woman's body, not to mention the bodies of young girls who are still developing and have not yet reached their full potential. They reduce lung capacity, they cause dyspepsia, fissures of the liver, gallstones and even constipation. It is tight lacing that can cause infertility, not swimming in the sea or exercising in the gymnasium. If men are so concerned about our procreative organs and tell us not to do heavy work or exercise, then why do they force us into these cages of horror which are proven to have caused miscarriages and even a high infant mortality? Tight lacing during pregnancy can cause that child to be born with organic weakness! Is that what fathers want?'"

"No, of course not," interrupted Harriet, "and it's important to make that clear. What sort of children do they want women to produce?"

"Just listen, Plum. 'I'm recommending that dress reform can take many paths to create attractive but sensible fashions. I advocate for the divided skirt as a wonderful garment for the active woman. Pregnant women could wear such a skirt with a waistline that could be expanded as the baby grew, just by shifting the buttons. Viscountess Harberton who invented the divided skirt back in 1882, has suggested thus:

I always have mine to button at each side, the front part being buttoned on to a calico bodice. I have flannel or merino drawers inside the skirt made the same way, but buttoned on to the divided band inside. I usually wear braces, but some people do not fancy them, in which case loops, for buttons on the bodice keep the dress from dragging on the hips.

"Our young women are so active," Alice continued reading, "and now demand the freedom to be so. Riding bicycles is the most wonderful and joyous physical exercise a woman can do. The best thing is, she is free to be completely on her own, within her own sphere and she can go as fast or as slow, as careful or as wild as she wishes – all unaccompanied!"

"Like swimming," mused Harriet, "I used to have the most amazing feelings when I swam. I was transported, almost beyond my physical limitations."

"It was never the sport for me though, Plum. I rather figure that I may try and get onto a bicycle."

"They recommend one starts with the tricycle."

"Pooh to them. I'll get on a bicycle, you watch if I don't. Why use three wheels when two will do? I'm not an invalid! I continue my piece thus: 'The male sex cannot seem to bear this thought – unshackled females abroad on the town! Unshackled bodies! Why gentlemen, where is the danger? Are you so weak, in mind and in body that you see these free women as a threat? Men might have to learn to be brave all over again! The ridiculous argument that we become unsexed by these clothes and that we appear immodest or 'unfeminine' is one of the oldest arguments of the seemingly superior male mind. Do women working in the mines, in the laundries or on the factory floor wear corsets? No. If these hard-working females did so they would not last long. Is it therefore that women who are engaged in hard physical labour do not qualify as 'real women'; are they unsexed by their labour? And is not giving birth the hardest labour of all? All mothers become classless in giving birth whilst at the same time reaching the highest power on this earth.'

"Oh, and one more thing I found, a good word for a certain doctor who practiced in England and only died in the 1830s. His name was Dr Abernethy – I believe he founded St Bartholomews – but listen to this, Plum. He is recorded as saying to a woman whose sick daughter, encased in a corset was brought to him: 'Why madam, do you know there are upwards of thirty yards of bowels squeezed underneath that girdle of your daughter's? Go home and cut it; let Nature have fair play and you will have no need of my advice.'"

"Wonderful! A man who supports our beliefs. You are a clever writer, Alice. Perhaps that's where you belong." And that, thought Harriet, will be a very dangerous thing for me. She had a premonition that something else was coming, something unbearable.

CHAPTER 23

The Train Wreck

WERRIBEE, 1884

Harriet and Alice left Melbourne by train the next morning of Wednesday, 2 April 1884, for their regular classes in Ballarat. They had a successful day's teaching despite Alice's ever-increasing boredom with the lessons. There was no doubt that Harriet was an excellent trainer. Much better than me, thought Alice as they sat in the warmed waiting room at Ballarat station waiting to return to Melbourne. It was cold outside, much colder than Melbourne and there was a long trip ahead of them. Their train would not reach Melbourne until 10.45 pm. Eventually, the train from Horsham pulled in, but it had a ten-minute wait before they could board. A lady hurried out of the train and walked quickly into the café waiting room.

"I've time for a quick cuppa, I'm sure," she said as she signalled the girl behind the counter.

"Don't miss getting back on though, Mrs …?" Alice advised in a friendly gesture.

"Mrs Johnston. No, I'll be quick. I've been visiting my brother in Horsham. I miss the farm, I used to ride horses as a young girl.

I miss the freedom – on the farm you could do anything."

"I agree with that. Where's home now then?" Alice enquired.

"South Melbourne, Raglan Street," she replied.

"Ah. I know it well."

Harriet nudged Alice to come along.

"Well, bye-bye, see you in Melbourne."

"Cheerio." Mrs Johnston gave them a gentle wave as she returned to her second-class carriage, directly behind the engine. They settled into their own carriage, a few carriages further back behind Mrs Johnston's. They were both tired and short-tempered with each other. They chose to sit on either side of the aisle, giving each other a little more space. Seated beside them were two women and Harriet exchanged niceties with them, a Mrs Cummins and her sister, Mrs Milne. They chatted a little, Harriet more vocal than Alice who was not in a happy mood. It was already dark and the journey ahead to Melbourne would take a few hours. Next stop was Little River where they had to wait for the line to be cleared at Werribee before the last leg up to Melbourne. A leg they never made.[31]

Meanwhile, at the Werribee station, Mr Biddle, the station master, ordered his 17-year-old daughter, Jessie that, as he's late for choir practice she must operate the signals for the night. He tells her that if the goods train coming through from Melbourne is late she must hold it there, on the siding, and send the 'all clear' to Little River station so the train from Ballarat can come through first.

"When are we due at Little River?" asked Mrs Cummins as the train rumbled into the night.

"About 8.15 pm," answered Harriet. Alice, seated by the window was still not talking. She was tired, it had been a long day, full of altercations and disagreements. Her mind was far away at the property in Beaconsfield where her new house was becoming a reality.

The station master's daughter waited alone in the Werribee station, an oil lamp burning in the window. The clock on the wall read 8.10 pm.

The Ballarat train slowed down as it pulled into Little River Station.

"We usually have to wait here for some time for the 'all clear' from Werribee. There's a goods train that comes through first," Harriet informed the other women.

At Werribee, the station master's daughter glanced at the clock. She was well trained at this post. The clock read 8.18 pm. Then she heard the Melbourne goods train whistle as it pulled into the station. The 35 empty sheep trucks wheeled screeching to a stop. The fireman of the goods train, Robert Walker, received the staff from her which indicated that the line ahead was all clear and he gave it to the driver, Kitchen, signalling the goods train was now clear to leave Werribee.

Jessie sat still in the silence and read her father's instructions again. She frowned. The clock now read 8.40 pm. Confused, she suddenly jumped up and telegraphed the 'all clear' signal to Little River. What on earth was she thinking? At Little River the signal came through as a telegram. The station master handed it to Mr Craik the engine driver. "Looks like the goods train is late again, when it comes in they'll be holding it at Werribee. You can get on now. The line's clear." The whistle blew and the passenger train pulled out from the station heading for Melbourne. The goods train from Werribee, heading for Little River hurtles on into the night straight towards the passenger train coming in the opposite direction. The two trains are set inevitably on a collision course.

At 10.00 pm it happens. All hell breaks loose. The second-class carriage where Ellen Johnson was seated was uprooted, with smashed timbers everywhere. One piece of frame has struck Ellen in the stomach. She screams in terrible pain but death is upon her. In her carriage further back, Alice, who was asleep, is knocked unconscious. Blood runs from a terrible gash on her forehead. Harriet has been thrown against the timber wall opposite. Almost concussed, she is quickly alert and doesn't scream; she is incredibly cool. She just keeps saying, "Don't die. Don't die," as she cradles Alice's bloody head, and pulls her clear of the wreckage of roof timbers and broken glass. In the pouring rain she also manages to get two more ladies out of the wreck and tend to them on the ground. Mrs Cummins is in shock with an injury to her leg and cuts and bruises about her body and head. Mrs Milne has concussion, cuts and bruises, and is in shock. The roof of their carriage was damaged. People are shouting and screaming in the tearing rain and the pitch darkness. People soon arrive and the place begins to resemble Dante's *Inferno*. They have set fire to all the smashed wood to provide heat and light for both the wounded and those wandering in shock. The rescue operation is disorganised and fraught. Two dead. It is not until 2 am that the wounded are finally able to be transported to Melbourne hospitals. Harriet and Alice are taken straight home after Dr George Teague has examined them and stitched Alice's forehead. He confines them to the house for at least three days.

CHAPTER 24

Abbotsford

THURSDAY 3 APRIL, 1884

Harriet is at Alice's bedside, talking quietly to her. Alice is pale and her head and right eye are heavily bandaged. She is quite distraught as, with difficulty, she reads the *The Age* newspaper.

"Heavens, that poor woman died! Did you see her, Plum?"

"No. I was too busy trying to get you out. You were unconscious and I was in Hell."

"Dearest Plum. My rescuer! I can just remember the noise. The falling. I think I was on the other side of the carriage?"

"I was thrown across the carriage as we crashed. I have a hematoma the size of the Brighton Pavilion! Luckily, I stayed conscious and could pull you free. Everything was disintegrating. I rather think my hat saved me."

"That hat! Praise be for the ridiculous hats that you wear!"

"Perhaps if you'd have had one? You'd not have 12 stitches in your head, my dear. It's your eye that I'm so worried about."

"No wonder it feels so painful," and she lifted her hand to her forehead, but cried out in pain. "Oh! My shoulder!"

"It's very bruised dearest, that's all. I'll rub some arnica tincture into it. Dr Teague has thoroughly checked you over. You are to stay in bed for at least three days, I rather trust a bit more. You were lucky my love. That woman, the one who died, apparently received a piece of timber right into her stomach. It was a terrible death for her. I'm sure I heard her scream. Both the drivers are dead, it was a tragedy. We were so close to death."

"I think I'm going to be ill."

Alice pushed herself to the edge of the bed ready to vomit on the floor but Harriet grabbed the pan on the table and managed to get there in time. Alice's spasms turned into dry retching.

"Can you take some water, dearest? If you keep vomiting I must call the doctor. We don't want you with concussion."

Alice lay back exhausted and closed her eyes. She turned around towards Harriet and spoke slowly, with her eyes closed, "I had the strangest of dreams last night. I was riding a horse, a great stallion." Her mouth was dry and her words whispered. "He was black with a golden mane, he was pounding the earth with his enormous hooves. I was astride his wide back, there was white foam, sweat on his flanks and belly, it covered my thighs." She paused. "I could feel him throbbing between my legs, he kept on calling out to me, 'Say my name. Say my name!' Over and over. 'King, you're the King,' I kept crying out. He laughed and laughed. Then he threw me off his back, as if I were a flea, a mere nuisance."

"That's very vivid," said Harriet a little disconcerted. She never remembered her dreams.

"There was something else – I can't remember – something else. What day is it?"

"Thursday. It was only yesterday."

"Seems more …" And she was asleep.

∞

Alice turned her nose up at the soup bowl in Harriet's hands.

"My love, it's beef broth, the very best thing for you." Harriet's patience was not quite so unbounded.

"Have we finished the chicken?"

"Yes, we've finished the chicken."

"Don't like beef as much as chicken."

"Well, I'm sorry Miss Moon, I'll make sure you have chicken for dinner."

"Sorry to be such an awful pill for you, Plum."

"No matter. How do you feel about going for a walk?" Silence. "Just down the street perhaps, look at the river, then back?"

"Maybe later this afternoon. Have you got a paper I could read?"

"There's more news of the crash in this one, and here's a copy of the *Illustrated Weekly*, that should keep you amused."

"I can't wait to be well enough to journey out to see how our new home is growing."

The building of The Steyne in 1884 at Beaconsfield was slowly coming along but Alice and Harriet stayed on in St Heliers Street continuing their work. Though Alice had involved herself in organising Harriet's lectures with the AHS from 1885, she was far more committed to the realisation of the Beaconsfield property and her blossoming interest in raising poultry. Her original aim in joining the Society had been to bring the beliefs and the knowledge embodied in the Society to a class of people who would not necessarily be members of the same class, but most of the time it felt more like a chore than a calling. Thanks to Harriet's acumen when it came to self-promotion, her talks were usually fully reported in the press, as she had become a media favourite.

They had the town house and they had the farm. If Alice was still tied to teaching, it was by a very thin thread, while Harriet, along with Josephine, remained fully committed to the gymnasium and the schools.

Gymnastics class 1890, Methodist Ladies' College.

27 October 1885. A note from Miss Dick and Miss Moon appeared in the amusement column of *The Argus* thanking those who had been responsible for the gift of the silver tea service, presented to them the day before at the annual display at the Melbourne Town Hall.[32]

Directly below this was an advertisement which said that Alice Moon was offering for sale her share in the gymnasium.[33]

So finally, for Alice it was time to split, not necessarily from Harriet but from the work of teaching. She was over it. For Harriet, teaching was and always would be her passion, her raison d'être and she never lost sight of her mission. Josephine had been teaching at the gymnasium since the early 1880s. She was a natural. She was trained in the Ling Method, but also showed an affinity for working with damaged bodies, especially people with spinal problems. She would be an obvious buyer of Alice's share but that didn't happen straight away.

CHAPTER 25

The Steyne

BEACONSFIELD, 1884–1887

It was more than a two-hour journey for Harriet to the Melbourne gymnasium – not to mention the schools and other lessons. Ruyton School in Studley Park, Kew, was advertising Misses Dick and Moon as teachers of gymnastics prior to 9 February 1886. It's not clear when Alice actually left the gymnasium, but she had definitely left and given over her share to Josephine by 1887.[34]

Josephine advertised her services as a teacher of dancing early in 1887. The McCormicks, Josephine and her mother, Anna, and her older sister, Ellen, were still living in St Heliers Street. It is possible that they moved into The Steyne, as Alice was not successful in selling it when she made the move to Beaconsfield. After Alice died, Josephine was listed as living in Alice's house with her mother and sister up to the time she herself passed away in 1924, aged 66.[35] I've been unable to find a record of Josephine's purchase of St Heliers, but own it she did. Josephine probably would have had enough money to buy the house herself, along with her mother and sister who both outlived her.

A country paradise, Beaconsfield was a famous retreat for artists and professionals. The 'tree-change' between 1884 and 1887 was a time of great joy and happiness for Alice – the freedom she could now experience was unlimited. With Harriet she cleared the land, and, keeping the little cottage, built a new house for themselves. Called 'the amazons' by the locals, both she and Harriet learnt to ride bicycles, wear their divided skirts and tramp along roads in their bloomer styled trouser-suits.

Beaconsfield expanded rapidly in the 1880s. Many Melbourne residents took up either 320-acre blocks, or 20-acre blocks, and soon Beaconsfield had a summer society of professors, lawyers, doctors and well-to-do business men, some of whom left their families here all year round. There were 100 substantial private houses within a circle of two miles, along with two stores, a state school and an excellent public hall built by subscription and used for religious services, balls and other social entertainments. A ladies' college was built. Local industries were represented by timber getters, carpenters and a brickfield. The area was subdivided which included major road improvements and the erection of farmhouses. Alice's 40 acres was about four miles from the station and two miles from the township with a coach service link. Alice named her property The Steyne as she did with every property she ever owned.

CHAPTER 26

On the Road

BEACONSFIELD, 1886

Visualise eight men on the dusty road with pick axes, shovels, horses and carts under strain, stones falling into trays, masculine shouting, camaraderie in swearing, smoking, urinating where they stood … and suddenly them all seeing two women, dressed in britches and wearing men's hats and boots, one with her hands firmly in her pockets, a most unusual and rather intimidating stance making her appear quite boyishly nonchalant, even unfazeable, and the other swinging her arms akimbo, most unladylike, and both marching freely along the road towards them. The day is hot, the flies are buzzing in their hundreds, crawling into eyes and mouths, the dust is rising and the sniggers and wolfish comments start to come.

"Mornin' *ladies.*"

"Them's not ladies, them's laddies, lookit their'n trousers there!"

"Here's trouble," growled Harriet. "Perhaps we should make a detour here?"

"Nay! Here's fun, I'd say. Stride forth, Plum let's show 'em the Swedish waltz!"

They do stride forth in a masterly fashion with arms swinging in Ling Method time. Alice as always can't resist a confrontation.

"Good mornin' gentlemen, having your way with nature are you?"

"Beg pardon *sir!* Can't say as I've seen such a sweet face on so many's a young lad what gets around here on foot – *sir.*"

Alice came to a halt. Harriet was not happy – oh dear, here we go again.

"I don't know, Plum; d'ye think it's a sure mark o' respect they address me as 'sir'?"

"Yes m'dear." Harriet relinquished and entered the game. "They recognise their masters right quick on the road."

"Hey there lads!" He was calling to his mates for backup. "Ladies dressin' up as gentlemen! Next they'll be wantin' to make our roads!"

"Oh no, no, no." Harriet waved, "we're quite happy to watch, but perhaps we could *design* you a road or two and of course walk upon't when it's finished."

"Aye. A grand solution." Alice backing her up now.

A new voice comes in, sarcastic and a touch of crude. "If my missus dressed like that, I'd have her flogged."

But Alice was quick to the mark, "If your missus dressed like this, you'd have no chance of catchin' her to lay your brutish hands upon her, so fast could she run away! Oho!" And she did a little quick step for their benefit. A large chap with an even larger beer pot-belly put in his tuppence worth.

"If god meant women to wear trousers, he would have given her more brains. God knows it takes brains to keep a pair of trousers up!"

The men all laughed in support of his clever remark. Alice observed in detail his pot-belly and large arse. "Well if that's so, it's obvious to us all where you keep your brains, sir."

"Thou'rt look right queer with thine legs all parted, lassie," a hard edge to his voice backed up by a threatening move forward.

"I'd have her legs parted afore long!" A savage thrust from another burly chap, sweat running down his neck to meet the soiled collar of his shirt.

"Thou'rt look even more queer with a skirt draggin' you down into the dust," said Alice calmly, "how would you work?"

"Man was born to work, born for trousers!"

"Don't be naïve, sir," shot back Harriet, "we're all born the same – stark naked!"

"You take those trousers off, lassie and you won't look t'same as me! Haw, haw, haw." Supporting growls and snide laughter.

"She ain't got no sex at all like that!" The crowd had gathered and now all the men surrounded them.

"Where be thy husbands?" Howls and whistles.

"We have no need of husbands." Alice and Harriet back to back together, arms crossed firmly!

"If I be thy husband, I'd have thee in the lock-up!"

Alice swung round on him, "If you be my husband I'd rather *be* in the lock-up!" Both women laugh but they realise they are now treading on dangerous ground and are greatly outnumbered.

Just then a coach and four appeared and rolled slowly past, raising more dust, breaking the tension. Inside the coach were two ladies, a mother and daughter. They're agog at the sight of the women in bloomers. The mother noticed her adolescent daughter's look of keen interest and savagely pulled down the blind admonishing her, "Agatha! Don't let such a sinful sight taint yer mind! Joseph, drive faster!" She tapped the roof with her walking stick.

The coach passed turning slightly, following the bend in the road. The daughter lifted the blind, leaning out her side to not lose sight of the spectacle, her mouth open and eyes wide with disbelief. Or was it envy? Harriet and Alice waved to her. That brought a delightful reaction which was cut off by the blind being thrust down again. The distraction of the coach had allowed our brave marchers to move on and get past the workers who continued rather desperately to whistle and cat-call after them.

"They're off to earn their keep in the cat house!"

"Pair of whores!"

"What man'd want to bed that lot!"

CHAPTER 27

Under Pressure

BEACONSFIELD, 1886

Harriet had had a hard time accepting that Alice would not return to the gymnasium but she hoped that she would continue to teach at the schools. Ruyton was still advertising their presence prior to 9 February 1886. But Alice had another idea altogether, "When this road gets finished it will only take 15 minutes to get to the station. But it's still a good two hours to Melbourne. I really want more time out here. I've got so many plans for the farm, Plum. I just don't have enough hours in the day."

"But I need you there, I can't manage on my own. It's the schools – I can't let them go."

"Josephine is quite capable of stepping into my shoes. You'll still be the captain! It will always be your gymnasium."

"I always felt we would be together …"

"We'll still be together! Josephine has already shown you that she can take over from me. She said so."

"It seems to me she says quite a lot to you." Harriet couldn't hold back the bitter jealousy, all her fears rising into her mouth. Alice didn't react to it.

"You've got to let her in, Plum, let someone else in." They walked on in silence. "I'm talking her into buying my share."

"Really?" Harriet did not know how to react to this. It seemed the tables were turning. Josephine and Harriet at the gym and Alice out at the farm.

And thus it came about but they kept the name A.C. Moon for a while in their advertisements. And of course Josephine came out often to stay at Beaconsfield once the new house was finished. Harriet was always the one to get the limelight, but this time it was Alice who managed to get The Steyne, Beaconsfield, into the news. Writing under the pen name 'The Vagabond', an article by Julian Thomas entitled 'Picturesque Victoria' appeared in *The Argus* on Saturday 28 November 1885:

> Anon, in fault of not possessing the Big House, I would prefer Professor Halford's bungalow, and after that 'The Hut', belonging to Messrs Smith and Johnson, where the green sward in front, and the honeysuckle embowered verandah, tempt me to linger. The next best view is, perhaps, from Mr. Elms, but from every site there is a grand panorama. Mr. Walford is known as possessing a capital spring of freshwater.
>
> I shall always remember with the greatest of pleasure the kind reception given me by the ladies of Beaconsfield, and especially at Miss Moon's poultry farm, The Steyne, a name she says which recalls memories of Brighton. Up and down hill you drive past Mr. Bullen's towards Mr. A. Beckett's. The new cottage is on the left of the road. There is an older residence with a few acres of ground opposite it for sale. I wish I could purchase this. At 'The Steyne', white Hamburgs, Polands, game, and other pure-bred domestic fowls have a good time of it. Corralled in small yards, they have shelter sheds from the sun, cool water, dust baths, and everything a fowl could desire. The only want they cannot satisfy is to sit. The incubator does that for most of them. It is a luxury reserved only for a few favourite fowls. This establishment is evidently conducted on first class business principles. The motto

'mens sana in corpore sano' is illustrated by the fact that here a lady who for some years has devoted herself to successfully cultivating the muscle of female young Victorians has a home in which there are the most charming traces of artistic culture. I should like to buy Miss Moon out, and devote my energies to chicken raising.[36]

CHAPTER 28

An Imagined Summer

BEACONSFIELD, 1887

A soft warm light fell on the tomatoes which floated in a bowl of boiled water, their skins splitting. Red tomatoes, some green, different sizes, all home grown. Alice was peeling skins, putting pulp into another bowl, making tomato jam. She worked in the soft light while gazing out of the window to the garden where, digging over a bed with shovel and pitchfork, Josephine and Harriet were stripped down to camisoles and basic underwear sweating it out. Alice's thumbs dug into the flesh of tomato, it spurted seeds – red and orange. It was a hot, hot morning in this amazing summer of 1886 to 1887.

Alice's breasts thrust against the soft white muslin bodice of her shift, her hair was pushed up, some wispy bits clinging to her neck, sweat on her breasts, which rose and fell as she watched Josephine bend from the waist to shake out weeds from the soil. Jo was strong and supple and slightly taller than Harriet. Alice moved outside and leant against the doorframe, watching.

"Who would like some lemon barley water?"

Harriet looked up briefly. "Wonderful! Jo, time for a rest."

And she thrust her spade into the rich red soil and wiped her forehead with the back of her hand. She was sweaty and lightly tanned, her forearms streaked with dirt. With her bare legs in old lace-up boots she had a rather wild and sultry presence that stirred Alice deeply. Harriet approached Alice and then couldn't help laughing.

"Hello, Miss Moon."

"Hello Miss Dick."

They kissed, something they hadn't done for a long time, not like this anyway. Alice slid her hand under Harriet's shift and up her thigh. Harriet resisted, embarrassed and then suddenly she screamed! Alice was holding a peeled tomato in her hand and it now dripped down Harriet 's thigh. Josephine watched the two women chase each other round the side of the house, her eyes narrowed in her desire to be free like them, unaware that her hands were clutching and unclutching the handle of the garden fork.

Christmas break brought hot summer days to Beaconsfield and the three women created their own world away from the eyes of men. As days flowed one into another, the beautiful, eager Josephine was drawn closer and closer to the seductive nature of The Steyne and the challenging energy of Alice. Despite their newfound closeness, Harriet's jealousy did not abate and rightly so, for Alice was deeply attracted to Jo and this summer seemed to be the time when her fidelity to Harriet was put to the test. Alice and Josephine were falling in love, neither of them able to express it, both guilty in front of Harriet who suspected the balance had shifted, but she had to continue to focus all her energy on her crusade in the gymnasium and the schools.

Another hot late summer's morning and the heat of day was pushing the thermometer up fast. They were all three picking blackberries. A huge rambling bush, growing against a wooden fence along the bottom paddock. Alice and Josephine, together on one side of the bush and Harriet on the other.

"You must keep whistling, Jo, or I shall never trust you not to eat them all," Harriet called.

"I have to eat them all!" screamed Jo.

"Plum! She's being hopeless!" Alice is in fits of laughter.

"Don't worry. I've heaps and heaps round here. We shall have enough."

"Heaps? Heaps? What does that mean?" laughed Jo.

"It's what the young girls say. Basketfuls then!" Harriet snorted.

"Jo, look at your mouth, it's purple! Plum, her mouth is purple!"

"Look at my tongue!" Josephine lasciviously stuck her tongue out in Alice's face. Alice shrieked in mock horror. Then there was silence.

Harriet's heart lurched. "Are you being lewd, Josephine? Don't you know about tongues?"

Alice and Josephine's faces are touching. "Your lips are like crushed berries, all bloodied with juice," Alice whispered. They touched their lips together, then Alice pushed another juicy blackberry into Jo's mouth, allowing her fingers to linger there. Jo was falling into the abyss of sucking them.

"Do I hear silence? Are you devouring fruit?" Harriet asked from the other side.

"Forbidden fruit," whispered Alice.

"Oh!" Suddenly Harriet gasped out loud.

Alice quickly separated herself from Jo, expecting to turn and see Harriet there, but she wasn't. "What is it?" she called airily to Harriet.

"Oh, do come quick!" Harriet whispered hoarsely, "Sssh, careful!"

151

They both moved around to the other side of the brambles. Jo's face was flushed and hot. Alice was calm. Harriet was bending into the bush, her gloved hands holding some branches back. She whispered, "Look! A nest! Four baby blackbirds."

Three faces, flushed cheeks, straw hats, hair clinging to necks, sweat running salty, strong fingers, whispers, intimate closeness of the three women. They whisper to each other.

"Aaah, look."

"They're terrified."

"So quiet."

"Ssh, leave them. Don't disturb them."

"Their mother must be somewhere."

Harriet stood at the laundry window which looked out over the rear garden and extended to a wire fence where the fields and paddocks took over. Over the year, Josephine's presence on those weekends at Beaconsfield had been hard for her to manage. Through the window, Harriet's view extended at least ten miles. But Harriet was not looking at the view, she was watching Alice and Josephine picking wildflowers, almost out of sight at the bottom of the rambling garden. Beyond the home fence there was a huge chook run and housing for Alice's poultry where she was experimenting with various methods of incubation and raising chickens carefully within rules of what we now call organic farming. Harriet watched the two women picking bunches of jonquils, the last of the sweet smelling heralds of spring. They stood very close, sometimes bending reaching for the same flower and straightening up, laughing intimately.

The sky was powder blue with baby clouds floating as if in a dream. Harriet's mouth was a thin straight line. Her chest was tight. She was a silent spy. Her gloved hands gripped her riding crop, bending it, wanting it to break, wanting them to know she is about to break herself when she heard the rapping on the front door. Irish McSweeney had arrived to give her her riding lesson which will remove her physical presence from the property. She didn't want to go, yet she must, she must pretend trust, she must pretend and fake her nonchalance, her ignorance. With a last glance at the two women now seated in the field of bright grass she turned on her booted heel and passed through the kitchen and the cool, dimly lit hallway. McSweeney's large form was outlined in the stained glass door.

"Arr ye ready then, Miz Dick?" His hat in his hand, his red hair curling about his ears, and his Irish features nailing his colours to the mast.

"As ever I will be," Harriet replied, tersely.

This was not a good way to begin a relationship with a horse, she reminded herself as she saw the dear grey mare that McSweeney had selected for her. He himself rode a large black stallion, not young and frisky, but sedate and settled. Hmm, thought Harriet to herself, that one has definitely sowed his wild oats, much like his master. And that made her smile so that by the time she leant in to the neck of the mare, and smelt her earthy hide, she had let go her inner pain.

"Dat be your'n mount. She be a dapper lady, won't give thee any trouble. Now let me help tha' mount up."

But Harriet had already got her foot neatly into the stirrup and was up and over into the saddle. She had warned him that she would not want a side-saddle and was well-prepared, wearing bloomers beneath a split skirt. McSweeney made no comment, nor was he even bothered by her strength and control over the horse. He recognised her natural ability and was thus obliged to be honest.

"Roight den, dat be done easy, Miz Dick, th'art a natural!"

He admired how Harriet had swung herself, unaided, into the saddle. "Ah. Now you be an at'lete! Oi be forgettin' dat."

McSweeney mounted his stallion and headed off down the driveway that led to the road and up to the steep rise.

"Oi'm not fully practised at this yet, Mr McSweeney, so you don't be leavin' me behind!" Harriet was enjoying imitating his Irish brogue.

"No fear o' dat Miz Dick." He laughed heartily. "No fear o' dat. Now you keep your knees tight in there, dat's how she knows thee be in control and don't pull back on da' bridle see, like dat, not unless you're wantin' her to turn or stop – dat's better, dat's th' way. Ah now, th'art a natural!"

Let us turn our attention back to the farm where Alice and Josephine, amid the grass and flowers, could hear the retreating riders' voices disappearing up the road. Alice waved and called, "Goodbye! Plum!"

"She can't hear you now."

"Nor see me either." Alice looked at Josephine who blushed and turned aside, her heart pounding, her head bent away. Alice gently placed a finger to Josephine's exposed neck and traced around her cheek to her lips. "Do you want to go for a dip?"

Josephine, overcome with the sensuality of what was being proposed, removed Alice's hand from her cheek. "In the creek, you mean?"

"Yes," Alice laughed, "in the creek."

"It's hot enough."

"I'm very hot," and she laughed again.

"Just like this?"

"Well, we will take our clothes off, won't we?"

With that Alice leapt up and ran, calling to Josephine to not be a slow-coach, and she was over the post-and-rail fence and heading across the meadow and down to the creek, zig-zagging through the willow trees and wattles already in bright flower. Josephine hesitated briefly, then with one last look back over her shoulder, hoping not to see Harriet suddenly appearing behind her, followed.

Bare feet and legs in the waters of the creek. Josephine watched Alice stepping over stones to where the water was running deep. Both women had left their last layer on, their thin cotton chemise undergarments. Alice reached the deepest part of the creek. She swam well, her body clearly revealed through her chemise. She turned to watch Jo enter the water, her arms raised in excitement at the cold touch. As she too got wet, her pubic hair clinging to her undergarments, her breasts and nipples revealed as the wet cotton clung, then released. Alice trod water, never taking her eyes off Jo, watching, her mouth slightly open, as the crystal water flowed in and out across her lips.

Josephine shrieked in delight, "It's freezing!"

"Only for a moment!" Alice plunged under.

Jo joined her, then leapt up gasping, "Freezing!"

"Let me warm you up!"

Josephine's breasts were clearly outlined, nipples hard and erect. Alice came closer and manoeuvred so that her own nipples touched Josephine's. Both women gasped in erotic, dangerous pleasure. Heads thrown back their lips met and they plunged into each other's mouths. Falling into water, legs around waist, wet eyelashes, white chemise, mouths searching tongues.

Harriet's face was in deep concentration as if, in her mind, she had witnessed this last scene. Or did she imagine it?

"Come on, Miz Dick! Give 'er a nudge along dere!"

McSweeney had gone way ahead of Harriet who had fallen behind, lost in her fear and jealousy. "Th'art daydreamin' dere."

"Hardly," said Harriet under her breath. More like a nightmare, she thought. She dug her heels into the flanks of the old grey mare and kicked her to life, cantering up to the distant McSweeney and galloping on right past him.

" 'ere now you watch out dere, miz Dick, dat be no way to ride her home!"

But Harriet had gone. Leaving the mare in the yard she crossed the verandah and opened the front door of The Steyne. The afternoon sunlight silhouetted her form. Behind her McSweeney was disappearing up the lane, the exhausted mare trailing behind him on a lead. She pulled off her boots and striding down the hallway she shouted, "Hello! Hello! I'm home."

Josephine emerged from the kitchen, looking cool and innocent.

"Hello, how was the ride?"

"Let's just say I'm dying for a cup of tea. Where's Alice?"

"I think she's upstairs, asleep. She's been painting – I'll have some tea with you."

Josephine was relaxed and Harriet could get no sense of any subterfuge in her manner. It was her own imagination that was filled with betrayals. I'm in a desperate way she thought. "Fine," she replied nicely and followed Jo into the kitchen.

CHAPTER 29

Alice's Dream

BEACONSFIELD, 1887

Alice dreamt she was lying on her bed. Soft light and a strange mystical feeling in the room. A small lamb lay on the covers beside her, nuzzling her breast. She appeared to be semi-conscious. Two unknown women at the end of the bed were talking in hoarse whispers. They were the same age as Alice.

"There's no hope."

"But she's too young to die!"

The women are distraught. They cry and grasp each other's hands.

Pressed back against the far wall in the shadows, beside a gilt mirror, just discernible, stands the figure of a large bearded man. He holds a top hat. Watching.

Alice's breath comes in short gasps and then with great difficulty. She feels the gripping pain in her chest. Suddenly a small, deadly snake slides out from under the strewn bedclothes that lie fallen around the bed. It slithers away. Alice's eyes are just slits. She sees it and mouths silently, one word, almost inaudible.

"Charming." Then she is dead.

Alice woke up, sweat on her upper lip. Her heart was pounding. The room was hot and dark. Her throat was dry and felt sore.

"A terrible dream, just a terrible dream." And she fell back onto her pillow, sweat on her brow and strands of her hair clinging to her forehead. She moaned softly. Harriet woke and sat up. They slept in separate beds.

"What is it dearest? Are you ill?"

"No. I'm frightened, a dream has frightened me." And she related the dream to Harriet in great detail. Harriet, rather than dismissing it out of hand, had felt a shiver run down her spine. Her Marmie, despite her Christian attitude to life, had always placed great trust in dreams, especially ones that were so clear and full of such symbolism. A gilt mirror, a snake, a mysterious man in the shadows. She ruminated upon it all the next day and was quite distracted in her classes. It wasn't just the dream. She knew this. It was the hollowed out feeling in her gut that her predictable world was sliding away from under her feet, sliding away out of her control. It's been months since we had any intimacy. Alice seems to have built up an electrical charge around her that cannot be broached. It's true I'm obsessed with my work, but no more so than before when we worked together. We are so out of balance. I miss her spontaneous embraces. Now that's just a memory and she's always with the hens, or the cows, she deliberately puts them between us. It's ridiculous, isn't it, to take second place to a hen? And then there's Josephine. I believe she's coming out to the farm again next weekend. I'm glad I've given up on the riding and I can be there – but at this thought Harriet felt embarrassed and shallow and yes, weak. Self-hatred seeping into her heart.

CHAPTER 30

Alice Changes Direction

MELBOURNE, 1888

Alice sold the beautiful estate at Beaconsfield on 18 April 1888. Perhaps Harriet was relieved. The travelling had wearied her immensely, but really it could not have been as simple as that. It's hard to imagine that after all that work and effort in starting up an organic farm and delving into experimental poultry breeding, Alice could just throw it all away without a backward glance. But it says something about her personality and her sudden, quixotic changes of mind. She had another venture burning bright on her horizon. She was going to start a restaurant.

"A restaurant?" Harriet was dumbstruck. "Isn't that a bit beneath you?"

"Not the restaurant that I'm going to deliver. I've been thinking about it for ages. I've made enquiries already – yes, and I haven't involved you, Harriet, because this is my enterprise and a new start for me."

"I thought this farm was your 'new start'?"

"I've proved what one can do here and I'm perfectly happy to have someone else claim it now." She hesitated before adding,

"I've taken lodgings in Parkville."

"What about St Heliers?"

"It's too far out from the city and my restaurant will be right in the business district and I will need to be there all the time."

"Well I suppose it will be easier for both of us then."

Alice looked straight at Harriet, a flash of cruelty in her eyes, and a look of frustration in her expression. "Harriet, you are not hearing me. I have taken lodgings for myself in Parkville and I intend, for the time being, to live there alone."

Harriet could feel the blood draining from her face, her legs weakening. So here it was at last. "But, but we *will* still be together? Just not living together? With you back in the city our hours together could be so much better worked out." But her words fell on deaf ears.

Furious and unable to argue or explain anymore, Alice stomped out of the kitchen. Angrily pulling on her boots in the scullery, she disappeared across the yard to the poultry barn. Harriet watched her go, her mouth was dry and her eyes were pricking with tears. She stopped breathing. When she drew breath at last, she found she could not think any further than her next move, which was to catch the coach to Beaconsfield station and take her train to Melbourne where a killing schedule of school appointments awaited her.

The sale of The Steyne, Beaconsfield, signalled the end of their intimate relationship and a huge change in their partnership arrangements.[37] Alice had been totally disconnected from the world of gymnasiums and teachings for some years. I presume that the land that Harriet had bought in Beaconsfield was also sold around this time.

There is a strange reference to an A.C. Moon living in

Archibald Street, Caulfield in 1888–1889, but there was no Archibald Street then.[38] Alice is next listed as residing at 13 Benjamin Street, Parkville and this would make sense as she was in attendance every day at her new restaurant which she named The Central Luncheon and Tearooms. It was just a short trolley trip straight down Royal Parade to Elizabeth Street. There is no mention of Harriet at this Parkville address, although for many previous years, they had always been listed only under Alice's name. If Harriet wasn't there, then where did she live? Perhaps she remained at St Heliers Street? Perhaps Alice even did accommodate her in Parkville, but my instinct tells me no.

CHAPTER 31

Alice's Restaurant

MELBOURNE, 1888

The establishing of The Central Luncheon and Tearooms was a great achievement for Alice. She did it on her own. She decorated and supervised all the décor and the facilities, many of which had never been thought of before in a city restaurant. If one looks at the advertised menu, one can only imagine what a feat it was to run the establishment for luncheons, teas and dinners, seven days a week! Not to mention the extra services she provided for her business clientele which openly advertised facilities aimed at attracting female clients: a parcel service, a postal service and a telephone service.

At this time in Australia, the women's rights movement was heating up. The calls for women's suffrage pretty well followed the movements in America and England. The first American Women's Rights Convention had been held at Seneca Falls in 1848, and was, by comparison with later events, a very small affair. But the time had finally come, and the male establishment were rocked to their socks and shaking in their boots. In America, the movement had begun when the women fighting for the abolition of slavery and for the rights of slaves realised that their own position was actually worse than the black slaves – they at least could escape to Canada. But for women, there was no safe haven of equality.

In Australia, it was probably worse for women. Marcus Clarke wrote in February 1887: 'Australians are not a nation of snobs like the English or of extravagant boasters like the Americans or of reckless profligates like the French; they are simply a nation of Drunkards.' This observation was aimed at the male population. And in the same year, J.F. Archibald, founder of the Archibald Prize and founder and editor of *The Bulletin*, wrote: 'Women's enfranchisement just now means men's enslavement.' Such was the word on the street.

Back in June of 1884 an article had appeared, headed: 'Suffrage for the Clever', which read as follows:

> Women who want to join Victoria's newly formed Women's Suffrage Society will have to pass an educational test to receive membership. The society was formed at a meeting last night to work to provide women with the same political privileges as men. Around 50 women and 20 men attended the meeting and voted for the restrictive test for membership.[39]

It seems that neither Alice nor Harriet ever had time to go to the meetings and demonstrations for women's suffrage. Their own work schedules were prohibitive, but within their gymnasium classes, they had proselytised for women's rights from day one.

Alice opened the Central Luncheon and Tea Rooms on 1 November 1888 in the basement of the newly built City of Melbourne Chambers, at 114 Elizabeth Street on the corner of Little Collins Street.[40] From my investigations it seems that the modern entrance to the basement of the building is now from Little Collins Street and the Elizabeth Street entrance seems to have disappeared. At the same time, the Ladies' Gymnasium

City of Melbourne Chambers today, Elizabeth Street.
Alice's restaurant was in the basement.

was in Hansen's Buildings, directly opposite the Melbourne Chambers on the north side of Little Collins. Alice obtained the services of a French chef and catered for balls, picnics and private functions. She was determined to break down the barriers to catering for women in the city by encouraging them to come to her restaurant to both eat and relax, or to conduct business there by providing them with writing tables, courier services and a telephone: No.1151! For most of the women this was the first time they had held a telephone in their hand! They kept coming back just to use it, even though they didn't know anyone to whom they could make a call.

The entrance to the Central was down a flight of steps off Elizabeth Street. Alice's innate sense of art and design was evident everywhere. The rooms were beautifully arranged; everything was most excellently outfitted, from the handsomely draped gasaliers to the basement windows which, though grated, were filled inside with graceful ferns. During lunchtime, the place was full; it was a mecca not only for merchants and professional gentlemen, but also for an equivalent number of upper-class ladies. Alice employed and groomed her waitresses very carefully. She dressed them in starched white calf-length aprons over the usual black stiff full-length skirts and bodices, white cuffs and high collars, and a pleated headdress. Alice was often complimented on the superior class of young women that she employed, and on their swift and accurate service. Alice's innovations stood out once patrons realised that they were, for their convenience, provided with ample restrooms, writing tables, a parcel and postal service and a public telephone.

Let us follow two elegantly dressed ladies as they, for their first time, descend the staircase into the Central. Wearing full length gowns, bustled and cloaked, tiny-waisted thanks to the iron corsets beneath the silken splendour of rûches and bows, their hats are masterpieces of frivolity. It is quite a feat of balance that they remain on their heads as they make their way down the terrazzo stairway. They carry small dilly bags and parasols, as above ground it is a bright, hot Melbourne day. They hesitate at the foot of the stairs, gasping in admiration at the sumptuous decor, the carpeted floor, the gentle gaslight, the aspidistras and ferns in brass pots, the curtains, the elegant waitresses, the soft murmur of the clientele, tables of men in frock coats, all enjoying their luncheon and the heavenly smells. They are quickly approached by an immaculately dressed Alice Moon who glides to their side to welcome them.

"Ladies, welcome to the Central. I am the proprietor, Alice Moon. Would I be right in saying this your first visit?"

"Why yes, Mrs Moon, we've all heard so much about it. What is that beautiful smell?" Catherine was gushing.

"Freshly brewed coffee, madam, and please – it's Miss Moon."

"Do forgive me. How charming it is, Miss Moon – Lottie, would you like to take a coffee?"

"Coffee? Oh no, dear Catherine. No. I shall have tea. I never drink coffee. Coffee is a man's beverage."

"Well, we play at being men here," laughed Alice lightly. "Perhaps you both would you like to take luncheon?" She started to lead them to the dining room where the tables were beautifully laid with silver cutlery, damask napkins and fresh flowers in a centre bowl. At the dining room entrance, the two ladies hesitated to see the telephone booth next to the private writing tables in the foyer.

"Look here, Lottie! They've got a telephone!"

"A telephone! Good heavens, Catherine, don't go too near it. I understand they can make you quite sick."

"Really? I know that Charles uses his all the time."

"Well so does Randolph, but he told me that women can become quite ill if they use them."

"Really? Excuse me, Miss Moon?" Catherine called Alice back to the booth.

"Yes, madam?"

"That is a telephone, is it not?"

"Why yes, I believe it is." Alice was used to dealing with her clientele's curiosity.

"A dangerous thing to have in a restaurant, Miss Moon, where there are ladies present?" Catherine was severe and determined to prove Charlotte at fault.

"Dangerous? In what way, may I enquire?" Alice knew what was coming.

Charlotte assumed her mistress-of-the-house voice, taking

166

charge. "Well, I've been told women can become quite faint if they use one."

"What a quaint idea – and you would have been told this by your husband, perhaps?" Alice was grinning inside.

"Why yes, it was my husband."

"And he is in the city, in business, no doubt?"

"Oh yes, Miss Moon. He is a barrister."

"Ah, a barrister. Using the telephone all day I shouldn't wonder."

"Yes," agreed Charlotte quite vehemently, "I believe it's a very important part of his work."

"And is he quite well?"

"Oh yes, quite well thank you – robust I would say."

"The telephone not affecting him at all?"

"Well, no." She hesitated, unsure of her ground now. "I don't believe so."

"Woman's blood is no different to man's. Women's hands are no different to man's; eyes, mouth, ears –"

"But Miss Moon, a woman's brain is utterly different, quite susceptible to instruments of a mechanical nature!" Charlotte was lecturing again.

"Ah yes, our brain – and, if I may be so bold as to ask, what do you do with your brain, Mrs …?"

"Brewster, Mrs Randolph Brewster," and she held out her hand to Alice who took it gently, then let it go.

"May I call you by your name?"

"That is my name."

"I feel as though that is more your husband's name, I meant your Christian name?"

"Oh yes, I see. Charlotte. Charlotte Brewster."

"I am Alice. Your brain, forgive my impertinence, would get a lot of use would it not?"

"Oh dear, my brain? Well, I don't know."

"Yes, yes, you do. How many children do you have, Charlotte?"

"I have four sons."

"Four sons! My goodness, how marvellous! And you have conceived and borne these four men, fed them, nurtured them, run a household, advised, taught, mended, aided, cleaned their bodies, and also, I imagine, cared for their spiritual wellbeing?"

"Well, yes, I suppose I have …"

"Without a brain in your head?"

"Oh! When you put it like that – but it's not the sort of work that Randolph does – men are so different."

"In their work, yes. Different. Creating pieces of paper, crises, failures, successes, profits and losses, poverty and wealth, war and peace. But, Charlotte, you have created *real* things of flesh and blood. You have created men!"

Catherine burst out loud, "Lottie, this woman is astounding!"

Alice laughed and took Charlotte by the elbow and steered her into the booth. "Now don't tell me that your magnificent brain cannot deal with a telephone! Come. Let me show you how it's done."

"Oh, oh, I am quite excited now, Catherine. Do let us have an experience!"

Charlotte entered the booth. "Oh dear, who on earth shall I make a telephone call to?"

"If I may suggest, you possibly might call your husband?" Alice smiled invitingly.

"Oh, what fun! Yes. Now, I have his number written somewhere, but wait, I *remember* his number, you see Miss Moon, I do have a brain! It's 15–23, the same as the ages of two of my sons!"

Guided by Alice, Charlotte lifted the receiver and waited. "Hello? Oh dear, someone's speaking! How extraordinary!" She looked at the earpiece to see the voice coming out of it. She laughed again out of sheer terror and excitement. The voice asked her what number she wanted. Catherine was leaning in, hearing every word too.

"That's a *woman* talking Lottie, so you see, it can't be too bad!"

"1-5-2-3. Fifteen and twenty-three, thank you." Charlotte drew herself up to her full height, totally in command now.

"One moment madam."

They waited and heard a buzzing sound then a female voice spoke.

"Good Morning. This is Brewster and Gammon, how may I help you?" Both Alice and Catherine motioned Charlotte to speak.

"Oh hello, yes, hello. I wish to speak with Mr Randolph Brewster."

"Yes ma'am. Who shall I say is calling?"

"*Whom* shall I say is calling."

"Pardon, ma'am?"

"It's whom, dear." Lottie turned to Catherine, frowning, "This is really not good enough, Catherine. The girl can't speak the Queen's English."

"She can hear you, Lottie!" Catherine whispered.

"Oh dear, Mr Brewster please."

"Yes ma'am."

There were two clicks and eventually a man's voice came on the line.

"Hello?"

Charlotte, recognising her husband's voice suddenly became quite soft and almost embarrassed, "Hello? Randolph? Hello?"

"Hello! Who is this? Is this you, Flo? How do like your new telephone, eh? But I've told you not ring me here, you naughty girl. You just can't get enough can you? Eh? I'll see you this evening, poppet. I can get away around nine o'clock."

Charlotte's face drained of blood. Her hand started shaking. Both Catherine and Alice couldn't help but hear what he had said.

"Flo? Can you hear me?"

"Yes." She was almost inaudible.

"All right, my lovey dovey, I'll be there at nine. Keep it wet and warm for me, won't you. Ha ha." He clicked off.

Silence. Charlotte didn't move but the receiver dropped from her gloved hand and hung on its cord. "He called me Flo. We don't know anyone called Flo? He said … he said he would see me tonight at nine. But tonight's the night he stays at his club."

Catherine helped her trembling friend out of the booth. She put her arm around her and supported her to a chair in the lobby. Charlotte was stunned, speechless and breathless and the corset wasn't helping.

Alice picked up the dangling instrument and hung it back on its hook. "Perhaps he's right," she said. "Telephones can be dangerous things."

CHAPTER 32

Love Ends

MELBOURNE, 1889

I t was June 1889. Harriet, always keen to extend her influence and her work schedule or perhaps financially stretched, applied for a position instructing gymnastics at the Teachers Training College in Spring Street, Melbourne. She and Josephine gave a demonstration lesson to 30 women trainee teachers while Mr Charles Topp, the examiner, subsequently gave the following critique. He didn't like her work – she was 'too soft spoken, didn't use military terms or sharp words.' She fatigued them, two girls had to stay home the following day. "Miss Dick has overestimated the strength of women engaged in serious study all day." He also criticised her skill as organiser and maintained her exercises were 'too difficult for children.'[41]

Sounds like she got right up his nose. Don't forget, by 1889 Harriet had successfully been running her own gymnasium for ten years! Her teaching methods – which obviously were opposite to the 'male methods' which for so long had gone unquestioned, being designed for men only and considered the 'norm' – simply did not make any sense to Mr Topp. Harriet's focus was always on women and here she bravely (and sensibly) departed from the universally accepted rules. All these training schools were run on militaristic lines, for they had never had to encompass or accommodate female students. For the most part when women entered or attempted to enter their domain, the odds were skewed against them, which proved, to the men's great satisfaction, that women simply 'weren't up to the task'. Should they ever prove their equality, or be allowed entry into those sacred halls, they were accused of being 'intruders on the rights of men'.

Harriet did one last display at the Melbourne Town Hall in 1890, but then started to devote her time to remedial work with damaged people. Josephine was in her element here. She had a natural talent for it and an increasing love of the work. With the public separation of Harriet and Alice, Jo felt more at ease spending time with Alice, although it was incredible how Harriet clung to the old regime, regularly taking meals at the Central, probably testing Alice's patience to the nth degree.

Alice's meeting with the Parker-Leary family created a mutual and instant rapport. Mary Rose, Florence's sister, would have boasted of the opportunities to be had in Sydney and would no doubt have offered Alice a place to come and live with her family in her beautiful house in Double Bay "right on the harbour water! You would always be welcome to come and stay, we have many rooms!"

Once Alice heard about the vibrant scene in Sydney, referred to as the era of the New Woman, a label that was applied mainly to female writers, her heart was set on escaping Melbourne and, I would suggest, the ongoing influence of Harriet. The promise inherent in being able to meet Mary Rose's Sydney inner circle of female friends which included published novelist, Evelyn Dickinson and her partner, Louisa Macdonald (later the head of the Women's College at the University of Sydney), and other political revolutionary intellectuals like Rose Scott, Maybanke Wolstenholme (Anderson) and Lady Windeyer and her daughter, Margaret, would have confirmed for her that now was the time to make the final break from Harriet.

She confided to Josephine, "I've been talking to Florence about becoming a real journalist. Apparently in Sydney they are hiring females called 'pen-ladies', at *The Sydney Morning Herald*. They seem to be much more advanced than here in Melbourne. I know Mary Rose's friends are already renowned published writers and are intimately connected to William Curnow, the editor of *The Sydney Morning Herald*."

Josephine recognised that Alice's plans to become a professional writer, to extend herself beyond menus, meals and newspaper advertisements, would release Alice from the complicated emotions that they were both entangled in. She appreciated Alice's bright, enquiring mind, and saw the suffocating influence of Harriet's claims upon her. They could not still have been living together during the time of the restaurant. It would have been truly awful as Alice and Josephine could continually meet at the restaurant which was right opposite the gymnasium. Harriet, although intelligent and steadfast in her commitment to her crusade for women's health, could be domineering and often quite self-centred. But she loved Alice like no other. Because of their close connection, both personal and commercial, there had to come a time when Alice finally broached the subject of moving to Sydney, far away from Melbourne, and completely away from Harriet.

Late one afternoon, Alice turned up at the Ladies' Gymnasium when Josephine was absent. Finally, she had found the strength to tell Harriet that she was selling the Central and moving to Sydney.

Harriet was completely devastated. In the past months she

had struggled with their separation, never accepting that it was a permanent decision. Living apart was surely just a temporary glitch in Alice's always turbulent behaviour. They had had no intimacy since Alice had created the Central, but Harriet was a stubborn woman and while there was life, there was surely hope? But this news was frightening. It was her own life's work to be in the gymnasium. Alice owned the lease on the gymnasium. With that gone, would she have to start all over again in Sydney?

"You just expect me to throw away my gymnasium and trot off to Sydney to start afresh, just because you want to be a writer?"

"You seem to forget that it was *my* money that set up *your* gymnasium in the first place!" retorted the furious Alice. "And I am in no way expecting that you should come with me! We really have not shared our life for a long time!"

"You can be a writer here, can't you? Where will we live?"

"I know where *I* can live, Harriet, and where *you* live can no longer be of my concern. In fact, I see this as the break that has been stirring away beneath us for over a year. You must acknowledge this, surely? Ever since we left the farm and I admitted to you that I no longer feel about us the way I used to. I have been unfaithful to you – that I admit – and I'm sure that you were well aware of this. That lie has been living with us for more than six years."

Harriet knew the truth, for she would have had to have been incredibly gullible to never have suspected it. Ever since those uneasy days at Beaconsfield and now, all this time that Josephine was in the gymnasium with her, being kind and caring, and all this time deceiving her! But she had been deceiving herself.

"No. You are wrong in accusing Jo. I was the one who was deceiving you," admonished Alice. "Josephine never wanted that. I have made a profitable business of The Central and I can now sell it into good hands."

Harriet was speechless. Alice left the gymnasium also without a word. Harriet knew that once Alice had made a decision she always acted upon it, no matter how destructive or cold-hearted it might be. As for her own emotions, they were shattered. It made no difference that for so long she had consciously turned a blind eye to what she knew. Alice was her life partner, her soul mate. Images of the angel girl in white waiting on the pier, the adoring eyes upon her as she triumphed in the water, lost in time. I cannot just let her go. I will fight for her. Can she be in love with Mrs Merewether? Or with Florence Parker? Is this the result of the trips to Tasmania with Josephine? Doesn't she care for Josephine? Josephine won't leave Melbourne. Her mother depends on her and besides, she loves the gymnasium and she wants it to be great. How have I lost touch with Alice? I've been so ambitious but that was for both of us, wasn't it?

Such recriminations tormented her. That night Harriet stayed back alone in the gymnasium. She took herself through a most extraordinary workout. Alone and in full flight she ran, she leapt, she pulled the weights, she tossed the clubs, she swung on the trapeze. All in silence. Just the sound of her own breath. Sweat on her brow, sweat running down her back, her arms and neck, she tried to reach a state of oblivion of the mind through the exhaustion of the body. Her exhaustion ended in tears but also seemed to empty her of any doubt. Against Alice's wishes and in some sort of blind terror, Harriet decided that she too, must move to Sydney, or lose Alice completely. She talked to Josephine. She proposed to make the move and try to open a gymnasium up there, but still maintain her influence at the Melbourne gym, which would be run by Josephine and her assistants. The schools' lessons would also be taken over by Josephine. The name of Miss Elphinstone Dick would stay with the Melbourne business.

CHAPTER 33

Goodbye Melbourne, Hello Sydney

1890

One has to wonder at Harriet's blindness or should we call it stubbornness? Could she absolutely not accept that the relationship was over? I believe she did never really accept that she and Alice were not to be together for ever. She also was to have no idea of the contents of Alice's will, where she was not included as a beneficiary nor even mentioned. [A stipulation in the will, written in Sydney in 1891 presumably with the help of Walton Merewether, was that the women were never to share any of their inheritance with their husbands.] Alice saw no need to disillusion Harriet, she was on her own path and, as always, financially independent. And at last she was allowing herself to claim her secret belief that she was a writer.

She moved to Sydney sometime in 1890 or 1891, and straight into the home of Mary Rose Merewether and her family. It is common knowledge amongst the descendants of Florence Parker that Walton Merewether was not an easy man. No doubt that was the reason why his marriage to Mary Rose ended in separation. But at that time, the Merewethers were living together as stated, at Lurlie in Double Bay. The house still stands today.

Back in Melbourne, the restaurant menus ceased to be advertised in 1890, the new owner obviously trying to save money. Meanwhile Alice, with never a thought for her first love or their shared history, was happily settled in Double Bay. Mary Rose wasted no time in showing her off to all her friends. Those friends, as already mentioned, were of an elite group of women, not necessarily wealthy but certainly free thinkers and revolutionary minded, committed to women's suffrage, women's rights, the temperance movement, the cause of raising the age of consent, the lack of education for women – the list was endless.

It is most likely that Matilda Curnow, a good friend of Mary Rose and the wife of William Curnow,[42] gave Alice a foot in the door of becoming a pen lady – a lady journalist. So it was that one morning William Curnow sat at his overflowing desk, interviewing Miss Alice Moon.

"So, you want to be a pen lady, Miss Moon. I'm quite partial to women working for *The Herald*. Gives the men a bit of a push on. What about starting with some book reviews, eh? Then we'll chart your progress from there."

Alice is in. She's thrilled. She has her own desk, and the other two women on the secretarial staff feel a little miffed by her presence. She cares not about her appearance and wears masculine clothes. And obviously, she has ditched the corset! The men study her with open curiosity and some disdain. They soon learn that she will not get tea for them, nor will she cop any innuendo, her tongue being as quick as her fingers which fly across the page, scribbling away, or upon her Remington typewriter.

Alice quickly became quite well known as a pen lady and

soon moved in a literary circle of friends including Sydney's leading feminist writers. She began to write creatively, working on romantic short stories that eventually got into print in such publications as *Freeman's Journal*.[43]

Harriet's doings were of no interest to her, but she never did completely sever their connection. Either at home in Double Bay, or taking advantage of her office space in the city, she was writing creatively and excelling as a journalist. Her knowledge of the bush, so beautifully expressed in her original stories, could have been gleaned from visiting Louisa Macdonald's brother's farm in rural NSW. Her friendship with Evelyn Dickinson certainly deepened.[44]

Accepted into this exciting world of women's literature, she took advantage of the intellectual, educational and political activities that Sydney offered. With her friends she soon became active in a range of women's organisations, including the Womanhood Suffrage League and the Women's Literary Society. Enjoying a new sense of freedom within the public sphere, these 'New Women' gave speeches, petitioned parliament, walked through Sydney's streets unchaperoned, and wrote articles for newspapers.[45] This was a far cry from the company of Harriet and the Ladies' Gymnasium.

CHAPTER 34

Harriet's New Gymnasium

SYDNEY, 1893

Harriet stood patiently watching while a workman removed the sign:

Miss Mary FOSTER. Principal Ladies' Gymnasium.
177 Liverpool Street, Hyde Park (under Unitarian Church)

and erected her own sign,

Miss H. Elphinstone DICK. Principal Ladies' Gymnasium.
177 Liverpool Street, Hyde Park (under Unitarian Church)

As he worked, the man talked about the Depression and hard times which had put Miss Foster out of business, and how '93 looked like being worse than ever ... and him with his wife pregnant again "an' there 'aint no way of stopping that!"

Grim-faced, she gave him a look and under her breath murmured, "I know *one* way of stopping it." She knew all too well that her clientele would drop away in a recession. "I've been teaching at a private school and they are certainly beginning to feel the pinch. I've got the bruises all over my bank account." She also had bruises all over her soul. It must have been hell for her,

179

and one wonders about this woman's determination and strength to just keep on going in the face of such adversity. Despite there seemingly being no hope for Alice and her to be reunited, Harriet too had moved to Sydney.

In May 1893, it is recorded that Harriet left the port of Melbourne on *The Bucephalus II* and sailed up the coast to Sydney. It amused her to think that she was riding the famous wild black stallion that Alexander the Great had tamed. She knew the story: how he had tamed the horse by turning it away from its shadow which had disturbed it. Thus, he won ownership of the horse. If I could only turn Alice away from her shadow, perhaps she could see me again in a new light? Alone and with no contacts, she sought accommodation and soon rented a house in Randwick. Her next move, a fortuitous one at that, saw her taking over a Miss Foster's Women's Gymnasium along with its existing clientele and thus, plunging right into keeping herself busy, she again managed to find teaching work at a girls' school. She'd left all her friends, her supporters, and her wealthy clients behind just to be near Alice, in the strangeness of Sydney, in spite of being humiliated by Alice's silences and her dismissive coldness whenever she arranged to meet her, which was not often despite the fact that they were both working in the centre of Sydney. Harriet often caught the trolley bus from Randwick to Bondi Beach where she found great solace in the sea, the element that nurtured her spirit and physically supported her. It was there that she was happy to be alone, enraptured by the glorious sight of rolling ocean surf and white sands, the striped bathing tents and little wooden bathing boxes on wheels, parked at the water's edge, some with wooden fences that went out into the water. These contraptions enabled women to change and get down into the water both privately and safely. Most people were heavily dressed. Intrepid male bathers splashed about further out to sea. That always brought a smile to her face. She swam like an amazon, drawing admiring glances from the other bathers. The ever-present cries of the gulls took her home to Brighton, and a great sadness would sweep over her. Her tears were disguised by the waves. She often wondered what her life would have been if she had stayed in Brighton. Would she have had the success, the kudos and rewards she had achieved thus far in this new land? She was now 41, but when she looked around at the feisty women of her own age, she saw that she could go on to greater achievements. Perhaps she should become involved in the Womanhood Suffrage League? Through Mary Rose and Louisa Macdonald she had met a few of those active women, and she admired them greatly.

Harriet was sometimes included in parties at Lurlie despite the fact that she and Alice were no longer a couple. An invitation would come from Mary Rose who, out of compassion and a genuine liking of Harriet, insisted on honouring Alice's original friendship with her. Often it would be Alice who would pour cold water on that idea, for whenever Harriet was included, Alice became awkward, not embracing her, nor even kissing her with a friendly greeting. It's easy to guess why. She would have harboured guilt for, having already written her Will, she had omitted Harriet completely. Alice's new life, her independence and her blossoming beauty which came with her new happiness, made Harriet feel even more bereft. Despite this, Harriet discovered that she was quite at ease with Alice's literary chums and found it natural to share her stories of thwarted feminism and disastrous meetings with men, for in truth she'd lived a life of deep political commitment to women's rights and was an impressive talker. She kept the group enthralled one afternoon when she interrupted Alice who was giving a serious lecture on the Rational Dress Society, with her own views on the implications of 'pocketless women', and how men would continue to hold sway over the female sex and civilisation itself while they had all the pockets and women had none! Louisa Macdonald enjoyed her company a lot and they became good friends. So much so that when Harriet took a trip home to England in 1893,[46] it is recorded that she delivered a gift from Louisa Macdonald to that lady's friend, Eleanor Grove.[47] She must have returned quite quickly as she was back in Sydney when Alice died in April 1894.

From 1892 onwards, life for Alice at the Merewether's was akin to landing in another country. Her days were busy and filled with exciting and intelligent new acquaintances, writers and artists, and more specifically Mary Rose's female friends, a contingent of women whose ideas and lives were intellectually and socially in advance of any Alice had ever known. These were women who argued clearly against all the male laws and constrictions of this Victorian age. Alice had stopped going to church back in Beaconsfield, but in the discussions on religion amongst these intelligent dames, her mind opened to the lies and the ridiculousness of the laws of Christianity and the writings of the Bible. She had always been alert to the church's control over ideas of dress and control of women's sexuality, but the arguments she now heard were scholarly, and an intellectual criticism of religions based on all-male authority. She embraced her new friends not only for their freedom of thought, but also for the way they lived their beliefs. Watching Evelyn Dickinson and Louisa Macdonald's close relationship made her yearn for a lover who was unafraid to demonstrate that love openly. Harriet had always had a puritan streak in her that warned her about expressing the physical closeness that Alice wanted her to openly demonstrate. Perhaps not having had a mother around as she grew up meant that Alice owed no allegiance to anyone in these matters. On the other hand, Harriet's loyalty to her

Marmie's beliefs had carved out a path for her that she could not stray from.

It became a regular affair for Matilda Curnow to organise a luncheon *au plein air* on the foreshore of Sydney Harbour at Rose Bay with her intimates, Rose Scott, Louisa and Evelyn, Mary Rose, and now Alice. On this particular day, as on many others, the group did not include Harriet.

Alice was gloating over a review that she had written of Louisa's book, a monograph on Cypriot antiquities.[48]

"Give me your book, Evelyn, as soon as it's finished and I'll write the review *and* get it in the paper!" Alice was in her element, it seemed as if all her dreams had come true at last. She felt that she had finally landed where she belonged. Stuffing her mouth with chicken and slices of cucumber, she leapt up, ran a few paces, and to hers and everyone else's shocked surprise, performed a perfect cartwheel on the grass. With gasps of delight, her friends all applauded in stark contrast to the walkers in the park who looked as though they'd been hit with a pie in their face, as Alice later commented. "I don't know whether it was the sight of my bloomers, or my ankles, which disturbed them the most! It's a glorious day! What a picture! Little sailboats on the harbour! Sometimes I think I should go back to painting – I am trained you know!"

"We knooww!" came a chorus of voices followed by laughter as Alice collapsed in a heap, choking on chicken sandwiches and laughing until her eyes watered.

Later, Alice walked Evelyn down to the water where her little skiff, *The Lark*, was moored. She and Mary Rose had actually arrived by boat for the picnic. Casting off, they sailed out on the sparkling harbour. They were soul sisters, their joy in each other's company was positively effervescent. There may have been a frisson of attraction between them, but Evelyn was Louisa's life partner, and Alice would have never done anything to interfere with that.

"You would never know there was a Depression out here," sighed Evelyn.

"There isn't!" was Alice's sharp reply. Skilfully, she whipped the sail around, tacking to increase the speed of the boat.

Alice wrote often to Josephine in Melbourne and her letters, and the little drawings that accompanied them, were full of lightness and of genuine loving friendship. She never wrote about her deeper feelings, the feelings which she and Jo had shared in those summer days at The Steyne in Beaconsfield, and later in her restaurant days. There was one week late in December 1893 when Jo came to have a holiday in Sydney. Florence Parker was also there, newly pregnant with her sixth child who was due to be born in July 1894. Josephine and Florence were both staying with Edith Louise Leary, Mary Rose and Florence's younger sister. Gatherings at the Merewether's were full of gaiety and rich talk.

Alice quickly found that her feelings for Jo were still the same, but there was no way that Josephine was going to give up the Ladies' Gymnasium now, and she certainly would not leave her beloved mother alone in Melbourne. It made Alice feel bereft, but the tyranny of distance brought home the reality of their physical separation and had to be acknowledged. She knew she would never return to Melbourne, just as she knew she would always love Josephine. She proved that love in her will, bequeathing everything to be dispersed among Florence, Mary Rose and Josephine.

CHAPTER 35

Afternoon Tea at Quong Tart Tearooms

SYDNEY, 1893

Louisa Macdonald, Evelyn Dickinson and Rose Scott have already settled themselves at the round table of polished wood, set in the Chinese style with a crystal vase of fresh flowers and Christmas holly utterly pleasing to their judicious gaze. There is a low buzz of conversation and polite laughter as ladies and the occasional gentleman enjoy the exciting oriental flavour of the famous Quong Tart Tearoom establishment in the Royal Arcade of Sydney.

"Aren't they a little late?" queried Evelyn as she turned to set her gaze on the front door to the establishment.

"Yes, a little, but they may have had trouble securing a cab from Double Bay – the rain always does that. Not just yet, we will wait until our companions arrive, thank you," said Louisa, turning to the waitress who had arrived at their table asking for their order. The menu was extensive, but the ladies were gathering today simply for tea and the famous Quong Tart scones.

"Here they are!" said Evelyn waving a gloved hand. She signalled across the room to Alice and Mary Rose who had made their way into the restaurant, shaking umbrellas and flicking off rain from their long skirts. Alice as usual looked exuberant, hatless and rosy-cheeked, her dark hair now cut short like a young boy, her simple overcoat – pale grey gabardine hanging loosely at ankle length – revealing her smart black boots. Mary Rose, more matronly and formally dressed, donned a large feathered hat, dressy overcoat over ankle-length gown, now slightly muddied, and wet boots. They were laughing out loud as they disrobed their outer garments, assisted by the maître d'. Alice, greatly amused by something she had said to their cabbie, shook her head, not minding the least when a few wet drops flicked across her beloved companion's cheek for she loved the dishevelled look, knowing how it enhanced her larrikin nature.

"Tarah!" she called from the doorway across the ornately hatted heads of patrons. "Hello, we have practically swum from Double Bay! Spring rain? Spring deluge!"

Much laughter as they seated themselves, all five women sharing enthusiastic embraces and kisses. They were all, including Rose Scott, fast friends by now in this early spring of 1893, and outings of this nature did not always occur that often.

"What do you think of our Quong Tart, then?" Evelyn was eager to impress Alice as she gestured about the room, as if it was she who owned the establishment, and not the celebrated Chinese gentleman.

"It's heavenly, celestially heavenly," laughed Alice removing her gloves and attending to her recalcitrant strands of damp hair.

"Hats keep your hair dry, dearest!" admonished Mary Rose, all composure and decorum.

"Yes, but I do hate them, I hate their ridiculous design. I'd rather wear a bowler! Why do men get all the simplicity in their clothing? Why don't we have pockets in our coats – and fewer buttons!"

"At least, my dear friend, you have thrown the corset back in their faces!" Evelyn adored her and her larrikin ways.

"I am still looking for some kind of undergarment that will support me, but not destroy me!" laughed Rose Scott.

"They're out there, dear Rose. A slightly reinforced chemise is the answer. We shall find one together!"

Alice was very much in awe of Rose Scott. All the women were regular attendees at Rose's weekly salons held at her home Lynton in Jersey Road, Woollahra (the house that Florence Parker would eventually come to live and die in). Rose lived there with her invalid mother, Sarah, and her adopted son, Helenus (her deceased sister's child). She was already one of the most famous and well-known reformers in New South Wales, with a sweetness of nature wedded to a powerhouse of activity. She was incredibly intelligent, entertaining and beautiful. Rose had started the Womanhood Suffrage League (WSL) in 1891, and had met Louisa not long after Louisa's appointment as the head of the new the University of Sydney Women's College. Rose was brilliant at inviting into WSL leading feminists of the day including Lady Windeyer. Their manifesto was to achieve votes for women. Through her salons, Rose had become well known amongst politicians, judges, philanthropists, writers and poets.[49]

"Now we must order!" Louisa was taking control. The waitress was there in a minute, her starched floor length apron over her long black skirt almost crackled with dutiful obeisance. How she drank in the energy of these five women who were not lowering their voices in public, nor laughing behind their hands. How in love with life they seemed, how wild and happy.

Tea soon arrived, served in Quong Tart's famous Chinese porcelain teapots and then came the scones. Oh, the smell and the delight and the attack! Melted butter, jam and even, upon special request from Louisa, clotted cream! This is what they came for! This is what caused queues outside the Quong Tart establishments of which there were two in central Sydney.

The gossip continued between mouthfuls of rich jam and cream, and sips of hot tea. Finally, fully replete, they all breathed a sigh of relief and asked for one more pot of tea.

"I shall never eat again," squirmed Mary Rose, easing her stays.

"I feel the same," agreed Rose. Alice laughed. She raised her arms up and stretched them wide, expanding her chest and remarked, "I, on the other hand, could probably accommodate another round or two!"

"Stop it!" laughed Evelyn. "As I have promised you, I have ceased to wear the corset except for a few occasions and this is one of them." She tapped her stomach, "but I have only half done it up!"

"Bravo." Alice clapped her hands.

"Now we have satisfied our appetites, I must bring you up to date on progress at the university. The college will be completed early next year and we are looking to have the official opening hopefully in May, only seven months away, and of course you shall all be invited, along with the Governor and the State President of the Legislative Assembly and ..."

"Oh, not too many politicians, please!" scolded Alice.

"Only the ones we have to have. But certainly, the whole coterie of our glorious female companions will be there! Vida will be coming up from Melbourne, and Alice, will Josephine be able to attend?"

"I will write immediately. I need a definite date?"

"Of course. Oh, I nearly forgot. Our esteemed companion here has a rather exciting tale to tell about the ghastly snake man!" Louisa directed her gaze to Rose Scott.

"Oh Rose, do share it then!" Alice clapped her hands.

"Yes please, I'm ready for a horror story!" Mary Rose screwed up her pretty face.

"Only too happy to oblige, although did I not mention this at the last salon? Perhaps not."

She began to tell her tale of a visit she had made with a medical friend of hers, Dr Cedric Bowker. He had invited her to accompany him on a visit to the scientific laboratory of a Mr John McGarvie Smith. This man was apparently a clever bacteriologist, and as Rose proceeded to describe his most appalling laboratory in Woollahra which had a snake factory where he kept hundreds of the poisonous creatures, Alice felt the hairs rise on the back of her neck.

"I would describe him as a patriarch of the worst order. A devil of a man whose every effort to seduce me was not in the least hampered by the physical presence of the good Dr Bowker! He owns a most strange laboratory which he has built behind his premises in Denison Street. Yes, he is married, strangely enough to the widow of Daniel Deniehy. Yes, the infamous drunken Irish orator. She was most gracious in her welcome, but he swiftly steered us away to the rear of their house. He has the most extraordinary facilities, my dears. Thousands of pounds worth of equipment, no less. Eventually we were taken upstairs into a room where he keeps a menagerie of snakes. The smell was utterly repellent. He then challenged me to hold a snake in my hand!"

Everyone around the table gasped. Not Alice. Dealing with snakes had become a commonplace occurrence for her out at Beaconsfield.

"I'm no shrinking violet as you all know, but let me tell you, the manner in which he did so was utterly revolting. I'll never forget the words he used as he thrust the black, squirming serpent at me. 'Every woman loves to hold a snake in her hand.' It might as well have been his masculine appendage, my dears!"

"And did you take the snake?" asked Alice.

"No, I didn't. His sexual innuendo was very clear, hardly disguised as entertainment. I politely said, 'I'd never willingly hold a man's snake in my hand sir; my advice to you is that you and you alone should grasp it and hold it tight, all day long if necessary!'"

The women shrieked. Other patrons turned to look in disgust at their outburst.

"Dr Bowker apologised profusely to me afterwards for putting me in such an invidious position, but it was the taunting of the man, the inference of his superior, irresistible sexual power over women, and his contempt for us that disgusted me. There was a journalist present at this meeting and no doubt he will write about it."

The women all agreed, but before they could chat amongst themselves, Louisa declared an end to the gathering. "Now, if we have finished our tea, shall we wander off to Paddy's Market and find ourselves some bargains?"

They rose as one to gather their skirts, cloaks, gowns, gloves, reticules, umbrellas and all the rest of their paraphernalia, and proceeded to the exit where Louisa had already prepaid *l'addition*. Outside, the rain had ceased, the sun was out and the world glistened anew.

CHAPTER 36

Meeting John McGarvie Smith

SYDNEY, FEBRUARY 1894

Alice, having completed a treatise on 'Health in the Home', wanted to go deeper and write a treatise on bacteriology designed to be used in the home, encouraging women to become more scientifically knowledgeable about managing the hygiene of their physical surroundings. Through her journalistic skills she knew she could demystify the language of male science, opening it out to the average woman, but she needed some guidance. In Melbourne she had been lucky in her acquaintance with Professor Halford who had certainly broadened her scientific knowledge, but since hearing of McGarvie Smith and researching a little about his early scientific studies on sewerage and bacteria, she thought it would be quite an interesting challenge to see if he would be willing to guide her in her own research. Wasn't it just like Alice to choose to throw herself into the lion's den? She asked William Curnow about the man and, being acquainted with him, he convinced her that McGarvie Smith was indeed the only knowledgeable scientist in the area that she wished to investigate. And what's more he lived a mere stone's throw from Double Bay. She asked if he could arrange an introduction for her. Working in *The Sydney Morning Herald*'s office would give her a certain amount of kudos. Curnow agreed immediately and organised for a meeting to take place between Alice and McGarvie Smith in his own office.

Alice was at her desk when she observed a large, muscular man enter the outside office. He was thickly bearded and strode into the space like a lion tamer entering the cage of beasts. His loud, jovial laugh had a certain familiarity to it, perhaps an over-familiarity, as if everyone should know him, or at least have heard of him. It had to be Smith. Yes, he was directed into Curnow's office and shortly after, Margaret, Curnow's personal secretary, came across the floor to Alice's desk, signalling her to join them.

Upon meeting, John McGarvie Smith said, "Call me McGarvie, my dear!"

Alice had felt the hairs again rise on the back of her neck as a strange feeling of déjà-vu passed right through her body.

"I'm sorry. I thought you were Mr Smith?"

"I prefer McGarvie and I shall call you Alice!"

Coldly, Alice gave a short laugh. "I think we should keep this on a professional footing. I am Miss Moon and you are Mr Smith. It is not as though I could forget that, being such a common name."

"Charming. Professional, of course." And he grasped her hand and bored his unflinching black eyes into hers. His hand was hot and smelt funny, an unfamiliar bitter odour rising from it.

"My friend Mr Curnow has nothing but high praise for you, Miss Moon. It seems I shall have to bow down to your feminine wiles in order to share my deepest secrets with you!"

"Really? I don't think I would have you bow down to me at all, Mr Smith. I would rather we meet each other eye-to-eye and proceed in a professional manner."

"But naturally," he cut her off, bluffly strutting across the room, "I expect nothing but professionalism and commitment to accuracy and diligence, eh Curnow?" It was as if he shared a private joke with Curnow who frowned slightly not understanding the inference at all.

"Miss Moon is all of that, John, I assure you. You may call me when you are ready for her to begin. I can supervise her times to fit with her commitments here." Dismissively, he rose and held out his hand to McGarvie Smith. The meeting was over.

Smith swung round, his booted heel disturbing the rug beneath it, and despite what had just been said, he swooped a low bow before Alice, rising so near to her face that she could feel his breath. His smile was not at all pleasant, more of a leer. When he had gone, Curnow sighed and retook his chair saying, "All bluster and a huge ego but you should be able to deal with that, Alice. I know of no other more suited to match you, his reputation in science precedes him!"

Despite the nature of the man, Alice was excited and felt her old daring-do-self coming to the fore. A few weeks later she arrived in a hansom cab at Ginevra in Denison Street, Woollahra, Smith's residence. The large, bearded figure met her at the front door. He was dressed in duck breeches and knee-length leather boots, his open-necked shirt revealing his black chest hair reminding her of a pirate, but his over familiar, leering, and chauvinistic manner, full of sexual innuendo, repulsed her. If she had any doubts of her judgement after her first meeting with him, they were quickly erased. His patronising attitude and stance were the very traits that simply strengthened Alice's life decisions. She was confident enough in her own self to take him on, and if his training meant the publication of her book, the promise of enhancing her reputation in the literary world, then why should she refuse?

Avoiding any introductions to his wife or stepdaughters who were somewhere in the front rooms of the main house, McGarvie Smith swiftly guided her along the side of the house to the back courtyard wherein lay his two-storey laboratory. She was led through a small parlour-like room which contained a couch. Obviously where he sleeps, thought Alice, remembering in her brief research it had named him as a man who never stopped working. From there he walked her through a room that housed a library of scientific works which he boasted were priceless in value. Another laboratory contained such an array of scientific instruments as to baffle the uninitiated of which Alice was not one; microscopes, photographic lenses, electric batteries, and all the complementary appliances were in evidence, as were incubators, furnaces, blowpipes, assay balances, reagents, and the thousand and one other articles necessary to ensure perfectly successful operations and determinations. All the while he made sure she got the monetary value for all his equipment drummed into her.

He boasted, as she paused to inspect the intricate scales, that he had so perfected the art of weighing that he could determine the weight of any substance to the 10,000th part of a grain. She hesitated, recalling that a weight the bulk of which is so infinitesimal was to be simply inconceivable.

"Nothing for me is inconceivable, Miss Moon." His reply insinuated a whole other agenda to Alice, one which she was acutely alert to. "Rather than waste time collecting the specimens that I require for my research," he continued, directing her towards a staircase that led to the upper floor, "I keep them all in here." He unlocked the heavily panelled door at the top of the stairs and stood aside to allow her to enter first.

Alice was repulsed by the smell that hit her as she entered. Rose Scott's account was alive in her mind. Even though forewarned, she hesitated briefly when she saw the origin of the foul odour. This inner sanctum was where he kept over 500 poisonous snakes in cages. McGarvie caught her momentary hesitation and congratulated himself on how easy it would be to get the better of this frustrating female. In echoes of McGarvie Smith's appearance and manner, we are reminded of Alice's dream. Unfortunately, however, she is not.

Mr J. McGarvie Smith experimented with live snakes.

"There's upwards of 200 venomous specimens in here, but never fear, Miss Moon, for they are all carefully stowed in my specially designed cages, so that even the shrinkage caused by the hottest of weather shall not result in gaps through which any one of them might crawl. As you can see, I've all the species I need: black, brown, tiger, and broad-headed snakes, as well as death-adders. And here is their food." He pointed across to other cages where she saw entrapped rabbits and guinea pigs.

It wasn't long before Smith had taken a snake from its cage and, almost to the word, said to her what he had said to Rose Scott, and therefore to every woman he managed to lure into his inner sanctum: "You must hold my snake, Miss Moon, men don't like to, but I've never found a woman who is afraid to hold a snake in her hand."

Thus challenged to hold the python he'd cleverly snatched from its cage and completely alert to the innuendo – his making an offer to her to hold his penis – and without hesitation or fear, she complied. Summers at Beaconsfield meant that she didn't flinch, but caught the snake firmly in her right hand, happy that her gloves afforded some protection from the smell of the reptile. Smith watched her as a cat would eye a mouse coming unwittingly into its power. Little did he realise that Miss Moon was no mouse.

"Why, what a strong hand you have, Miss Moon, so firm a stroke. And no fear?"

"What is there to fear, Mr Smith?" She was quite happy to feel the python wrap itself about her arm. "I have done away with many a snake that invaded my space. I have no fear of snakes, sir. In fact, I find them to be quite beautiful creatures, unlike many other similar, much smaller things that seem to imagine they are bigger than they really are, who poke their unwanted heads in where they are not wanted." Cleverly, she unwrapped the reptile from her arm and holding its head in one hand and its tail in the other she offered it back to him. Having expertly disengaged it from her hands, she was amused to see him caught off guard, to not so expertly receive it. His eyes narrowed and his nostrils flared as he cleared his throat of phlegm and robustly spat into a spittoon at his feet. Alice boldly held his gaze, hiding any obvious show of the disgust she was feeling.

"So," she continued, sounding a little bored, "I believe your present research is bound up with discovery of an antivenene for snakebite? How is that progressing?"

"Ah," Smith replied, almost dropping the reptile but then getting it clumsily back to its cage, "I've found that there is no universal panacea for the bite of a snake. Individual species all have their unique poison, and therefore each need a unique antivenene. Here is a specimen of snake poison." He took a glass receptacle from a drawer. "It looks like a crystal, but it is in reality albumen, and is impossible to analyse. It can be administered, without loss of potency, in any solution."

What a pumped-up, self-important boaster, thought Alice. He is deliberately inveigling me, baiting me all the time. But unlike his snakes, I will not bite!

He passed behind her, deliberately brushing her skirt with his open hand, "Snakes are like women, Miss Moon – you can never tell their age and they look good until they die."

Turning to face him she cut him short, instead directing his attention to the information she hoped to gain from him for her paper on the health dangers of sewerage, and the lack of ventilation in modern homes.

"Why, my dear Miss Moon, my scientific discoveries remain my own of course, but I'm only too happy to extend your knowledge of an area of which I am already an expert. It's a race to the top, my dear Miss Moon."

"Oh, I'm not interested in being first in anything, Mr Smith. I want to disseminate knowledge as fast as possible to make the world a safer place."

"Certainly. Very admirable. But first a little more about my laboratory, yes? As you shall see, I keep all the poisons in their concentrated form here in a fire-proof safe." Grandiosely, he opened the safe to reveal an extraordinary array of phials in which were the spores or germs of anthrax and typhoid, cholera, leprosy, consumption, and other fatal maladies, in quanteous amounts. "Enough to vacate half of Sydney!" he laughed, "and now, my dear, let me demonstrate how I milk the venom from the snake."

"If you must, sir but I would rather have more information regarding how I am to further my learning in the basic principles of bacteriology in relation to my project on safe levels in the air of domestic homes. How do you propose we advance together to achieve my aims?"

Ignoring her remark, what followed was a well-executed demonstration of milking a snake. From its cage, he expertly caught one specimen with a lasso and then manoeuvered the head so that it plunged its fangs into the rubber cap on top of a glass cylinder, and the poison dripped down into the glass dish at the bottom. Alice resigned herself to play the waiting game and made no comment.

He then placed the glass of liquid poison over chloride of calcium in a desiccator. "This is where it dries without heat and assumes a crystal form. I find," he continued, gripping her strongly under her elbow and steering her away to another partitioned room where he kept a menagerie of animals, guinea-pigs, dogs, and rabbits all doomed for experimentation, "that the dried venom of the black snake, and that of the tiger snake, are exactly alike in poisonous properties. I have demonstrated this to my fullest satisfaction by injecting the one thousandth part of a grain of each kind, dissolved in water, into the medium veins in the ears of two rabbits five pounds in weight. They died in about 110 seconds."

McGarvie Smith disliked her attitude and was rattled by her disinterest in him. He over-compensated by parading around the laboratory, talking loudly, boasting about how much he knew and how he had progressed his science further than any other.

"It seems that since you have enough of this dry poison in your laboratory to kill half of Sydney, you should erect some 'danger within' signs on your front gate." Alice stood her ground, her head tilted quizzically to one side, with almost a snide twist to her mouth.

"Ha, ha. Of no doubt." Not entirely sure of what she was referring to he pushed on, "and, my dear Miss Moon, the venom will keep for all time. In water, it becomes a perfectly clear solution, passing through the finest hypodermic needle. I can carry out a series of experiments and repeat them at any time on my guinea-pigs, dogs, and rabbits."

"That must make you feel very powerful, holding all those small innocent lives in your hands." Does he think he is threatening me?

"But I have moved on to other interests now. There is a great need to rid this country of the rabbit plague, and the farmer will pay a lot for a formula that would, *en masse*, do away with the vermin that they are."

"I see. Do you work alone on this?"

"I prefer it that way." Smith hesitated. "I do have certain connections with other scientists at present and I will of course inform you of that. Dr Katz, of the Pasteur Institute in Paris, has been working with me. We too have been looking at the anthrax vaccine."

She cut him short, directing his attention again as to how he proposed they should proceed should she agree to his terms. She had had enough.

"Why, my dear Miss Moon, it will be quite simple."

Alice bit her tongue. *If he calls me his 'dear' one more time, I shall protest.*

"I propose we make a timetable wherein you attend my laboratory downstairs and I set you to work with some specimens and explanations of the bacteriology that is good, and of that which is bad. I will first have to teach you the mastery of the microscope."

"No need sir, I have owned my own microscope since the age of 13. I'm already quite at home with it." Alice sucked in her breath, her equilibrium rapidly disappearing. "I really expect to be able to progress deeper into bacteriological structures and chemical compositions. I have studied with Professor Halford at the University of Melbourne."

"I'm most impressed. I will deliver some lectures to you, set you some tasks, you answer the questions, write them up and return them to me so that I can correct your mistakes."

"Let's hope there will be few mistakes, Mr Smith." She apologised that she had another meeting to attend and would await his call regarding commencement of the training. She turned abruptly and left the way she had come, saying she could find her own way out, and that her cab was waiting for her. He let her go, a strange smile on his face, aware that she was not so short of a quid that she could keep a cab waiting at his door.

CHAPTER 37

To Please a Man?

WOOLLAHRA, 1894

McGarvie Smith looked forward to the day when he could get the better of Miss Alice Moon, but at their next meeting her sharp wit and her 'New Woman' ideas angered and frustrated him into a state of despondency. Her mannish haircut that tended to make her look like a young boy affected him in ways most unguarded and unsettling. He imagined how she might have looked with a head of abundant hair, prettily braided in order to have it unbound and let loose in a sexual passion that he was sure he could invoke.

"Good morning, Miss Moon. It has been troubling me to think what a pity it is that you have cut off your beautiful hair." This criticism welcomed her as he opened the door. "There's nothing that pleases a man more than the crowning glory of a woman's long tresses." Smith hated her look as much as he hated the stirrings in his own body for her young boyish appearance.

"But I am not here to please a man, Mr Smith, there's nothing further from my mind."

"You really don't know what you are missing out on, Miss

Moon, do you?"

"If being made to feel a lesser human being than the man next to me, being made to obey someone whose intelligence is less that my own, whose brutish strength can maim and kill me, were I to stand up for my God-given freedoms – simple human needs and justice – to live in freedom as a man does – those are the things I will gladly lose." Alice in her usual sharp manner was clearly unafraid to reveal where her politics and her sexual interests lay. There is no worse thing for a man than to feel irrelevant, and this is what she did to him.

Her second visit included another journey upstairs to the snake cages. This time Smith had decided to rattle her completely.

"I want you to experience something, Miss Moon."

Alice stood calmly in the middle of the room while Smith opened a cage door and withdrew from it the ugliest and most poisonous of reptiles, the death adder. Alice tensed as she had no idea of his malicious intentions. It didn't take long for him to reveal his purpose. He threw the reptile onto the floor and it slithered and slipped quite slowly around, unable to seize a purchase for itself. The floor, she had noticed before, was a shiny, polished tiled surface designed of course to limit a snake's powers of escape. She couldn't help herself, but she swiftly withdrew to the bench, intending, if need be, to climb up on it and out of the snake's path. But the reptile headed the other way, its skin in the pattern of a Fair Isle sweater rippling as it panicked and threw itself at the far wall, still unable to grip anything. Smith was laughing. Enjoying her discomfort and her obvious fear, he strode across and deftly caught the snake in his lasso and returned it to its cage, slamming the door securely.

Alice recovered her breath. Her eyes hardened as she acidly asked, "So now that Adam has tamed the serpent, he really has no need of Eve?"

"Very perspicacious of you, Miss Moon, but I think that my Eve would need to have a few more attributes along feminine lines, don't you?"

"I agree. Long tresses, a soft voice, an unenquiring mind and a helpless stance, perhaps even a scream or two?"

Smith regarded her, not quite sure that he had won the round after all ...

"I have another two hours committed to you here, Mr Smith and if there's any actual work you have prepared for me to do, may I suggest you reveal it to me now and leave biblical matters to the priests?" She turned and left the laboratory and made her own way downstairs to where they should have been working.

CHAPTER 38

This Man Is the Very Devil

SYDNEY, 1894

Harriet received an invitation to the opening of the University of Sydney's Women's College, to be held on 4 May 1894. It was a personal invitation from Louisa. How kind of her, she thought. Perhaps I can arrange to go with Alice and Mary Rose. Surely the whole crowd will be going? It'd be so much nicer to arrive with a friend. She telephoned the Merewether's on the evening of Friday, 20 April to put her suggestion to Alice, but Mary Rose explained that she had retired early as she had a morning appointment with a scientist with whom she was working. She would get her to return her call on Saturday afternoon. Why had Harriet decided to call that night? She could have rung her at any time with her request, but something in her had triggered a need to talk to Alice right then. It had been nearly a month since they had seen one another. There is no doubt that Harriet was intuitively closer to Alice than Alice was to her. The promised return call on Saturday was never to be made.

Alice had regularly confided to Mary Rose and the other

women, word for word, her conversations with McGarvie Smith. All of them were disgusted by his inferences, but were also a little worried by Alice's bravado – much the same as Harriet, fearing for her safety, had also been made to feel uncomfortable all those years back.

On the Saturday mid-morning of 21 April 1894, Alice arrived at the Smith residence, Ginevra in Denison Street, for her pre-arranged session with the scientist. She had already made great advances in her knowledge and had started to write the first two chapters of her book. Since Saturday was yet another working day, she thought she could bring Smith up to date with her progress. Smith was prepared for her, having decided that today was to be the day he would break her down. He settled her at the desk downstairs where she usually took notes from him, and while she was unpacking her valise, ready to have him correct her last chapter, she turned to notice he had left the room. He soon returned.

"Are we ready to begin? Your last work was extremely impressive, my dear. Just a few suggestions on the order of things."

"Good. Can I have your corrections?"

He stood immobile looking at her, his face growing red, his eyes narrowing. Then he turned abruptly to another desk and retrieved her papers. She settled herself at her books, not realising that he was silently approaching her from behind. In a moment he had wrapped his arms fast around her, pinning her own arms to her side.

"You have no right to deliberately seduce a man with your wiles and then refuse his advances," he whispered harshly in her ear, his grip firm across her breast, his breath stale from whisky.

Alice froze. "Take your arms from my body!" she hissed at him. "Your imagination has got the better of you, sir, and your desires are entirely misplaced!"

The fact that she did not cry for mercy as he had expected, nor did she shrink from his grasp but seemed to grow stronger against him, made him falter and he released her, laughing that it was just a bad joke, that he accusingly knew she preferred women to men. He just thought for a moment that perhaps he could change her mind. He laughed again but Alice was not fooled.

"I think that we will not work today, Mr Smith, nor any other day, sir. You will send me your final invoice and it shall be paid. You have revealed yourself to be the lesser man, or perhaps just the normal run-of-the-mill arrogant male who happily oppresses us all. Would you be so kind as to call me a cab, sir? I do not need to publicly complain of this unwarranted attack, but know this, you sir, are now a marked man."

"Yes, quite correct, Miss Moon. You are quite correct. I apologise. I'm just a foolish man. I shall call a cab and as a peace offering perhaps take some tea with me whilst we wait."

"Thank you, no. A glass of water shall suffice."

He left her alone and she heard him ask his manservant to hail a cab straight away for Miss Moon. He returned after a few minutes with a tea for himself and a tumbler of water for her. In the meantime she had put on her jacket and gathered her notebooks and gloves.

"Thank you." She refused to sit but stood at the window that looked out on the courtyard, but not the road. She drank but a few mouthfuls of the water. Smith drank his tea and stared at her all the while, but she refused his gaze.

"I'm sorry to see you go and this has been a most unfortunate misunderstanding. I am a passionate man and have never before found myself to be so aroused, against all my better judgements, by one such as you, Miss Moon."

Alice remained silent and there was no further conversation until the cab arrived. Alice followed the manservant across the yard and through the house and out to Denison Street. Smith went with them and offered his hand to help her into the cab. She turned and looked at him with disdain.

"Your hand is not needed here, Mr Smith. It is a hand that needs to be re-trained so as not to threaten a woman, but to serve and honour her." And with this, she shut the door in his face. She missed seeing the smile that appeared on his lips.

It is a short trip to Lurlie not so many blocks away in Double Bay and mostly downhill. Traffic was light as it was an early Saturday afternoon. Upon arriving home, Alice complained to Mary Rose that she was feeling unwell, dizzy and breathless and she retired to her bed for a rest. Mary Rose did not query the fact that she was home early.

CHAPTER 39

The Worst News in the World

DOUBLE BAY, 21 APRIL 1894

That same Saturday early in the evening, Harriet was disturbed by a loud knocking on her door. She opened it to find Walton Merewether standing dishevelled and in a state of terrible distress.

"You must come with me now, there's been a terrible tragedy. My dear Harriet, Alice is … Alice is dead." Alice had been discovered dead in her bed around 3 pm in the afternoon. "She came back in a cab from visiting Mr McGarvie Smith this afternoon and upon arriving home she complained of chest pains and took to her bed. Sometime after, Mary Rose heard her moaning. She ran to her room but found her to be deceased. It is shocking. Shocking!"

Harriet, distraught and in shock, allowed Merewether to take her to Lurlie in his cab. She kept saying, "She is only 37, she is young and fit and beautiful, in the prime of her life and now she lies dead in her bed?" Upon arrival at the Merewether home, she was met by Mary Rose and Evelyn Dickinson who wept uncontrollably. Walton guided Evelyn back to the parlour for some tea while Mary Rose, her own face pale with anguish and her eyes red from crying, held out her hands to embrace Harriet.

But the telephone interrupted and she had to excuse herself to take the call. Walton issued quiet commands to the servants and explained to Harriet, "The doctor is still upstairs, please can you just wait 'til Mary Rose is back?" Muffled sounds of weeping were coming from the kitchen where the maids gathered, distraught with grief. As soon as Mary Rose returned, she took Harriet upstairs to Alice's room. Harriet breathed deeply, she did not want to live this moment, she did not want to ever have to live this moment. Her beloved Alice lying cold and still, her face drained of life, her skin grey. Louisa Macdonald, her hand on the counterpane seated by her bedside, was gently weeping. She turned to acknowledge Harriet.

"He says she suffered a heart attack, Harriet. He cannot pinpoint any other reason."

"No other reason," echoed Mary Rose.

Harriet felt her heart freeze, her hands were immobile, her breath was gone, then it came back in a dry cough as her insides cramped. She was frozen to the spot. In horror, her mind was churning, what am I seeing? What is happening here? Like a bombshell she remembered the dream that Alice had had so many years ago at Beaconsfield. The scene was almost as in that dream. The women weeping at the bedside, there was even a gilt mirror on the wall like the one in Alice's dream, and the doctor standing attentively back from the bed in the shadows, as in the dream. Except in the dream the male figure was bearded and this man had only a moustache and whiskers. Her breath was caught in utter fright.

"Please, can I have a moment with her?" she whispered hoarsely to Mary Rose.

209

"Of course, of course. Louisa dearest come down, Evelyn needs you. Doctor, can we please talk with you now?"

They all quit the room, leaving Harriet alone with Alice.

"My angel in white." She took the cold hand in hers. She shuddered at death's touch. "Ah, you're not there, are you? Gone. The miracle of you is gone. We are not the body, oh how suddenly clear it is. What a shocking thing to understand. We are not the body, we are in the body, but not of it. Oh, my sweet warrior, my beloved, for I shall have no other, not in this world, not in this lifetime. Oh, dear saints above, what else was in that dream of yours? What must I remember? There was something else." But her tears would not come, just dry sobs, gasping for breath, such a pain in her chest. Mary Rose soon returned and put her arm around her in comfort and compassion.

"Come with me, my dearest Harriet. You need a whisky. We all do."

"Just give me a little more time with her please."

"Of course. I just wanted to make sure you're all right, my dear. Come down when you're ready."

I shall never be ready. Losing you once was unbearable. But death is untenable. While you had breath, I had hope. I always had hope. I hate this place. I hate Sydney. It seduced you away from me. You have pricked your finger on its spindle, but you will not awake from this sleep.

And Harriet bent and placed her warm lips on the frozen lips of her beloved. Hard to know if she felt guilt or anger? Perhaps even a terrifying thought passed through her at that moment? Mine, now. Forever mine.

Mary Rose was waiting for Harriet at the bottom of the staircase. She led her to a small study and poured her a whisky from Walton's private cabinet. Without the others there, she quietly related to her what had happened that day. Harriet, who knew nothing of Alice's work with McGarvie Smith, sat in horror as she listened to all that Mary Rose could relate. A trembling arose in her very being as she knew, she knew what Alice must have done to this abusive man. She knew only too well her wicked tongue, her bravado, her clever demolition process of any man's ego. Now Alice had met with malevolence and evil. Harriet felt it in her bones.

"How could he have hurt her though? He was miles away?"

"Not so far, Harriet. He lives in Woollahra, it's a 20 minute cab ride. She arrived home just after two, breathless and angry; she told me he had attacked her! I told her to go to bed. I'd bring her a drink. She went to her room. I left her a while to perhaps rest and calm herself. Then I arranged some tea for her. I was carrying it up myself as I felt the need to get more information about the event. As I came up the stairs I could hear her moaning. I found her unconscious on the bed, lying still, so still, her face was awful ..." Mary Rose was sobbing. Harriet grasped her hand.

"Something must be able to be done, surely?"

"How do we prove anything? She was alone with him, she was always alone with him."

"How long did this go on for?"

"She has been working there for a few months now. Probably half a dozen visits. I'm not sure."

"Why? Why would she take such work?"

"No, she was studying with him. He's a scientist. She was writing a book or something on hygiene or health in the home. She was so scientifically clever you know. And she loved writing."

Harriet didn't want to hear any more. She already could see Alice's ego being pumped up as usual. But who could foresee death? She drained the tumbler of pure malt and felt something shrivel inside her.

∞

The news travelled fast between the friends. That night the women gathered at Lurlie. Evelyn Dickinson, Louisa Macdonald, Rose Scott, Harriet and later Maybanke Wolstenholme, and Edith Leary. Mary Rose greeted Edith at the door. "Come in Lulu and sit down, my dearest. Let us all gather calmly. I have rung our Florence, as you know. I don't know what I'm saying, of course you know!" Gently, she steered her tearful sister towards the parlour as she called to the parlour maid, "Annie, please make some fresh tea for us all." Her husband entered the room then turned back – too many women for him to feel at ease – but Mary called to him, "Walton dear, could you please ring Maybanke for me. She already knows, but ask if it's possible for her to come over here tonight?"

"Of course, Dolly," he nodded and gratefully left the room. Mary Rose introduced Edith to the group, but of course she already knew everyone. It was simply that Mary Rose seemed to have lost her bearings.

"I've already spoken to Florence, she cannot travel because of her confinement. I've talked to Josephine. She wants to talk with you, Harriet, you can ring her from here if you wish?" Harriet nodded, her brain still trying to clear, her mind locked into Alice's coldness in death. "And Kate will be back soon," continued Mary Rose.

"Kate?" queried Harriet.

"Yes, Kate Leary, our sister. She lives just over in Lancaster Villas in Jersey Road. Haven't you met her here? You know Lulu of course." She gestured to Edith. "Dr Ellis says it was heart failure. They want to do an autopsy on Sunday morning, and we are burying her on Monday afternoon. Reverend Stiles has already been, but he will come back on Sunday, that's tomorrow of course. I can't think clearly at all. Harriet, my dear, I'm not sure how familiar you are with the work that Alice was involved in with that dreadful man, Smith?"

"Smith? No. I'm not." Harriet felt sick. Her stomach gripped, she thought she might vomit. "Who is he?"

A groan rent the air and the women sucked in their breath and someone moaned – a despairing sound.

Tea was served, Kate arrived and on her heels came Matilda Curnow. They all resettled in the library where a fire was burning, the evening having become cold. Mary Rose began to relate the events of Alice's work with McGarvie Smith. Matilda told how her husband William Curnow knew the man, but none of them realised what a tyrant he was.

"A brute, Blackbeard the pirate, a pompous brute." Evelyn was seething in anger and despair. They told Harriet of Alice's work with McGarvie Smith, each interrupting the other, their words tumbling out, his laboratory of snakes and poisons and animals intertwined with Alice's stories of her baiting his male ego.

Harriet drew in her breath. Snakes! That was what she had forgotten. The snake. Alice, Alice you just could never stop, could you? "Please let me speak now." She gathered her thoughts together. "I have to tell you about a terrible dream that Alice had many years ago."

The conversation came to an abrupt halt. Everyone looked at her. Evelyn spoke first, "A dream? She never told me about any dream."

"No, probably not. It was years ago. She told me because we were partners, we were together, we lived together for 14 years. I met her when she was just 14 herself. You know that, all of you?" The women nodded and murmured agreements and 'of course', 'we understand'. Harriet wanted to scream, she wanted to weep and cry out, you know nothing about us! You know nothing of my angel in white. I'm all alone here and you know nothing about my Alice Moon!

Mary Rose took her hand and gently said, "Dearest Harriet, forgive us. Your pain is so different to ours. Your years with her are precious memories. We never had those years."

Harriet didn't cry. Instead, she related the dream as best she could. And in so doing, she deliberately emphasised the part that she'd forgotten. The snake! "There was a black snake that slid out from under the bed. And Alice said one word."

"What word did she say?" begged Evelyn.

"*Charming*. That was the word."

Louisa gasped and Evelyn shrieked and held her hand to her mouth.

"What? What does it mean? What aren't you telling me? For pity's sake, Mary Rose help me to understand?" Harriet was on a knife edge.

"People speak of him as a snake-charmer," she answered, "his self-made reputation of being a charmer of both women and snakes is well-known." Her face was pale. Harriet felt a cold fear creep into her heart.

The conversation erupted. Talk of clairvoyants and dreams, and communicating with the dead, perhaps visiting someone who could help them talk to Alice's spirit? Louisa took control. She proposed that the possibility of Alice being poisoned by Smith had gained credibility and that the facts seem to support this theory. Alice had been at McGarvie Smith's laboratory that Saturday afternoon and had left, according to Mary Rose, vowing not to return. But where was the proof of murder? What would the autopsy reveal, if anything? They were due to have it done on the morrow, Sunday, and they were going to bury her on the Monday. The doctor had diagnosed heart failure. Well, didn't that coincide with poisoning? They knew so little of snakebite.

"But she would have said if she'd been bitten by a snake,

wouldn't she Dolly?" Evelyn's hands were gripped tight, her knuckles were white.

But then Mary Rose remembered Alice's story of the crystals of venom that could be dissolved in water – tasteless and untraceable. So now they talked in undertones, their anger and frustration at their helplessness, knowing that to gain any proof or evidence of their suspicions would be impossible. Harriet, left out again, reminded them that they must let Alice's family in England know about her death. Her mother and father were both gone, but there were other members there, siblings.

"Of course, Harriet. How lax of me. Thank you, we must telegraph Myra, she is her half-sister is she not?" Harriet nodded. "Would you help me with that Harriet?'"

"Yes. I'm sure you know her father is dead and her own mother died long ago, a year before I met her in fact. I must also tell my family. They adored her."

"Then we shall telegraph them too. As I said, I've already telephoned Josephine in Melbourne. She knows. She cannot get here in time for the funeral on Monday, but says she will come as soon as she can." Mary Rose held Harriet's hands in hers. But by now Harriet was far away. She was running up the stairs of Castle Square where she found her Marmie sewing in the sunlight. She cried when she saw her there, she fell to her knees and laid her head in her beloved mother's lap. And she wept and wept until she felt the gentle hand of her mother stroking her head and crooning a soft lullaby to her. Mary Rose held her warmly and rocked her until her breathing eased.[50]

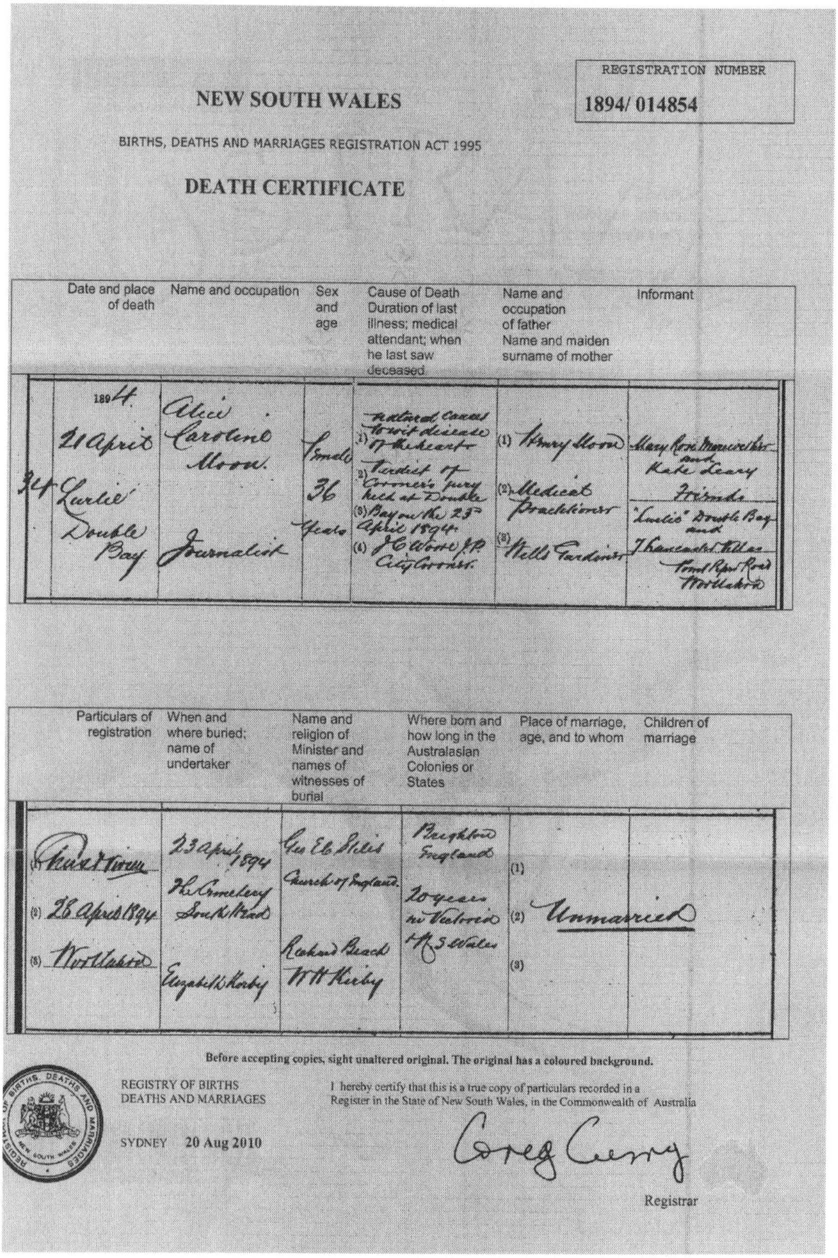

REGISTRATION NUMBER
1894/ 014854

NEW SOUTH WALES

BIRTHS, DEATHS AND MARRIAGES REGISTRATION ACT 1995

DEATH CERTIFICATE

	Date and place of death	Name and occupation	Sex and age	Cause of Death Duration of last illness; medical attendant; when he last saw deceased	Name and occupation of father Name and maiden surname of mother	Informant
364	1894 21 April "Lurlie" Double Bay	Alice Caroline Moon. Journalist	Female 36 Years	(1) natural causes to wit disease of the heart (2) Verdict of Coroner's jury held at Double (3) Bay on the 23rd April 1894. (4) J C Woore J.P. City Coroner.	(1) Henry Moon (2) Medical Practitioner (3) Nelly Gardiner	Mary Rose Manwaring and Kate Leary Friends "Lurlie" Double Bay and 7 Lancaster Villas Point Piper Road Woollahra

Particulars of registration	When and where buried; name of undertaker	Name and religion of Minister and names of witnesses of burial	Where born and how long in the Australasian Colonies or States	Place of marriage, age, and to whom	Children of marriage
(1) [illegible] (2) 26 April 1894 (3) Woollahra	23 April 1894 The Cemetery South Head Elizabeth Kirby	Geo Ed Stiles Church of England Richard Beach W H Kirby	Brighton England 20 years in Victoria & N S Wales	(1) (2) Unmarried (3)	

Before accepting copies, sight unaltered original. The original has a coloured background.

REGISTRY OF BIRTHS DEATHS AND MARRIAGES

SYDNEY 20 Aug 2010

I hereby certify that this is a true copy of particulars recorded in a Register in the State of New South Wales, in the Commonwealth of Australia

Greg Curry

Registrar

Extract of Alice C. Moon's Death Certificate.

CHAPTER 40

The Funeral

SOUTH HEAD CEMETERY,
23 APRIL 1894

After Alice's body was returned to them on Monday, Harriet and the women and their friends followed the cortège to South Head Cemetery where the Reverend Stiles conducted a service. McGarvie Smith, dressed in a black frockcoat but still booted and black-bearded, was there. For all the women, it was the first time they had seen him. None wanted to meet him, and they turned away and kept to their intimate group.

The groundswell of anger among them was palpable. Harriet knew only the women she had met at the Merewether's and even then, save for Mary Rose and Louisa, she felt isolated from them. Like the rest, she stared at McGarvie Smith, boring her dark eyes into him, wishing her stare could turn him to stone. She held him in her rage, wanting to confront him, whereas the men in the group seemed to be happy to chum him, and this was because of his reputation, notoriety and appearances in local magazines. It was an Anglican service and Evelyn gave a beautiful, emotional speech along with William Curnow who was a wonderful orator. As people were breaking up into groups, or leaving in cabs for the long ride back to Lurlie, Mary Rose took her aside and whispered that Dr Ellis had confided, when quizzed, that causes of heart failure could be brought on by many things, amongst them tachycardia which was a seizure effect on the heart organ. Her husband had a medical encyclopaedia and in it she had found an obscure reference to tachycardia being a symptom of poisoning by snake venom.[51]

"But what can we do, dear Harriet? There was an autopsy, they said she had a fatty heart, but surely, some sort of poison …?" She couldn't finish.

For Harriet, this information was enough to make her vomit. She retreated to a clump of yew trees near the south wall and hiding her distress, she dry-retched into the long grass. No one noticed. She couldn't stop shaking and heaving, yet she was still unable to cry. Her eyes were dry. She was troubled by an intense pain in the middle of her chest and her breathing became difficult. "Dear Lord, save me," she whispered to the east wind that had now whipped up from the sea. Suddenly, four seagulls swooped low over the cemetery, crying their mournful complaints. It rattled her. But it made her straighten, look up, feel her heart lift out of her body. "Oh, my heart, my heart, it's gone with you, Alice!"

Harriet couldn't bear to go back to Lurlie where everyone would be gathering for sustenance and fellowship. She stayed separated at the edge of the cemetery and waited until the mourners had all departed. The gravediggers came and methodically filled in the grave, aware of her guardian-like presence.

Finally, left alone beside the newly-mounded earth, now covered by the wreaths and flowers that the diggers had carefully placed there, she talked to her beloved. She got no answers and as the sun began to set, and the ocean wind grew cold and unfriendly, she walked to the main road and hailed a hansom cab. The horses' breath was white on the evening air, and the steady sound of their clip-clopping lulled her into an exhausted sleep all the way back to Randwick and complete emptiness.

CHAPTER 41

The Will

DOUBLE BAY, JUNE 1894

Later that week, Harriet was invited to Mary Rose's to hear the reading of Alice's Will.[52] Josephine was there. Harriet felt herself crack open after being so stoic these past few days. Jo hugged her close and kissed her cheek.

"Oh Harriet, dearest Harriet, I can't believe this. I can't believe it." Jo had been trying to glean information from the women but she had become overloaded with all their confused suspicions and misgivings. "Is there nothing to be done? Did you know this man? I want to confront him. I could do it!"

Harriet held her hands. "I too could confront him. But I've never met him. He is so well-known, there are rumours of his arrogance and hubris, but there's not a man among them who would confront him – even if we were to suggest such a thing. It's so good to have you here, Jo. I have truly missed you."

"I have hardly any time, the gymnasium is so busy. I regret I never came up for Christmas. She begged me to come, but I decided to go to Tasmania instead to be with Florence. She's distraught you know, she's due to give birth in six weeks and

220

they won't let her travel even though I know she could, she's very strong. She so wanted to be at the funeral, as did I. Such short notice."

Walton Merewether read the will to the gathering. Beneficiaries were named as Florence Agnes Parker – Alice deliberately refused to call her Mrs Erskine Parker – as well as Mary Rose Merewether and Josephine McCormick. Only those three were mentioned. Harriet sat at the back utterly wretched, humiliated and ashamed. Not to be mentioned. Not even a memory. It was as if she and Alice had never existed, never been together, never loved. How to erase a life? Josephine was shocked and deeply embarrassed. What could she say? Not only was her infidelity marked by this extraordinary gift, but she had never thought that Harriet could be so coldly treated by Alice. Walton continued reading that the beneficiaries were left this money on the proviso that they never shared any of it with their husbands, present or future, nor with any man. For Harriet, in desperate financial need, her embarrassment was palpable; the other women whispered surreptitiously, avoiding her eyes, keeping amongst themselves, too embarrassed to converse with her. This drove her out of the house onto William Street to find a cab and get away, away anywhere to absorb the shock of what must have felt like the worst betrayal of all – to find herself and their relationship of some 20 years so heartlessly eradicated.

CHAPTER 42

Revenge

LURLIE, JULY 1894

Some weeks later, Mary Rose telephoned Harriet to invite her to Lurlie for a gathering at which they all wanted her attendance. Apart from her commiserations when Harriet arrived, Mary Rose seemed very excited. The women were gathered in the parlour. The talk was about choosing the headstone for Alice.

"We all want to know how you feel about this idea for the inscription, Harriet," said Evelyn.

"Thank you for asking me, but I'm sure you've all got the best ideas in the world." Harriet's embarrassment was rekindled in their presence. She almost felt as though she had been telling lies about Alice, their intimacies, their life's work together. Perhaps they didn't really believe her.

Mary Rose took the floor. "Let me start by saying that we asked Evelyn to think of the inscription, a quote or something which would be suitable," she said. "You know how we are all feeling so helpless and unable to accuse that man, but Evelyn has this wonderful idea. It's a quote from the Bible."

Harriet sucked in her breath and began to shake her head

negatively, but Mary Rose moved to her and gripped her hand, continuing, "I know, I know. Alice did not place a lot of importance on religion in her life, but listen to this quote and tell me what you think." She opened her notebook and read to the group. "It's a quote from the Book of Job, and it's not one that I was familiar with either. 'When he giveth quietness, who then can make trouble.' What do you think, Harriet?"

Harriet was silent. She realised it was an extraordinary message to have on a gravestone, a message that would reverberate down through the years. Injustice, surrender, silent anger and accusations all in one.

"It's very clever," said Harriet quietly. "It says so much without saying anything explicit. If he reads it, he will be forever watching his back."

"Well put, my dear, well put!" and they all clapped their hands.

When the headstone was raised, the women met again at the grave. Inscribed on the headstone are indeed the words:

"When He giveth quietness, who then can make trouble."
—Job C.34 V.29

"This will be a message for the women of the future," said Harriet softly.

"Perhaps. We can only hope that it is read and understood, and is not so well disguised that they will miss our intention," said Mary Rose.

"It's a sign both of our frustration and our acceptance, *now*." Evelyn added, taking Louisa's hand in hers and holding it tight.

"Will you not come back for tea at Lurlie, my dear Harriet?" Mary Rose took her by the elbow, guiding her to the waiting cabs.

"If you don't mind Dolly, I want to stay here for a while. Can you ask for one of the cabs to wait for me and then I'll join you as soon as I'm ready?"

Mary Rose squeezed her arm and nodded. "Of course."

CHAPTER 43

Alone

SYDNEY, 1894

Alone at the grave, Harriet considered the simple white stone cross and the writing. You're in there under that heavy load. I would have taken you out and cast you to the wind, my love, to the foam on the waves like the Little Mermaid.

Above her head, the seagulls called and wheeled in crazy circles. She closed her eyes and saw again the pier in Brighton on that wild, gusty day where she had cried out her love of the great oceans. There suddenly was the girl on the railings, that adoring look in her eyes, almost worshipping a goddess, she thought, smiling. I was a goddess then. I was a sea goddess and she was my sylph, my siren, my nymph, my angel and I lost her. I've lost that part of myself that was so free. I don't think I shall ever find it again. I must go on. I shall never stop working for women. I shall never give up. I have to believe things will change, and that I will see that happen.

In a letter to her friend, Eleanor Grove in England, dated 13 July 1894, Louisa Macdonald wrote:

> Evelyn is thinking of writing a short memoir of Miss Moon but I do not know if it will come to anything. She has not yet recovered from the shock or the sense of loss, and I am afraid she would find it most trying and painful work.

The Evelyn in this letter is of course Evelyn Dickinson. Louisa, Head of the Women's College at the University of Sydney since 1891, had to pull out all the stops to manage the grand opening of the College on 4 May, only two weeks after Alice's shocking death. It was a tough call for all those women. Louisa put on a brave face as she held the platform making her speech, welcoming Members of the Legislative Assembly, bankers to the College, professors, lords and ladies. Evelyn sat pale and wretched and still seething with anger and frustration. They all were.

A year later in 1895, in a boastful newspaper interview, McGarvie Smith revealed how he could measure microscopic amounts of snake poison in the form of crystals and dissolve them in water without the drinker suspecting.

CHAPTER 44

ℛeturn

MELBOURNE, 1898–1902

The years followed one upon another until 1898, when Harriet, deeply changed, sold her gymnasium, which by then had been re-housed in 281 Castlereagh Street, to a Miss Violet MacKenzie, and made the move back to Melbourne. She was by no means ready to quit. She still had plans.

The University of Melbourne continued to refuse to allow women into the Faculty of Medicine. Dr Constance Stone had to travel to America to get her medical degree and when she returned to Melbourne she set the wheels in motion to revolutionise the non-existent women's health services. The Royal Women's Hospital was about to become a reality.

The Shilling Fund was established to which the people of Victoria would donate and raise money for the building of the first lying-in hospital for women, the Queen Victoria Hospital, a hospital designed to give medical service to all women, with ten (honorary) women doctors led by Dr Constance Stone in attendance. In 1899 it is opened. Harriet and Josephine McCormick applied and were given honorary positions, providing services in a new method of medical therapeutic massage – the beginnings of physiotherapy – and a special exercise program of medical gymnastics for the women. I find it truly wonderful that Harriet and Josephine remained close and successfully worked side by side after all that had happened. After Harriet's death, Josephine continued working at the Queen Victoria until 1908.[53]

Early in 1900, Harriet set out again to visit her homeland. It was the beginning of a new century, surely one that would bring about enormous change for women. Her mother had long since died, but her father, George Rowell, was still alive but very frail. Her brothers had married and had children. Some had emigrated to New Zealand and Georgie, as promised, had emigrated to live in Perth. They all wanted her to remain in England.

She took long walks on the pebbly windswept beach of Brighton, remembering, 25 years ago, the extraordinary swim in the sea from Shoreham that she and Helen Saigeman had attempted and that she had won. The sight of Alice dressed in white, brave and smiling, waving to her, the crowds shouting, pushing, all wanting her. The beach was now cold and utterly empty. Attended always by the unmanageable gulls, she knew she had to return to Australia and keep going. It was a painful farewell to her beloved Pa. "Take all my strength with you, my dearest daughter. You have suffered a lot."

With a Miss Gaunt she opened another women's gymnasium in Melbourne. She met with Vida Goldstein who was about to publish the first edition of the *Australian Women's Sphere*,[54] a magazine which was to become one of the most revolutionary publications for women's rights and suffrage which by then, in 1900, was close to becoming a reality in Victoria. Suffrage had already been granted in South Australia. Harriet agreed to place a large advertisement in the first edition of the magazine in September 1900. It appeared on page five.[55]

Harriet (left) and Miss Montgomery.

There is a beautiful Falk Studio photograph of Harriet posed with her 'pupil', a Miss Montgomery, taken in Sydney sometime between 1895 and 1898. It is archived in the State Library of NSW.[56] Harriet, standing, appears to have lost weight and her calm expression reveals a gentle, happy mood. She wears one of her big hats, a habit she never fell out of, while Miss Montgomery, seated in front of her and dressed in the lesbian fashion of high collar, fancy tie and masculine tailored jacket, wears the very fashionable sharp boater style straw hat. She appears to be about the same age as Harriet, although it is hard to tell. Because of the location and dates, I would dare to guess that Harriet met Margaret in Sydney. I can confirm that they moved to Melbourne together sometime after 1898.

In Harriet's will, which was never registered, but was legitimised and recorded for probate, Harriet left everything she had to Miss Margaret Montgomery, or Peggy as she called her. Reading the probate document which was created after her death on 15 July 1902, it records that on the 29 August 1902, two women were signatories to the 'paper' – Harriet's will – and they made the affidavit for probate concerning its probity and veracity. They attest that in 1900, they, Mrs Harriett Tabitha Noot of Derham Street, Hawthorn, and Miss Annie Seely of Highett, had been asked by Harriet to witness her handwritten will.[57]

According to the witnesses, a Miss Margaret Montgomery, who was living in East Malvern at the time, was present in another room and after the signing, Harriet took the Will in to show her.

At the end of the probate document, finalised on 27 March 1903, one can read the lawyer's fees and an outline of services provided, along with a record of meetings with the witness, Harriett Noot including meeting with Harriet's brother, Frederick Rowell, who was by then living in Australia. All but last, there's an interesting note where, on 25 March, the solicitor was asked to approach Miss McCormick to return a clock and finalise payments due to the estate!

From the probate information it is natural to believe that Harriet found another loving relationship with Miss Margaret Montgomery. I believe that Harriet's deepest wound came from Alice, her angel in white, and that this wound of love never really healed. To have fought all her life for change and yet to see no end to the battleground must have been so sad. She was tired. She was living in Highett, a bayside suburb of Melbourne, and at 50 she suffered a heart attack.[58]

Huge advances in the world of men and the continual battleground of the sexes, failing women on every level, denying full equality or relief from patriarchal control, surely pushed our women to a point of exhaustion. Despite most women gaining the vote across the Commonwealth of Australia in 1902 nothing changed. I quote Emma Goldman who later said: "Politics is the reflex of the business and industrial world whose mottos are: 'to take is more blessed than to give, one soiled hand washes the other, buy cheap and sell dear.' There is no way that women's power to vote will ever purify politics."[59]

The following death notice for Harriet was published in the month after her death:

> We regret to have to report the death of Miss E [sic]. Elphinstone Dick from heart disease. It is chiefly owing to Miss Dick that the importance for physical culture for growing womanhood is as well understood as it is today in Victoria. In partnership with the late Miss A.C. Moon, she devoted her life to the systematic physical culture of girls, first in the teaching of swimming and then by course of general physical training on the Swedish principle. She will be remembered gratefully by the several hundred of Victorian women, who benefitted from her training and sympathetic kindness. Miss Dick was a very capable business woman, and successfully managed a farm; she was a strong advocate of woman's advancement.
>
> —*The Australian Woman's Sphere*: Notice. August 10, 1902, p. 190

Harriet lies buried in Cheltenham Pioneer Cemetery[60] in Melbourne. Though her grave is plain and uncared for, she is surrounded on many sides by the most extraordinary collection of life-size statues of guardian angels carved in stone. And yes, there are seagulls in attendance, calling and happily weaving overhead.

The simple headstone inscription is something that Harriet would have been angry about, for they misspelled her name with two Ts. The inscription reads:

IN
Loving Memory
HARRIETT. E. ROWELL
BORN BRIGHTON. SUSSEX
ENGLAND

Harriet Elphinstone Dick has been erased. That unexplained mystery name that she appropriated for herself, a name which embraced all that this magnificent, brave and intelligent woman stood for. Her creed was to fearlessly commit to loving and rescuing women of all ages. Her courage drove her to break all the rules of men, fully accepting that a woman seeking freedom can only be making trouble.

ENDNOTES

Prologue

1 Lois Young, 'Feminism and the physical sex education, physical education and dress reform in Victoria, 1880–1930'. Masters Thesis, Monash University, 1984.

2 See my story 'A Letter to Roxane' in the 1997 book *Motherlove 2*, edited by Debra Adelaide, Milsons Point, NSW: Random House Australia.

3 Obituary in *The Bulletin*, 19 May 1894.

4 This proved to be untrue in my later research, a great lie perpetrated on history. This research, and the history of John McGarvie Smith, is included as an Afterword.

Chapter 7

5 This report appeared in the *Brighton Gazette* on 4 September 1875: "Another great swimming feat was performed on Wednesday, when Miss Agnes Alice Beckwith, the daughter of the famous professor of swimming, and well known in Brighton, swam from London Bridge to Greenwich, a distance of five miles, in 63 minutes. The feat was witnessed by immense crowds, who were enthusiastic in their applause of the young lady, who protested she was not in the least fatigued, and could have done another five miles with ease."

Chapter 8

6 A detailed report of Harriet's swim appeared in the *Brighton Gazette* 9 September 1875. Here is an excerpt:
"The first mile was accomplished in about 13 minutes ... In another half hour, more than half the distance had been accomplished and both swimmers were apparently undaunted ... Miss Saigeman was seized with cramp, and was obliged to leave the water. Miss Dick, still being fresh and undaunted continued on her journey and was accompanied for half an hour by Mr Giles, the swimming master of Brill's Baths. By this time the party had arrived off the head of the Pier where Miss Dick was taken on board, having accomplished the distance of nearly six miles, in rough sea, in 2 hours and 43 minutes ... these young ladies have accomplished the greatest swimming feat of the present day with the exception of Captain Webb's Channel trip."

Chapter 11

7 The address is now a Thai massage parlour and the original front has been built over with a new shopfront.

Chapter 12

8   William Kenney was born in Essex, England in 1820. Having 'gone to sea' as a youth, he arrived in Melbourne 32 years later with the apparent aim to settle in Australia. In 1854, he took the brig *Nancy* to the St Kilda foreshore where he took possession of Mrs Ford's bathing area just south of the main pier. The brig was scuttled and was linked to the shore by a rope that had threaded on it a large iron ring. To the ring was attached the painter of the boat. Intending bathers on the shore entered the boat, and pulled themselves, by aid of the connecting rope, to the brig. The ship was subsequently moored to a landing stage. There were fenced swimming enclosures offering 'protection from predatory marine life'. In those early days, swimming was mostly undertaken only by men, often swimming naked. In 1858, the St Kilda Royal Gymnasium Baths and Sea Bathing Company was formed and baths erected at a cost of £6,500. Women were required to be well covered and curtained when swimming. In the years that followed, there were about six bathing establishments along the St Kilda shore, at least two bearing Kenney's name. In 1918, the St Kilda Council bought the establishment known as Kenney's Ladies Bath from Captain Kenney's surviving children for £1,250.

9   See *The Women's Encyclopedia of Myths and Secrets* by Barbara Walker, San Francisco: Harper & Row, 1983.

Chapter 14

10 Two differing reports of the events covered in this chapter appeared in Melbourne newspapers. In *The Age*, on page 3 of the 15 January 1877 edition, an article 'The Big Swimming Match', stated that the cup was awarded to Miss Dick after her competitor, Mr McGonigal, was taken out of the water showing signs of exhaustion. The report which appeared in *The Argus* on 18 December 1876 said that the event was a "very uninteresting affair" and that spectators believed Mr McGonigal should have been awarded the prize.

Chapter 15

11 On the ship's passenger lists, their names are given as: Miss Rowell, 30 (actual age 24). Miss Moon, 23 (actual age 21).

Chapter 16

12 *The Argus*, Saturday 5 April 1879, p. 8. <https://trove.nla.gov.au/newspaper/article/5938489>

13 Charles Pearson, headmaster of the Ladies College (which later became PLC in 1889) never promoted physical education yet one of his daughters, Hilda, attended the gym. Hilda won medals in 1885 and 1886–1887 and Charles Pearson actually attended the displays along with other dignitaries.

14 Lois Young, 'Feminism and the physical sex education, physical education

and dress reform in Victoria, 1880–1930'. Masters Thesis, Monash University, 1984, pp. 85–86.

Chapter 17
15 Here is the Melbourne Sands Directory listings for the gymnasium:
   1880   Moon Miss Alice at 11 Rupert Street, Collingwood.
   1880   DICK Miss ELPHINSTONE, ladies' gymnasium, Mutual Provident, Collins Street West
           Moon: Miss A.C. (Moon and Rowell) 2 St Heliers Street (Coll) Abbotsford
           Rowell: Miss H. E (Moon and Rowell) "The Steyne" St Heliers Street, Abbotsford.
   1881-82 DICK Miss ELPHINSTONE, ladies' gymnasium, 6 Mutual Provident Buildings, Collins Street West.
   1883   DICK Miss ELPHINSTONE and MOON Miss A.C. Ladies' Gymnasium, 6 Mutual Provident Buildings, Collins Street West.
   1884-85 DICK Miss ELPHINSTONE and MOON Miss A.C. Ladies' Gymnasium, Little Collins Street East, Melbourne. (Hansen's Blgs Opp Melb Chambers, north side).
   1899   St Heliers 16 Max Kreitmeyer. Mrs Anna McCormick 18 St Heliers Street Abbotsford (Josephine's mother).
16 News about the Geelong classes appeared in the *Geelong Advertiser* on Wednesday 2 August 1882 on p. 3, advising that ladies' classes are held every Thursday at 4.30, for the cost of one guinea per quarter. A public notice appeared in the same newspaper on 27 March the following year, advising of the formation of a calisthenics and gymnastics class, also for women.
17 Lois Young, 'Feminism and the physical sex education, physical education and dress reform in Victoria, 1880–1930'. Masters Thesis, Monash University, 1984, p. 11.
18 On 27 September 1887, an article on the Australian Health Society appeared in *The Herald*, citing its formation in 1875 at the instigation of Unitarian Minister Martha Turner. It was a sanitary association along the lines of similar ones in Britain, and it promoted hygiene. In Melbourne at the time there was a high incidence of diphtheria, measles, typhoid and other contagious diseases responsible for epidemics and many deaths, often among children and young adults. Other issues raised by the society included ophthalmia (conjunctivitis), sunstroke and 'preservation of the teeth'. The society comprised doctors, prominent citizens and politicians. In 1880–1882 it targeted poorer districts and women. Public meetings 'for wives and daughters' were held in Collingwood, Carlton, Richmond and South Melbourne.
19 *Australasian Schoolmaster*, Aug 1882, p. 32.

20   *Ballarat Courier*, 8 April 1884, and *The Argus* 4 April 1884.

Chapter 18

21   The Wives and Daughters Lecture Series, and the lecture given by Harriet, was reported in *The Argus* on 27 July 1887.

Chapter 19

22   The Sands directories were annual publications in Australia that listed household, business, society and Government contacts, The first Melbourne directory was published in 1857. The 1860 directory was more than 400 pages long and had over 10,000 entries. It continued being published until 1974.

23   The Parker-Leary family tree can be accessed through the Births, Deaths and Marriages databases available online through the State Library of Victoria. <https://www.slv.vic.gov.au> Florence Parker and Edith Leary are both in the same grave as Alice Moon.

24   Lynton, the house at 294 Jersey Rd, Woollahra, was the home of Rose Scott from the 1870s to 1925. It was the home of the Learys from 1925 to 1969 and was demolished in 1970. Clara Leary, Edith (Lulu), and Florence Parker all died at Lynton. Selma (Parker) Stewart Younger died elsewhere.

25   Lois Young, 'Feminism and the physical sex education, physical education and dress reform in Victoria, 1880–1930'. Masters Thesis, Monash University, 1984, p. 112.

26   'Blos: A Tasmanian River Study' by A. C. Moon appeared in the *Sydney Mail* and in the *New South Wales Advertiser* on Saturday 16 December 1893, on p. 6. <https://trove.nla.gov.au/newspaper/article/164369518?searchTerm=tasmanian%20river%20study&searchLimits=>

27   I've been unable to find any reference to this hotel in Falmouth.

Chapter 20

28   Lois Young, 'Feminism and the physical sex education, physical education and dress reform in Victoria, 1880–1930'. Masters Thesis, Monash University, 1984.

29   A report in *The Herald* on 5 October 1886 said that: "… a similar dress to that donned on former occasions was worn by those who took part in the gymnastics display on Saturday afternoon. This costume consisted of pleated skirts and Garibaldi jackets of white satin the latter made sailor-fashion at the neck with sashes and back draperies of navy blue or pale blue sateen…" and a report in *Bohemia* on 9 October 1890 said that "the girls wore no corsets and this was one reason why they could exercise so long without flagging, like a troop of the Priestesses of Hygeia." <http://nla.gov.au/nla.news-pages5739327>

Chapter 21

30 The information in this section comes from the then Shire of Berwick
rate books 1883–1888, as reported by Lois Young in her thesis on page 94.
The property 'The Steyne' was later changed to Newstead Forest, Upper
Beaconsfield.

Chapter 23

31 An article appeared in *The Argus* on page 6 of the Friday 4 April 1884 edition
reporting on the accident, under the title 'The Railway Disaster at Little
River'. <https://trove.nla.gov.au/newspaper/article/6046962/267372#>

Chapter 24

32 An article, 'The Melbourne Ladies' Gymnasium', appeared on page 5 in
The Age on Thursday 29 October 1885, in which it reported on the crowd
that came to witness the annual competition involving 100 members. It took
place at the Melbourne Town Hall.

33 The sale notice appeared in *The Argus* on 27 October 1885, p. 12.

Chapter 25

34 Lois Young details these facts in her thesis on pp. 95–98. Harriet and Alice
and later, Josephine, taught gymnastics in at least 16 different ladies colleges
in Melbourne between 1880 and 1892, charging one guinea per student per
quarter. The first school advertising Miss Dick's gym classes was Brunswick
Park House in 1880 and here she also gave 'lectures'. These were undoubtedly in health and physiology and prepared students for the Australian
Health Society's exam of that year. When MLC began in 1882, they were
both employed and remained there until 1887. Harriet taught on her own
there in 1888 which continued perhaps until around 1892. Gym classes were
interrupted due to the train smash.

35 There are various articles in which Josephine McCormick is mentioned,
including in the 24 February 1904 edition of *Critic*, in an interview with her
conducted by Inez Bensusan, which appeared in the *Brighton Southern Cross*
on page 2 of the edition published in Saturday 6 May 1899, and in an article
in *The Argus* on 2 August 1917.

Death notices also appeared after her death on 1 October 1924 in
The Argus on 3 October and *The Australasian* on 4 October. An obituary
appeared in *The Argus* on 16 October. She was described as "a woman of
broad sympathies and winning personality" whose "career was taken up in
alleviating the bodily suffering of other people, and these included a great
number of children whose spinal and similar complaints necessitated special
treatment scientifically administered." Her connection to the 'Melbourne
Ladies' Medical Gymnasium' was noted, as was her membership of the

Lyceum Club, her religious devotion, and her "deep interest in literature and the arts."

Chapter 27

36 <https://trove.nla.gov.au/newspaper/article/6074505?>

Chapter 30

37 The sale of the property is documented on p. 107 of Lois Young's thesis and comes from the Shire of Berwick's 1888 rate book. Alice sold Beaconsfield to a Richard Noble in April 1888.

38 However, Lois Young's thesis puts them there.

Chapter 31

39 <https://trove.nla.gov.au/newspaper/article/6052008?>

40 Details of the restaurant appeared in the column 'Our Ladies Melbourne Letter' in the Tasmanian newspaper *The Mercury* on Wednesday 20 March 1889. <https://trove.nla.gov.au/newspaper/article/9208806 ?searchTerm=our%20ladies%20melbourne%20letter&searchLimits=dateFr om=1889-01-01|||dateTo=1889-12-31>

Chapter 32

41 This information can be found on p. 108 of Lois Young's thesis.

Chapter 33

42 William Curnow (1832–1903) was a clergyman and journalist. He loved music and was a frequent theatre goer. His wife, Matilda Curnow, who died in 1921, helped establish free kindergartens and was a founder of the Women's Literary Society and the Women's College, University of Sydney.

43 Two of Alice's stories, 'The Red-Haired Boy' and 'Unlucky George' were published in the *Freeman's Journal* on Saturday 5 May 1894.

44 A *Bulletin* critique of Dickinson's 1900 novel *Hearts Importunate* stated that while the new novel by the Sydney writer Evelyn Dickinson was "not a book of literary account" it was "skilfully written" and "agreeably" presented. By saying it was a "conventional love-motive against an Australian background," the review took the typical stance of denigrating female romance genre writing. Alice would have received the same sort of criticisms about her writing.

45 This information comes from the PhD thesis of Gilliam Sykes, 'The New Woman in the New World: Fin-de-Siecle Writing and Feminism in Australia' which was completed through the School of English, Art History, Film and Media at the University of Sydney in 2002.

Chapter 34

46 This information comes from Lois Young's Masters Thesis, 'Feminism and the physical sex education, physical education and dress reform in Victoria, 1880–1930'. Monash University, 1984.

47 Eleanor Grove was the First Principal of College Hall, Byng Place, from 1882–1900, and Life Governor of University College London for the promotion and encouragement of the study of, and proficiency in, German. She was a German scholar and translated many German classics.

48 Alice's review of Louisa MacDonald's book, *Inscriptions Relating to Sorcery in Cyprus,* appeared in *The Sydney Morning Herald* on p. 5 of the Saturday 23 April 1892 edition. The article was headed 'Miss MacDonald on Antiquities in Cyprus'.

Chapter 35

49 It was not until 1910, after a campaign of almost 20 years by Rose Scott and others, that the age of consent for girls was raised from 14 to 16 in the *Girls' Protection Act.* In 1896, a Sydney newspaper argued against the campaign and questioned what was being done to protect boys: "There are impressionable youths who are as easily led astray as the impressionable girls, and in view of the terrible punishment awarded on account of crimes against females, and the easy opportunity for blackmail that would be afforded unscrupulous persons, the public will no doubt consider long and seriously before they place in the power of any hysterical or unscrupulous female of 16 or 17 the means of working such widespread mischief. With the age of consent at 18 many young men might be forced into marriages or fleeced by immoral girls or their designing parents. There are grave dangers associated with raising of the age." <https://www.dailytelepgraph.com.au/news/socialite-rose-scotts-voice-of-dissent-won-rights-for-australian-women/news-story/5279d9c1adaca3afa1 3bdfa967adc8ff>

Chapter 39

50 An article about Alice Moon's death, 'Sudden Death of Lady Journalist', appeared on p. 37 in *The Leader* in Melbourne, on Saturday 5 May 1894. It was very complimentary of her accomplishments and reported on the sudden nature of her death. It was this article that reported the presence of Mr McGarvie Smith among the mourners at her burial. Other death notices appeared in *The Argus* (Tuesday 24 April, 1894), *The Sydney Morning Herald* (Tuesday 24 April, 1894), and *Freeman's Journal* (Saturday 28 April 1894, p. 16) which also noted that a coroner's inquest took place on the Monday morning after her death. Alice's death certificate lists the death as due to "natural causes."

Chapter 40

51 Tachycardia, which is a rapid increase in heartbeat, is one symptom of snake venom and is possible that this is what caused Alice's death. Recent studies have reported on the connection between snake venom and heart conditions. In 2012, an article was published in *The Pan African Medical Journal* 13:51, 'Takotsubo cardiomyopathy in a snake bite victim: a case report' by Kichiro Murase and Kenji Takagi, which advised physicians to "consider not only cardioinhibitory effect of snake venom but also takotsubo cardiomyopathy as a differential diagnosis if the patient develops cardiac dysfunction following snake bite."

Chapter 41

52 The details of Alice's Will are contained in the Lois Young thesis, and also on the history page of a website dedicated to recording the history of people who lived in the Upper Beaconsfield area. The original source is stated as "miscellaneous." <https://www.upperbeaconsfieldhistory.org.au/g0/p46.htm#c1372.18>

It listed the following items:
- left all estate and interest in property known as Viney's Hotel Falmouth Tasmania to Mary Rose Merewether of Sydney, and any sum due to me by Mary Rose of Walter Lockyer Merewether
- £1000 or same amount in shares/stocks held by me to Florence Agnes, wife of Erskine James Rainey Parker of Tasmania Squatter (in codocil changed to all shares held by me in Tasmania Silver Mining Co)
- Residue to Josephine Julia Anna McCormick of "The Steyne" Abbotsford Spinster
- Appointed George Peter Mills of Melbourne and Robert Alex Vaughan Rae of Melbourne Merchant as Executors – they renounced probate
- In Codicil 15 Nov 1892 revoked above, gave to Josephine Julia McCormick her reversionary interest in marriage settlement of late sister Grace Ethel Hall
- to Mary Rose Merewether her personal effects at "Lurlie", incl clothing, jewellery, books, pictures, papers and my boat "the Lark"

The Probate was valued at £45 (16 June 1894).

Chapter 44

53 Lois Young, 'Feminism and the physical sex education, physical education and dress reform in Victoria, 1880–1930'. Masters Thesis, Monash University, 1984, p. 118.

54 The new publication, *The Australian Woman's Sphere,* of which Vida Goldstein was both the editor and proprietor, was devoted to the interests of women suffragists and was issued monthly from September 1900. It met with

mixed reception from the established newspapers. The *McIvor Times and Rodney Advertiser* in its 16 December 1900 edition, decried that "woman's temperament does not fit her for business life. She is too sensitive and highly strung to feel happy and at home in the bustle and rush of commercial life." Of similar sentiment, the *North Melbourne Courier and West Melbourne Advertiser,* on 31 August 1900, said, "The first number of a newspaper under the above title has just come to hand, the object of which is to forward the female franchise movement now agitating the minds of some of the feminine portion of the community. The name is somewhat of a misnomer, as political articles comprise the main features of the present number, and to the great majority of women they are as so much Greek or Sanskrit."

55 The advertisement listed the business name as The School of Physical Culture and Medical Gymnastics, located at 243 Collins Street, and named Miss Dick and Miss Gaunt as the principals.

56 <http://acms.sl.nsw.gov.au//item/itemPopLarger.aspx?itemid=902125>

57 The Public Record Office, Victoria, has the probate document under the name Harriett [sic] Elizabeth Rowell, known as Harriett [sic] Elphinstone Dick, in which it states that the date of granting of probate was 19 September 1902. It records Harriet's occupation as spinster and says she resided in Highett. <http://access.prov.vic.gov.au/public/component/daPublicBaseContainer?component=daViewItem&entityId=4137613205>

58 An obituary for Harriet appeared in *The Argus* on Monday 21 July 1902. (Her name was misspelt as Harriett.) It noted her interest in swimming, although this was attributed to the fact that she had brothers: "she shared all their pursuits, and early imbibed a taste for and a knowledge of their recreations." Her swim from Shoreham to Brighton in 1875 was noted. The obituary also recognised her professional training and teaching of girls and her passion for "physical culture." It reported that she died suddenly of a heart attack.

59 See *Red Emma Speaks: An Emma Goldman Reader,* edited by Alix Kates Shulman, New York: Humanity Books, 1998.

60 Cheltenham Old Cemetery is at 233–237 Charman Road, Cheltenham, Victoria.

John McGarvie Smith.

John Alexander Gunn.

AFTERWORD

Who was John McGarvie Smith?

AND WHAT WAS HIS CONNECTION TO THE ANTHRAX VACCINE?

"Allegedly avaricious and secretive, and reputed to have amassed a fortune, McGarvie Smith was deeply patriotic and convivial with a wide circle of friends."

—*Australian Dictionary of Biography*

"The man is a devil neither more nor less and a mad one at that but with the cunning of the devil himself."

—John Gunn, 12 November 1906, letter to solicitor

I would never have heard of John McGarvie Smith (1844 –1918), nor been led to discover a hidden history of lies, greed, intrigue, coercion and fraud, if I had not been snatched from my life into the lives of Alice Caroline Moon and Harriet Elphinstone Dick. Extensive research into John McGarvie Smith confirmed my suspicions that this man had brought evil upon Alice, and, in some unknown way, contributed to her death. He had been well known to those female friends who, long after her burial, gathered to inscribe a message on her gravestone;

243

a challenge perhaps for a future generation of researchers to find and expose the truth. *When He giveth quietness, who then can make trouble* (Job 34: 29).

When the dead call for justice from another time beyond the grave, one must either surrender or learn *not* to close one's mind to that persistent rattling of the bones whose truth has been ignored.

It would have been abhorrent for a man such as McGarvie Smith to find himself in the position of collaborating with a clever, erudite, well-educated (enough to be conversant in his very own specific fields of research), female writer and artist such as Alice Moon. She would never kowtow or succumb to his born-to-rule stance, nor to his seductive wiles; she did not need a man and openly boasted of this, and of her independence and personal wealth. Alice Moon embodied that impossibility, to the male intellect, that lesbians could be sensual, sexy and alluring. Through her wit, resilience and intelligence she thwarted all his attempts at seduction. Her clever insults and torments, her disinterest in his manhood and his lewd inferences concerning both the 'power of his snakes in a woman's hand', and the power of his own 'one-eyed' snake in that same hand, drove his anger.

John McGarvie Smith was a patriarch: commanding, controlling, secretive, boastful, avaricious, aggressive and often disloyal. Disliking the commonality of his name 'Smith', he very quickly adopted a middle name taken from a Rev. McGarvie whom he had known when young. He added McGarvie to his name and forever after insisted that people call him McGarvie and, preferably, leave out the Smith part altogether. A vain man. A man's man. And as long as he was in control, he was conviviality itself. He refused to ever repeat anything twice, declaring that if you missed it the first time, then that was too bad. He made many enemies. In 1877, he married Adelaide Deniehy, 14 years his senior and the widow of the poet, orator and politico bad-boy inebriate, Daniel H. Deniehy.

The story of the Gunn and McGarvie Smith Anthrax Vaccine

John Alexander Gunn (1860–1910) was the originator of the Australian anthrax vaccine. Gunn had spent more than eight years on his discovery of the *one-dose* vaccine and had been successfully using it for years. French microbiologist Louis Pasteur (1822–1895) had in 1881 discovered the *two-dose* vaccine (administered with a gap of two weeks). But we must remember that, different to Europe, stock in Australia was distributed over many square miles. It was thus very difficult to get all the stock back for the second vaccination. And it was even more difficult to deliver the vaccine to the outward reaches of a station which would take days, so using Pasteur's two-dose method was impractical. John A. Gunn's one shot vaccination was much preferable. However, there was a small problem with Gunn's formula: it did not sustain its potency over a long period.

This is where John McGarvie Smith enters the story. In April 1895, with Smith's input, it took only two days to resolve the longevity issue. After this success, Smith insisted on a full partnership with Gunn. Despite the Gunn family's resistance, the fact that Smith now knew the secret formula meant Gunn had to acquiesce to his demand. As a consequence, John Gunn's deserved place in the annals of Australian science was, upon his early death at 50 years of age in 1910, erased by Smith. It is important to know this, as in the years that followed Gunn's death, Smith began to claim not only to have discovered the one-dose formula, but to have worked on it for years. But Gunn had been using his vaccine successfully on his own flocks with no deaths recorded for many years before Smith arrived on the scene.

After Gunn's death in 1910, and despite Smith changing the vaccine's name to 'McGarvie Smith Vaccine', it remained Gunn's original formula which had been successfully used to inoculate millions of sheep and cattle from 1895 right through to the 1920s when anthrax became less of a problem. No stock ever died from it and the success rate was 99%. McGarvie Smith boasted for years of the success of 'his' vaccine and it was only when John Gunn's widow, Jessie Gunn, offered the same formula, free of charge to the government of New South Wales (NSW) as early as 1916, did Smith pretend to have perfected a *better* version of the vaccine. Nevertheless, he continued to write to newspapers boasting about the success of the original vaccine, which he now named the McGarvie Smith Vaccine.

Smith's promotional forum for 'his' vaccine was his frequent letter writing to the dailies. Many of his letters were in fact replies to the letters of others, who, for example, tried to reinstate the name of the original inventor, John A. Gunn: 'honor where honor is due'. The NSW Government made many attempts to get Smith to transfer the secret formula to them, but never succeeded. Smith was avaricious and kept it a secret, but later as he became unwell and weaker of spirit, a cabal of highly placed men, pushing their own agenda of personal financial gain, intervened (see below), thus circumventing the government's pleas and gaining private access to Smith and the formula.

In 1918, uproar followed in the NSW parliament regarding the 'loss' of the vaccine to the government after it thought its negotiations with a Dr Wall had secured the formula from Smith. The argument was that Jessie Gunn's donation of the Gunn formula was cheaper and should have been taken up. It implied that Drs Wall and Tidswell were grossly overpricing their services, which of course they were. These two men had hatched a plan of making extra money by demanding that before the vaccine could be given to the government, it needed to be tested. As if 20 years of successful application needed confirmation! They billed the government an extraordinary amount for four months (unnecessary) testing of a formula that had already proven perfect. The insider joke was that they never intended, in the first place, to pass the formula over to the government. Mr Grahame MLA later took umbrage at Dr Wall and called him a fraud, because at a previous meeting, Wall had insisted he did not want remuneration for supplying the vaccine formula. This led to the uproar in parliament.[1]

Chronology[2]

1844

Birth of JOHN SMITH on 8 February to Isabella Young (1822 – 30 December 1896) and David Milne Smith (22 May 1822 – 1 August 1901).

Later Smith adopted the McGarvie name. Bacteriologist at Paddington, Sydney. Eldest of 13 children. Smith was apprenticed to a watchmaker at the age of 13. He studied chemistry at the University of Sydney and in his spare time interested himself in bacteriology, travelling in Europe and America.

1860

Birth of JOHN ALEXANDER GUNN, Victoria. He became the manager of the Goldsbrough Mort & Co. Ltd. Properties, Yalgogrin Station (Central Division of NSW) and Borambola (near Wagga), until 1905, when he acquired his own property, Braehour, in the Wagga district. There is a plaque in North Yalgogrin commemorating John A. Gunn "who experimented on this site and produced the first anthrax vaccine in Australia." Built his own laboratory in 1890 on Yalgogrin Run. Bacteriologist and Station Inspector, his sons went to Geelong College. He acquired a lot of property: four houses in Sydney and land in outer Geelong. Anthrax was the scourge of the sheep industry at the time, killing more than 30% of sheep flocks and other livestock with more than 270,000 sheep known to be lost to the disease in the Riverina District.

1877

Marriage notice appeared on 16 July 1877 in *The Sydney Morning Herald*. SMITH—DENIEHY, 7 July, by the Rev. James Milne, J. McGarvie Smith to Adelaide Elizabeth, widow of the late D.H. Deniehy, solicitor. Adelaide was born in 1830 and died on 31 December 1908.

1880–1918

89 Denison Street, Woollahra (later renamed Holdsworth Street) was leased to John McGarvie Smith and Frederick Gannon (as trustee for Adelaide Elizabeth neé Hoalls) for £600. The property presumably was acquired as their matrimonial home. It was leased until May 1889. Adelaide had four surviving daughters from her previous marriage living with her when she married McGarvie Smith. They were:

- Ginevra Deniehy died 12 April 1881 (four years after her mother married McGarvie);
- Mary Deniehy died 19 July 1929;
- Ada Deniehy, who offered music lessons from Denison Street (1890–1894); and
- Constance (Clarence) Deniehy, 1855–1932, who married bacteriologist Henry Waldron in 1899.

McGarvie is listed in the Sands Directory at 89 Holdsworth Street from 1882 until his death in 1918. This house was named Ginevra after his late stepdaughter.

1881

The *double-dose* vaccine anthrax was developed by Louis Pasteur in Paris but could not survive shipment or outback climatic conditions. The regime of two vaccinations administered 14 days apart was a particular problem on the sprawling Australia sheep runs. John Gunn had many supporters in his endeavour of creating a *single-dose* vaccine, including Frank Stewart of Bygoo Station, Ardlethan, and Arthur Devlin of Uarah Station near Grong Grong.

1890

Gunn first works on the anthrax vaccine in his lab at Yalgogrin.

1892

Wednesday 3 August, 'Venom of the Australian black snake'.

Paper read at the Royal Society NSW, published in December 1892. Authors: C. J. Martin, professor at the University of Sydney and J. McGarvie Smith.

1892

An article on McGarvie Smith appeared on Saturday 24 December, p. 1418, in *The Sydney Mail*, 'Experimenting with Live Snakes. A Colony of Venomous Reptiles. An Exciting Pastime'. Interviewer H.J.D., Illustrator Mr Norman Hardy.

1893

Gunn testing vaccines at Yalgogrin produces successful anthrax double-dose vaccine. Next he develops a single-dose vaccine but has trouble with keeping the longevity of serum.

1894

Saturday 21 April, ALICE'S DEATH.

1895

McGarvie Smith features in an article on Sunday 3 March, *Sunday Times*, p. 2, under the heading 'The Woollahra Wizard'.

1895

Gunn, as well as managing Yalgogrin, was made superintendent for all NSW stations. Gunn and Devlin working with him try to increase longevity of the anthrax vaccine. John McGarvie Smith was approached and within days, the keeping quality of the serum was markedly improved. McGarvie Smith had previously worked on snake anti-venene. There is a story that he would get snake collectors to release all their snakes into one room. Then they would have to accept McGarvie Smith's price or attempt to recapture all their stock.[3] The partnership prospered financially, but in human terms it was a disaster that got worse. Under the terms of the partnership, each was to maintain a laboratory – McGarvie Smith was to vaccinate north of Sydney, and Gunn was to vaccinate south of Sydney and in Victoria. The partnership was entered into in April 1895. Gunn wrote about the immediate seasons that followed:

> Last season we inoculated over a million sheep with one inoculation and though this was the first season of its use … less than 10% had to receive the second inoculation to render them absolutely immune. And this season, as we are more and more perfecting the material, out of another million not [even] 2% required a second vaccination. The President of the NSW Board of Health [Tidswell?] stated that vaccines under the most favourable of circumstances killed 5% of the sheep treated; he undoubtedly referred to the published results of Pasteur's process as under no circumstance whatever will our McGarvie Smith and Gunn vaccine kill a sheep and we offered to give him £1000 to any charities of Sydney if he can produce proof of any deaths having been caused by it out of 3,750,000 sheep treated by us.

The challenge was never taken up. Louis Pasteur's vaccine became irrelevant because a cheap and foolproof method was now available. Gunn continued to work for Goldsbrough Mort as well as working on the vaccine. Obviously, Gunn was making it in his lab while Smith was making it at his Denison Street laboratory.

1896

Friday 21 August. Smith works with Katz from Pasteur Institute.

Smith's reply to a letter stating that Gunn invented the vaccine is: "Last year our firm (McGarvie Smith and Gunn) treated most successfully half a million sheep ..."

1896

Friday 21 August, *The Sydney Stock and Station Journal*, p. 8.

Letter from McGarvie Smith in reply to the claim that Gunn invented the vaccine. Interesting that Gunn did not contradict him. Perhaps he did not see the letter or was too busy.

To the Editor, *The Sydney Stock and Station Journal*.

Sir, — I would esteem it a favor if you would kindly give space in your paper to the following. In your issue of July 10th, you state the following, from a correction to hand: "That it was not true that McGarvie Smith invented a vaccine; he invented a process for keeping vaccine. It appears Mr. Gunn invented the vaccine, &c."

To the noble Pasteur alone is due the honor of discovering [the vaccine against anthrax] *the only substance known* that gives immunity or renders sheep and cattle proof by inoculation against this terrible disease. He demonstrated his great discovery amidst much rejoicings and published to the world the basis of his labors on this important subject (see the literature relating thereto). That this substance can now be produced by others is no secret. Last year our firm (McGarvie Smith and Gunn) treated most successfully half a million sheep. Not, as would be inferred by your remarks, with Mr. Gunn's vaccines treated with Mr. McGarvie Smith's method of preserving them, but by vaccine produced by both Mr. McGarvie Smith and by Mr. Gunn, and these vaccines, *first* and *second* respectively, were treated by the method devised by myself, *by which they are preserved, retaining all their protective properties unimpaired for an indefinite period an achievement never before accomplished.* This is the *only* originality in our vaccines; all other vaccines I know of become quite inoperative after a very few days. This advance, when operating over such a vast territory as Australia, amidst severe climatic changes, is of *great importance.*

I refrained from treating commercially sheep and cattle against anthrax for several years, believing as I did that the Pasteur institute was represented here in this great work, and during that period I demonstrated the giving immunity to sheep by one inoculation. This our firm has confirmed on large flocks, and, I trust, ere long will deal commercially with this further advance. Its advantages are obvious. I should have addressed you sooner and expected that the *honor* of *discovering the vaccine* would have been corrected and given to whom it is due, viz, the *noble Pasteur,* to whom we are so very much indebted. Apologising for trespassing so much on your valuable space, yours, etc.

—J. McGarvie Smith. Woollahra, 17 August 1896.

1897

Gunn moved to Borambola, 18 miles from Wagga. Successfully vaccinated over one million sheep. Increasingly, Gunn was leaving the Wagga area in connection with his own business. He got his brother, Marcus, to run Borambola and cut his own salary to equal that of his brother: £350 to £150.

Beatrice Webb wrote of her visit to Gunn's Station, quoted from *The Webbs' Australian Diary,* edited by A.G. Austin, 1898, pp. 58–60.

> … flies swarmed through the room (Australians have not yet tumbled to wire netting over doorways and windows characteristic

of the fly devastated districts of America). Our host proved to be an unusually interesting man. Australian born, of Scotch extraction, a successful manager of stations in different districts in NSW, he has devoted his leisure to a scientific investigation of Anthrax and had invented and patented a vaccine named after him – the Gunn vaccine. Last year he had vaccinated over one million sheep, receiving from 1 1/2d. to 2d. for each animal and supplying his own operators as well as his own vaccine. He was delighted to show us over his laboratory and glad enough to find someone interested in his hobby. He was a thorough-going individualist, objecting altogether to government regulation and the necessity of taking out a license for his experimental work – a fine fellow for all that – hard working and upright, with that interesting combination of speculative intelligence and a keen commercial instinct which is so characteristic of the best type of Scotchman. For the rest he was a materialist in metaphysic, a reactionary in politics, and an autocrat in the home, keeping his womankind in due subordination to his own requirements, his sister, a good–natured raw, ugly Scotch girl, doing the housekeeping and looking after the children, and his wife, a delicate little bright minded Melbourne lady, devoting her whole time to keeping his laboratory in perfect order and watching, hour by hour, his incubating processes. As might have been expected, the elderly book-keeper was Scotch and the jackaroo was also Scotch and doubtless if we had enquired we would have discovered that the overseer was Scotch; this station was in fact a little bit of Scotland transplanted; only religion had disappeared and free and easy materialism has taken its place."[4]

1900

Tuesday 29 May, *The Sydney Stock and Station Journal,* p. 5.

This interview reveals that Smith and Gunn were a business partnership and were inoculating with the final secret formula. The partnership was terminated on Gunn's death in 1910 at which point Smith claims full ownership of the invention of the vaccine, naming it McGarvie Smith Vaccine, and keeping the formula secret from everyone. Subsequently, he gets all the glory and all the money.

1905

Gunn buys his own station, Braehour.

1905

Relationships within the partnership are very bad. Letters go through Gunn's solicitor to Smith.

1907

Gunn writes to the Tax Commissioner that his partner is withholding financial information. Gunn had paid his dues but Smith had not. Gunn was writing to the tax commissioners apologising for sending in an incomplete return but his partner [Smith] was not providing him with full financial information. (Interestingly, when the information did come, it seems that Gunn's income for the 1907 financial year was £3,100. An average income at this time could not have been much over £100.) The partnership was brought to arbitration in 1907 and it still required an arbitrator's services when Gunn died. When the figures were produced for the arbitrator it was shown that Gunn had vaccinated nearly 2,000,000 *more* sheep than McGarvie Smith and at a cost of more than £50 per 100,000 sheep *less* than Smith. Over 13,000,000 sheep had been vaccinated at this time as had other sundry stock. (This is incorrect; sheep were inoculated with the Smith and Gunn vaccine.) In 1908, Gunn became chairman of the Rabbit Destruction Fund Committee of the Pastures Protection Boards Advisory Council which sponsored the experiments of Dr Danysz aimed at developing an effective rabbit virus.

1908

Gunn's career culminates in his appointment to the Upper House of NSW Parliament on 10 July.

1909

Gunn tried to help the rural community by taking a major part on a Closer Settlement Bill 1909; he was on a select committee for a new Sydney abattoir and he tried to improve rolling stock to rural areas.

1909

Tuesday 5 January, the death of Smith's wife, Adelaide is reported in the *Sydney Morning Herald*.

1910

J. A. Gunn believed "McGarvie is simply green with jealousy and hatred." If so, he had hated Gunn for a long time.[5]

> Sudden death of John Gunn (aged 50) at Braehour. Gunn died in Sydney on the 21 September 1910 and was buried in the Presbyterian section of the Rookwood Cemetery. His wife, Jessie, and three children (Gladys, Alexander and Angus) succeeded him. A fourth child, Jessie lies buried at Yalgogrin, died aged one in 1891.
>
> <http://trove.nla.gov.au/newspaper/article/1517829>

Most obituaries fell into the category of not knowing Gunn's discovery of the *one-dose* anthrax vaccine. Smith had already done much damage to Gunn's reputation through his claim to the honour for himself.

1910

Tuesday 15 November, *The Sydney Morning Herald*, p. 6, 'A Grazier's Will'.

The estate of the late John Alexander Gunn, of Braehour, near Wagga, grazier and bacteriologist, has been valued for State purposes at £31,690, of which £24,219 12s 11d represented real estate.

1913

On Friday 7 November, in *The Sydney Stock and Station Journal*, Smith advertises the anthrax vaccine, claiming all as his invention.

Mr. J. McGARVIE SMITH has much pleasure in stating that the giving protection by one inoculation introduced by himself has, since its introduction, been successfully used on over 15,000,000 Sheep and Cattle. Full particulars on application to J. McGARVIE SMITH, Denison Street, Woollahra, Sydney.

ANTHRAX VACCINE

Approved of and used by the Governments of
N.S.W., Victoria, and New Caledonia.

PROTECTION BY ONE INOCULATION.
Over 10, 000, 000 Sheep and Cattle successfully treated.
Rates greatly reduced.

J. McGARVIE SMITH,
Sole surviving partner of the late firm
of McGARVIE SMITH and GUNN.

Mr. J. McGARVIE SMITH issues Certificates approved of by the Stock Department of Victoria to owners of stock vaccinated by him in New South Wales, which acts as a passport for such stock to cross the border into Victoria, or into New Caledonia, during the Anthrax Season.

Such Certificates remain operative for twelve months from date of vaccination.

References will be given on application to the owners of over 16,000,000 Sheep and Cattle successfully treated by the improved process.

Mr. J. McGARVIE SMITH has much pleasure in stating that the giving protection by one inoculation introduced by himself has, since its introduction, been successfully used on over 15,000,000 Sheep and Cattle.

Full particulars on application to—
J. McGARVIE SMITH,
Denison St., Woollahra, Sydney.

When the Glenfield Veterinary Research Station was opened in 1923, one wing was to become the Gunn wing to commemorate Jessie's 1918 gift of McGarvie Smith Gunn's vaccine. The only condition on the gift was that Gunn's name be associated with it. There is a wooden plaque over one door at Glenfield commemorating J.A. Gunn. In 2017, a new wing at Glenfield was opened and named the McGarvie Smith Wing. Insult to injury!

The State Cabinet was involved in the McGarvie Smith/Gunn dispute in 1918 – one newspaper was even headed: Anthrax vaccines manacling government. The dispute with McGarvie Smith was never satisfactorily resolved. We can see from documents of the time that Smith was never one to forgive; his narcissism and his greed for self-importance and power overriding everything he did.

Gunn was a man of strong character and major achievements; he was dedicated to science, pastoral work and his family. He was exceptionally hard-working but very popular. He was also a man who achieved much for the Australian pastoral industry – he invented the first mechanical poison bait layer for rabbit control which was manufactured in Sydney and widely copied. He attempted viral control of rabbits and he stopped anthrax from ruining the Australia livestock industry. He then went on to serve rural Australia from the parliament of NSW.

1916

Wednesday 2 February, *The Sydney Morning Herald*, p. 11, 'Anthrax Vaccine'. This article is very important as it shows how many pastoralist men were aware of Gunn's claim to the vaccine.

> That this board absolutely refuses to be a party to any testimonial or any form of recognition to be given to Mr. McGarvie Smith unless the name of the late J.A. Gunn is associated therewith as

the principal in the introduction of a successful vaccine for anthrax which gave such splendid results to the stock owners of Australia; but that the board is in favour of the proposed acquisition by the Government of the secret of the manufacture of the anthrax vaccine as supplied by the late firm of McGarvie Smith and Gunn.

<http://trove.nla.gov.au/newspaper/article/15652008>

1916

Saturday 5 February, *The Sydney Morning Herald,* 'Anthrax Vaccine'. In this, Mr McKenzie – one of Gunn's strongest supporters – fought hard for Jessie Gunn and recognition of Gunn's name.

> Mr T. A. Mackenzie chairman Pastures Board Committee of Advice writes: "I wish to correct a statement in your issue of 3rd inst. ascribed to the stock inspector at ..."
>
> <http://trove.nla.gov.au/newspaperarticle/ 141885352/15532763#>

The Creation of the McGarvie Smith Institute

From the McGarvie Smith Institute official website, 2018:

> The McGarvie Smith Institute was established in 1918 as a result of a gift to the State of NSW by John McGarvie Smith, who had developed a vaccine for Anthrax. The Institute was incorporated by the *McGarvie Smith Incorporation Act 1928.* The Institute focuses on making grants to fund research in the production livestock industries. The Institute has a limited capital base and seeks appropriate niche research projects. The Institute works closely with NSW Trade & Investment and the Faculty of Veterinary Science of the University of Sydney.

How the McGarvie Smith Institute was created, not by Smith, but by other interested parties can now be verified through my research. It means exposing the scramble for power by a few men which will serve to remind us all of how, where money and power are at stake, men can continue to act untruthfully and in collusion in order to secure their own financial futures. There are many direct parallels today.

The evidence has shown that by early 1916 Smith was still refusing to share his 'secret vaccine'. Smith was to suffer, at the age of 72, a debilitating illness in that year of 1916, an illness from which he never fully recovered and one that foreshadowed his death on 6 September 1918. When word was out that the bacteriologist 'was likely to die with his secret intact' NSW Government agents, who all along had desired ownership of the vaccine for the public good, made their move. Unfortunately, they were just a little too late since others were privately at work to secure ownership of the vaccine and its incredible profits before the government could lock it out of private hands.

1917

Mon 29 January, *Northern Star Lismore*, p. 4, 'A Noble Gift'.

> Mr. J. McGarvie-Smith, the well-known N.S.W. scientist, has generously handed over to Mr. Ashford (Minister for Lands) his plant and formulae for making anthrax vaccine, and he refuses to accept any compensation.

This article is written 20 months before his death. In fact, Smith never handed it over.

The conspirators set up the inference that the vaccine was different to the Smith/Gunn vaccine, saying that the Gunn Smith vaccine was McGarvie's invention. In January, they said they'd got it from Smith and now they reveal they don't have it.

1917

4 March, *Sunday Times Sydney*, p. 7. 'Protection of Stock Anthrax Vaccine' by J.T. Bull.

And the legislator-medico that Mr. Grahame and the Premier a few months ago, commissioned to get the secret from this remarkable man, so apparently backward and obstinate, but in reality the embodiment of good nature and public spiritedness, carried out his mission well. There was the essential mutuality of dispositions. And Dr. Wall had a highly skilled bacteriologist at the back of him, Dr. Frank Tidswell — to compass the complicated secret in all its hearings.

They daily collaborated and compared notes. This has proved fortunate for pastoral interests the world over.

It is really due to the pertinacity of the Minister for Agriculture, Mr. W. C. Grahame, of whom McGarvie was personally very fond, backed up by the efforts of the *Sunday Times* [Bull himself], that McGarvie carried out, through the medium of Dr. Frank Wall, MLC, an intention that was latent in his mind for many years ... Few have any conception of how McGarvie Smith guarded his anthrax vaccine secret. For fear that it might be stolen he would never, commit it to paper, and up till a few months ago it looked as if the discovery would go into the grave with him.

For many years efforts have been made to secure Mr. McGarvie Smith's discovery for men on the land, but the discoverer was unwilling to part with it. It is to the credit of the present Minister for Agriculture, Mr. Grahame, that he endeavored to procure for the State the benefit of the public-spiritedness that Mr. McGarvie Smith in his communications to the Department for years past has displayed.

J.T. Bull creates an extraordinary web of lies to conceal what later comes out in court, in 1932. The list of politicians who wanted their finger in the pie is long. Their sycophantic dribble is evidence of their desperation. Grahame did not achieve anything – he was merely at the receiving end.

W.C. Grahame was betrayed by Dr Wall (see Hansard). It was he who rejected Jessie Gunn's offer of 1916. He pretended to promise Jessie that Glenfield Research Centre would have a wing named after John Gunn but in reality they needed to bury Gunn and his vaccine as they were promoting their own future nest egg with Smith's vaccine (the same vaccine).

Who were the private entrepreneurs who were to manipulate the 'enfeebled' Smith and to set up, under false pretences, the McGarvie Smith Institute? Dr Frank Wall and Dr F. Tidswell were Members of the Legislative Council of NSW as well as being bacteriologists. Henry Waldron, Smith's son-in-law married to his stepdaughter Clarence, was a key figure, as was Mr Waddell. Another important member of this group was Mr James Towers Bull, a journalist and spin doctor who, for the part he played, was given the reward of being made the first Secretary of the McGarvie Smith Institute. His links to the powerful media allowed him to create 'fake news' regarding the reality of how the formula was 'freely' given to a certain Dr Frank Wall and not to the NSW Government and to perpetuate the lies about Smith's acquiescence to the 'gift'.

The 'Deed of Gift' (in fact there were two) which became the official document of where and how the secret vaccine formula was to end up (referred to in Parliament as an Indenture), was in truth not written by McGarvie Smith but by Dr F. Wall MLC, Mr Waddell, Mr Cape (a solicitor), and Mr J. T. Bull (journalist). At the time of its inception, a sick McGarvie Smith was unable to write, let alone speak. One thing is certain, he would never have agreed to Dr Tidswell being given any part to play in it. His hatred of the man is publicly documented.[6]

1918

Sunday 28 April, J.T. Bull, *Sunday Times* (Sydney), p. 9. 'Australian Scientist's Discovery: Mr McGarvie Smith makes noble gift to the state'.

> Mr. McGarvie Smith makes noble gift to the state. Mr. J. McGarvie Smith, the Australian scientist, whose bacteriological and mineralogical achievements are well known, has decided to make a gift to the State Government of his discovery of matured spore anthrax vaccine ... Latterly Mr. McGarvie Smith, who is now over 70 years of age, has not been in robust health, having undergone a severe operation, and this has prevented him doing the laboratory work customary with him for over a quarter of a century. He has communicated to the Minister for Agriculture, Mr. Grahame, his intention to present to the State, through Dr. Frank Wall, MLC, a knowledge of the means of making his matured spore anthrax vaccine. Mr. McGarvie Smith has since instructed Dr. Wall in the theory and practice of the manufacture of the vaccine , and they are now collaborating in carrying out the necessary tests. The aged scientist has kindly placed at the disposal of the doctor his Woollahra laboratory and scientific instruments. The Department of Agriculture, which is establishing a Stock Diseases Station, at Macquarie Fields, is also placing facilities at the disposal of Dr. Wall. Mr. T. Waddell, MLC, ex-Premier and Treasurer, who is a pastoralist, has taken a keen interest in this Australian discovery, and has been untiring in his efforts to see that the benefits of it might not be lost to the world. *The Sunday Times* has been urging for some time that the State Government should take steps to secure the McGarvie Smith secret, and this paper now congratulates the scientist on his generous and patriotic action in making a free gift of it to the State Government ... These experiments must necessarily take weeks to complete. As soon as the efficacy of the vaccine has been formally demonstrated in this way, the vaccine discovery will be presented to a trust, which will hold it for the State for all time. This trust is to control the McGarvie Smith Institute and will be administered jointly by the

Government and the pastoralists. The proceeds will go to the State Government.

The men involved in the McGarvie Smith vaccine scam and the establishment of the McGarvie Smith Institute

John McGarvie Smith
Smith was not of sound mind and body and lay in a comatose state when the men listed below presented for his signature a Deed of Gift which legally signed away his ownership of the 'secret' anthrax vaccine, the entire contents of his laboratory valued at £5000, and £10,000 in bonds, his own personal wealth to be used in the creation of the McGarvie Smith Institute.

Thomas Waddell MLC
1918 Chairman of the Institute's Board of Trustees. 1927–1928 General Manager of the Perpetual Trustee Coy. Also a Board Member.

On Sunday 5 May 1918, in the *Sunday Times* (Sydney), J.T. Bull writes of him:

> The importance to the country of acquiring the McGarvie Smith vaccine, remarked Mr. T. Waddell, MLC, "has at all times appealed to me as most urgent. The securing of this remedy by my fellow Councillor, Dr. Wall, has relieved me personally of a great anxiety, which all pastoralists have shared. I cannot adequately express the unbounded admiration in which the great discoverer of this vaccine is held by the pastoral community, whose regret is that for several years past he has been unable to continue his laboratory activities.

Dr Frank Edgar Wall MLC
Pastoralist, biologist and MLC member of the government. Board Member. He is given special considerations in Smith's Will: percentages of the £10,000 'gift'. Later in court he

attempted to get more money due to him from the Will's estate upon the demise of Smith's stepdaughters. Present at the signing of the 'Deed'. In partnership with Waldron in 1927–1932 in their transport company and a crucial witness at the Goode Enquiry and Royal Commission into the corruption of Goode who accepted bribes from Waldron and Wall to buy favouritism when transport jobs were handed out.

James Towers Bull

Journalist, spin doctor, made first Secretary of the McGarvie Smith Institute. Bull wrote propaganda, using his access to the media right up into the 1940s. He also considered himself responsible for the set up of the McGarvie Smith Institute (and boasted of this often) being the one who paved the way for all the crucial introductions to Smith of the men who would later get control of the vaccine and its financial rewards. He was present and a witness at the 'signing' of the 'Deed'.

Dr Frank Tidswell

Ex-Government bacteriologist. Brought in to verify the vaccine once the group got the formula. This was a fraud as they well knew there was nothing wrong with the vaccine, but it brought financial gain to Wall and Tidswell. He was a Board Member of the Institute.

Mr Henry Waldron

Bacteriologist and business man. Married to Smith's stepdaughter, Clarence. Present at the 'signing' of the 'Deed'. Board Member. Waldron blew the whistle on Dr Wall and all the others at the Goode Royal Commission in 1932. Nothing ever came of his revelations.

Mr Cape
Solicitor at Cape & Kent Lawyers, Mr Cape was John McGarvie Smith's solicitor. Present at the signing of the 'Deed'. Most probably he had a hand in the legal aspects of the creation of the 'Deed of Gift'.

Other people involved

Mr F. A. MacKenzie
Chairman of the Pastoral Protection Board's Council of Advice. MacKenzie championed J.A. Gunn and looked after his widow, Jessie Gunn. He tried to get Glenfield named after Gunn. Also tried to get the NSW Government to accept the Gunn vaccine.

Mr G. Valder
Under Secretary for Agriculture.

Mr W.C. Grahame
Minister for Agriculture who named Dr Wall in Parliament as having lied to him and committed a fraud.

Mr Ashford
Minister for Lands.

On that fateful day, sometime in April 1918, when comatose and almost on his deathbed, Smith's 'signature' was put on the 'Deed of Gift' by Dr Frank Wall who held Smith's inert hand and forced the mark. This was witnessed by journalist, J.T. Bull, Henry Waldron and Smith's own lawyer, Mr Cape, and thus, once attached to the Deed of Gift, a document which detailed Smith's supposed 'donation' of £10,000 (in bonds), all his lab equipment valued at £5,000, and the secret anthrax vaccine formula, the men had achieved their goal which was to keep the vaccine and its inherent wealth out of the hands of the NSW

Government and the people, locking it up for their personal gain. The £10,000 was set up so that interest on it would be paid to Smith as long as he lived (which was only four months). After his death, percentages were given to his stepdaughters, and, after their demise, to Dr Wall. The McGarvie Smith Institute was created from this fortune and designed to remain in the controlling hands of the Board and its Trustees. They told the world that "the noble Smith had generously donated the lot for the good of the nation." No one knew the truth of this and it has never been exposed. But in my research I happened to come upon a strange reference to McGarvie Smith in a Royal Commission held in NSW in 1932 named The Goode Royal Commission (see below).

1918

Friday 6 September JOHN McGARVIE SMITH DIES
On Sunday 8 September, J.T. Bull writes of the death in the *Sunday Times* (Sydney), p. 3, 'McGarvie Smith Secret: Misunderstood Australian Genius Guarded His Discovery Till He Could Give It to the State'.

> No one can appreciate the true inwardness of why McGarvie Smith so long kept his discovery of matured spore anthrax vaccine a jealously-guarded secret until he knows something of the psychology of the man. McGarvie was not only one of the most unique figures that Australia has produced, but probably one of its most puzzling psychological studies ... McGarvie is gone, but his secret is, fortunately, not locked in the casket with him. He nobly and unselfishly passed it on for the good of the State, and gave £10,000 with it, and in due time the formula of the secret is to be lodged by the Minister for Agriculture in the Mitchell Library for safekeeping. McGarvie Smith is dead, but his good work lives to immortalise him.

In response to J.T. Bull, F.A. Mackenzie wrote the following article which appeared on Friday 27 September, in the *Albury Banner and Wodonga Express*, p. 32, 'The J. A. Gunn Anthrax Vaccine Formula'.

> Mr. F. A. Mackenzie, chairman of the Pastures Protection Boards' council of advice who has interested himself in the endeavour to secure recognition of the work of the late J. A. Gunn in the discovery and successful use of anthrax vaccine, replied to the statements made a few days ago in these columns by Mr. J. Bull, secretary of the McGarvie Smith Institute. 'Mr. Bull would,' he said, 'do well to inquire into facts before rushing into print. I am neither afraid of stultifying my friend's name nor myself, having facts before I speak or write. To give a direct denial to an assertion of Mr. Bull I have been permitted to see the deed of partnership between J. A. Gunn and J. McGarvie Smith, and numerous other documents. The latter show clearly that Mr. Gunn himself vaccinated half a million sheep in 1893-1894, with excellent results, as evidenced by owners' complimentary letter. This was before he met and entered into partnership with Mr. McGarvie Smith, which was not till April 4, 1895. In the partnership deed no mention whatever is made (as stated by Mr. Bull) that only Mr. McGarvie Smith's vaccine was to be used. On the contrary, each partner was to make his own for their allotted districts. The value of the partnership was very properly nil, as it ceased at Mr. Gunn's death. I am indebted to the Chief Inspector of Stock in turning up the date of issue of the first licenses, viz. J. A. Gunn, August 27, 1891; J. McGarvie Smith, June 13, 1897. From the foregoing I think the stockowners can treat with contempt Mr. Bull's references to Mr. Gunn as a lay worker. I anticipate with pleasure the early gift to the Government by the trustees of the estate of the late J. A. Gunn of the formula they possess, with the condition that the name of Mr. Gunn be permanently associated therewith.

> <http://trove.nla.gov.au/newspaper/article/102145645>

1918

Friday 4 October, *The Albury Banner and Wodonga Express*, p. 17, 'Anthrax Vaccine'.

> The trustees of the estate of the late J. A. Gunn (Mr. M. D. Gunn, of Hawksview Albury, and Mrs. Jessie M. Gunn) write in reference to the statement recently published from Mr J. Bull (the Secretary of the McGarvie Smith Institute) regarding anthrax vaccine and the late J. A. Gunn:
>
> No more inaccurate or incorrect statement has ever been published. Mr. Bull first asserts that the reason the Government declined to accept the complete formula for the manufacture of anthrax vaccine was that the trustees had no secret to offer. The trustees never professed to possessing a secret, but they did and do.
>
> <http://trove.nla.gov.au/newspaper/article/102144558>

1918

The following letter, 'Anthrax Vaccine. Gunn and M'Garvie Smith: We are groping in the dark' by Edwin C. Pope, published on Tuesday 22 October, *The Sydney Stock and Station Journal*, p. 2 truthfully explains what really happened:

> [Mr. Edwin C. Pope, of Euronga, Ardlethan, writes]: I was not aware of the controversy re M'Garvie Smith and Gunn's anthrax vaccine, but my attention was drawn to two articles in your edition of the 1st instant, and as both articles contain misleading statements, perhaps you will allow the oldest friend of the late Hon. J. A. Gunn space in your paper to give a short account of the true history of the discovery of the vaccine in question. Mr. Badgery's statement that Mr. Gunn was helping Dr. Loir in his laboratory is entirely without foundation. Mr. Gunn took the management of South Yalgogrin in May 1886, when I was sent there to learn station experience. I think it was the summer of 1889-90 that anthrax broke out on Yalgogrin, a disease that at that time no-one on the place had seen. Mr. Gunn had sometime previously taken up microscopic work as a hobby. In a very short

time, Mr Gunn discovered the anthrax microbe in the blood of dead sheep, and so knew what this new disease was. The following year the whole of the Yalgogrin flock was vaccinated with Pasteur's vaccine. Not twice, but five times were 34,000 sheep vaccinated, and even then the result was unsatisfactory, the percentage of protected sheep in the various flocks ranging from 60 to 90 par cent. It was the failure of the Pasteur vaccine that made Mr. Gunn begin his experiments. For two years Mr. Gunn worked practically day and night, and well do I remember the day he told me he thought he had got a vaccine. That year Messrs. Goldsbrough, Mort and Co. consented to the Yalgogrin sheep being vaccinated with Gunn's Vaccine. The Company's confidence in Mr. Gunn was not misplaced, the result being the whole flock absolutely protected. Three neighbours, whose losses were ruinous, and where the Pasteur vaccine had also failed, begged Mr. Gunn to vaccinate their sheep; he consented and fully protected their flocks. The next year Mr. Gunn began operations on a large scale, and though the vaccine had to be used in a limited time, by good management and hard work, Mr. Gunn vaccinated and protected large numbers of sheep over a wide area of New South Wales and Victoria. It was, I think, in 1894, that Mr. Gunn first met Mr. M'Garvie Smith. Had Mr. Badgery stated that Mr. M'Garvie Smith had obtained his knowledge in the laboratory of Pasteur's agents, he would have been closer to the mark. Mr. M'Garvie Smith did discover 'the method of' keeping' the vaccine, and that was the reason Mr. Gunn took him into partnership, but that was his sole discovery of any real importance. It was Mr. Gunn who first made the single vaccine, and to him also was the honour of discovering a cure for anthrax by a serum, which perhaps Mr. Badgery will have the honesty to admit is a step further than the late Mr Pasteur achieved. Now, as to Mr. M'Garvie Smith's statements, as quoted in your article on page 5 of the same edition. It's true in one sense there is no secret; but, like the statements that Mr M'Garvie Smith is credited with suggesting to Mr. Gunn, that they should erect a modern laboratory, endow it and issue vaccine free, is only a half truth. Why did not Mr. M'Garvie Smith give his partner's real reason for not agreeing? For the same reason, Mr. M'Garvie Smith omitted to tell of the unaccountable difficulty he had met with in producing good vaccine, how in one season, I think 1895, he failed almost completely, and had to ask Mr. Gunn to fill his orders for nearly one million sheep, thus putting double work on his partner, for Mr. Gunn had to make all the vaccine, and test it as well as testing Mr. M'Garvie Smith's worthless production. Mr. Gunn vaccinated and protected two million sheep that season without a single failure. The following season Mr. M'Garvie Smith turned out faultless vaccine. The true reason Mr. Gunn refused to agree to Mr. M'Garvie Smith's proposals was that, though they could produce a perfect vaccine, they could not give a formula that would always give the same results. As Mr. Gunn said to me, 'The more we learn the less we find we know; we are like men groping in the dark'. There was no need to protect the secret; the secret would protect itself. It was the ceaseless work, worry, and anxiety that greatly helped to cut short the life of the late Mr. J. A. Gunn, but had it not been for his untiring energy, perseverance, and strength of character, the pastoral industry would have been ruined over a very large portion of New South Wales, not to mention other States. "Honor to whom honor is due."

The Goode Enquiry 1932

This was a Royal Commission to investigate the actions of Mr J. Goode of The NSW Railways who was accused of corruption and bribery. Involved in this enquiry, as witnesses, were Dr F. Wall and his ex-business partner, Henry Waldron. They were partners in a business that was failing acrimoniously, and, in desperation, were paying bribes to Mr Goode to get their transport business off the ground.

In court, Waldron is full of lies and panicking. He drops a bombshell describing how Dr Wall, himself, J.T. Bull, Mr Waddell and Mr Cape all coerced the enfeebled and comatose McGarvie Smith to sign the document they'd created in 1918 ('The Deed of Gift') to set up the McGarvie Smith Institute and to hand over his vaccine formula, his lab equipment and his savings (£10,000) to them. All else they say are lies and propaganda that they created after his death. Their false reporting that the vaccine was handed over in 1916–1917 was to lay a trail that Smith was coming around to the proposition to give up the formula. But this did not happen on his death bed but on or around 22 April 1918. They had time to construct their plan and the myth that McGarvie Smith was a true patriot which J. T. Bull continued to promote for years right up to the 1940s. This could happen in spite of the 1932 Goode enquiry and Waldron's revelation of their scam. It appears that no one ever picked up on it.

Upon the creation of the Institute, Dr Wall and Dr Tidswell made a lot of money by pretending that they had to first 'test' the vaccine formula to make sure it worked. They spent months being paid a huge salary for 'testing' a vaccine that was already proven to work, resulting in a great profit for themselves.[7]

But on that day in the Goode Royal Commission in 1932, Henry Waldron accused Dr Wall of stealing the formula from McGarvie Smith. He also let it be known that Mr James Towers Bull was the means by which the media continually received articles that referred to the above matter in an untrue way.[8]

H.A. Waldron was recalled and cross-examined by Mr Curtis on 29 June. He said that until 1927 he had held a very high opinion of Dr Wall and regarded him as an honourable and upright man. He changed his view of Dr Wall when he reviewed all events over a period of years. Dr Wall, he alleged, had tried to ruin him, and he [the witness] demanded an inquiry. The following excerpt/s show the cross-examination of H.A. Waldron by Mr Curtis

Mr. Curtis: You then decided to send a document to the Governor, the President of the Legislative Council, the Premier, the President of the British Medical Association and others.

Waldron: I did, but not to the B.M.A. I kept that one out for the specific reason that I did not want to interfere with his [Wall's] livelihood.

He added that he had also sent the document to Dr Wall, together with a covering letter. He gave Dr Wall time to answer, and when he did not reply, he sent it to the Governor.

Answering the Commissioner, Mr Waldron said he had also written to Thomas Waddell, General Manager of the Perpetual Trustee Company.

Waldron was asked questions concerning the secret of the serum of the late McGarvie Smith. He said he was not definite in his view that McGarvie Smith wanted the Government to pay £50,000 for the secret, nor could he remember that he had suggested it to any person. (He also added he had married the stepdaughter of the late McGarvie Smith.)

Mr. Curtis: If the Government bought the secret for £50,000 it might have benefited you through your wife?

Waldron: I really cannot say.

Mr. Curtis: Did you know that the payment might have benefited you considerably?

Waldron: It may have; I do not know.

During further cross-examination, the witness turned to the Commissioner and said he thought he had better have some counsel.

The Commissioner: Counsel will not assist you to answer questions. You are sworn to tell the truth, and I think you had better do so and answer questions.

Waldron then said that accompanying the letter he had forwarded to the Governor, was an 'allegory' written in 1921 on facts given by Dr Wall. Mr Curtis said that throughout the letter Waldron had referred to the diary of a person. He then asked if the diary was that of his late wife? "How dare you ask these questions of me," retorted the witness. "The allegory was written by me to embody the story of a designed infamy. This was Dr Wall's description of the people entrusted with forming the Board of Trustees of the McGarvie Smith Institute. Dr Wall is represented as the faithful dog, and I am the Pariah."

> Mr. Curtis: Dr Wall got the secret before McGarvie Smith's death for the Government?
>
> Waldron: Yes. He was successful when everyone else had failed.
>
> Mr. Curtis: You make the charge that Dr. Wall got McGarvie Smith, when almost dead, to sign a document?
>
> Waldron: Yes.
>
> Mr. Curtis: You described it like this, "Pathetic tragedy stalked into the room when that document was produced. Mr. McGarvie Smith was in a comatose condition, and repeated efforts to arouse him were unavailing. I, in common with others, endeavoured to restore the dying man's consciousness by speaking in his ear, and finally succeeded in obtaining a faint glimmer of consciousness from the already glazed eyes. A faint roll of the head on the pillow was taken as acquiescence that his signature should be attached. The helpless hand was placed upon the paper, and his name was traced by a guiding hand." Do you think that was an honest way of describing to the Governor what took place?
>
> Waldron: They are the actual facts.
>
> Mr. Curtis: Have you seen the document from that time?
>
> Waldron: No.
>
> <http://trove.nla.gov.au/newspaper/article/136575072>

Waldron added that Mr Cape, a solicitor (McGarvie's solicitor), Dr Wall, himself (Waldron) and J.T. Bull were present at the time. They were pleased when Wall was able to get details of McGarvie-Smith's vaccine. He made a very fine vaccine himself which had different effects. The document was for the purpose of attacking the character of Dr Wall and for the purpose of bringing about a criminal charge. He wanted Wall to get all he deserved.

During the examination, Judge Thompson had to frequently call on Waldron to answer questions and once declared it was difficult to understand what his brain was thinking about.

There I leave this story to the reader to ponder how history can thus be manipulated and truth overridden by the self-interest of greed.

ENDNOTES TO THE AFTERWORD

1   Hansard 126. VOTES AND PROCEEDINGS OF THE LEGISLATIVE
    ASSEMBLY 29 October 1918. DEBATE
    Mr. Oakes: I say that the Gunn people have every right to full consideration
    at the hands of the Government; and to complicate matters, the Gunn
    trustees, who are not anxious to make money out of it at all - because their
    action has been perfectly generous have, through Mrs. Gunn, offered to the
    Minister for Agriculture the formula they hold; and what is the difference
    in the position? The Department of Agriculture immediately negotiates
    with them, on behalf of the Government, I take it, accepts the formula,
    and the expert officers of the department immediately start to make the
    test necessary for the department's security. There is no question of paying
    £1,294 to test Mr. Gunn's formula; there is no question of engaging two
    experts at £3,500 per annum for the two, to make the vaccine. And let me
    point out here that among the papers a letter from Mr. Kidd shows that these
    gentlemen approached the institute for no less a sum than £2,000 a year each
    for ten years to make this vaccine. I say this, with all due respect to those
    two medical gentlemen, that their action in this matter is not in keeping
    with Mr. McGarvie Smith's spirit of generosity in handing it over when the
    Government asked them to look into the matter, they simply put themselves
    into this very strong position, saying: "We have got this secret, and we will
    dictate the terms under which we shall make the vaccine."

2   My research is largely dependent on newspaper reports. In addition to
    newspapers, I have also used *Scotland and Beyond: The Families of Donald
    Gunn (Tormsdale) and John Gunn (Dalnaha, Strathmore and Braehour)* by
    Alastair Gunn and Donald Gunn, Morrisville: Lulu Press, 2008 and *Bygoo
    and Beyond*, by Mr. R H Webster, Sydney: Halstead Press, 1956.

3   *Bygoo and Beyond*, p. 88.

4   Book ref: p. 457: *Scotland and Beyond*. Beatrice Webb wrote of her visit
    to Gunn's Station quoted from The Webbs' Australian Diary, edited by
    A.G. Austin, 1898. (pp. 58-60). These critics (Austen and Phillips) then
    poured doubt and condemnation on Beatrice's writings. It's what men did.
    Criticising women's writing where they obviously didn't like their feminist
    overtone; see Beatrice's references to Gunn's patriarchal rule: "it is an
    interesting picture of J.A. Gunn and his family but not, perhaps, entirely
    accurate." A.A. Phillips, a *distinguished* (my italics) Australian critic, was later
    to write that Beatrice Webb's "portraits are a little *unbalanced* (my italics) by
    her fondness for finding faults ... Nevertheless she has a waspish acumen,
    and she almost always adds a vividness to our image of these personalities."

Phillips begrudgingly backhands her a compliment! Women's writings were not to be taken seriously or be worthy of any contribution to men's history.

5   *Scotland and Beyond*, Letter to lawyer, July 1908 (available in ANU archives). <newspapers.nla.gov.au/ndp/del/article/15178029?searchterm=Gunn>

6   On Saturday 16 July 1898, in *The Australasian*, (Melbourne), p. 10, under the heading 'Anthrax Vaccine', there is a letter from Messrs M'Garvie Smith and Gunn who refuse the sale of the formula to the Stock Department of New South Wales, saying they would not "consider a proposition which involved our severance from our life work." Here McGarvie Smith exposes his distaste for Mr Tidswell.
<http://trove.nla.gov.au/newspaper/article/138601907>

7   See the full report in *The Medical Journal of Australia*. Saturday 9 November 1918, pp. 400–402 and Saturday 16 November 1918, pp. 419–421.

8   Amazingly, J.T. Bull was still promoting the lie right up into the early 1940s! Mr Bull writes in the Sydney newspaper *Truth* on Sunday 6 April 1941, p. 26:

> At this stage I can claim, with that modesty that sits so well on the generality of pressmen, the press successfully came to the assistance of the man on the land, and I undertook the long-trail and by no means easy task of inducing McGarvie Smith to make a magnanimous gift of his anthrax formula to the New South Wales Government. It was all to the good that I had bespoken the enthusiastic support of the Premier and the Attorney-General …
>
> So, undeterred, I approached a member of the Legislative Council, an ex-Premier himself and many years a Treasurer, Mr. Tom Waddell, a pastoralist also, whom I took out and introduced to McGarvie Smith. Mr. Waddell in turn interested Dr. Frank Wall, a fellow-member of the Council, in his quest, and here again I introduced Dr. Wall to McGarvie.

ACKNOWLEDGEMENTS

To the den of dames at Spinifex Press. Thank you for your generous and consistent enthusiasm and the hours of careful scrutiny you have bestowed upon me!

To Lois Young and her amazing work in her thesis, thank you.

Other books available from Spinifex Press

Ann Hannah, My (Un)Remarkable Grandmother: A Psychological Biography

Betty McLellan

Ann Hannah was an ordinary, no-nonsense practical woman. While a constant and caring presence in the life of her grand-daughter Betty McLellan, she remained emotionally distant.

In an effort to understand her grandmother, Betty has used Ann Hannah's everyday expressions as clues to a life that, like those of many working-class women in the early 1900s, was fraught with challenges and difficulties, and largely ignored by historians.

What did Ann Hannah mean when she said that she was forced to migrate to Australia from England in the 1920s? Why did she remember her husband as a 'wickid' man? How did she cope with the death of her son? How did she manage to overcome the disappointments that punctuated her life?

Written with compassion and a sharp feminist consciousness, this astute biography provides valuable insight into the lives of many (un)remarkable women whose lives may have gone unnoticed but whose experiences shed light on the lives of women.

ISBN: 9781925581287
AUD $26.95
180 pp
eBook available

Lillian's Eden

Cheryl Adam

Australian rural post-war life in the 1950s comes to life through the story of a family struggling to survive after their farm is destroyed by fire. Lillian agrees to the demands of her philandering, violent husband to move to the coastal town of Eden with their children to help look after his Aunt Maggie.

Juggling the demands of caring for her children and two households, and stoically enduring her husband's continued indiscretions, Lillian finds an unlikely ally and friend in the feisty, eccentric Aunt Maggie who lives next door.

With wonderfully drawn characters reminiscent of Ruth Park and Kylie Tennant, Cheryl Adam shows us the stark realities of rural life behind the closed front doors and scented rose-filled gardens. She highlights the endless physical and mental demands on women like Lillian who have to grapple with the challenges of a new homeland as well as never-ending family responsibilities.

This rich, raw novel pays homage to friendship and to the rural women whose remarkable resilience enabled them to find happiness in sometimes the most unlikely of places.

ISBN: 9781925581676
AUD $29.95
302 pp
eBook available

*If you would like to know more about
Spinifex Press, write to us for a free catalogue, visit our
website or email us for further information
on how to subscribe to our monthly newsletter.*

Spinifex Press
PO Box 105
Mission Beach QLD 4852
Australia

www.spinifexpress.com.au
women@spinifexpress.com.au